INTRODUCTION TO LEGAL THEORY

AUSTRALIA
The Law Book Company Ltd.
Sydney: Melbourne: Brisbane

CANADA AND U.S.A.
The Carswell Company Ltd.
Agincourt, Ontario

INDIA
N. M. Tripathi Private Ltd.
Bombay

ISRAEL
Steimatzky's Agency Ltd.
Jerusalem: Tel Aviv: Haifa

MALAYSIA: SINGAPORE: BRUNEI
Malayan Law Journal
Singapore

NEW ZEALAND
Sweet and Maxwell (N.Z.) Ltd.
Wellington

PAKISTAN
Pakistan Law House
Karachi

INTRODUCTION TO
LEGAL THEORY

by

JOHN FINCH, B.A., B.C.L.

of the Faculty of Law, University of Leicester

SECOND EDITION

LONDON
SWEET & MAXWELL
1974

Published in 1974 by
Sweet & Maxwell Limited of
11 New Fetter Lane, London
and printed in Great Britain
by Northumberland Press Limited,
Gateshead, Co. Durham.

SBN Hardback 421 19630 0
Paperback 421 19640 8

To Chrissy

FOREWORD

This book aims to present a short guide to some of the most significant aspects of that very large part of jurisprudence which has to do with legal theory. Its purpose is to introduce some major features of the development of juristic thought, and to provide an initial understanding of the work of some principal contributors to this field. To this end the book should certainly be regarded as a primer and not as a reference volume. Of course, the following chapters necessarily contain a considerable amount of detail bearing on certain aspects of this very wide area of study. What is of paramount importance, however, is not so much the learning of such detail as its creative interpretation. The views and analyses of a limited number of jurists will be examined and compared in a manner which, it is hoped, will serve to lend some degree of continuity and cohesion to the reader's study.

An introductory primer such as this must try to avoid too great a simplification of the subject-matter, for despite the initial attractions of simplicity and ease of comprehension, the readers' needs would not ultimately be fulfilled by deliberate avoidance of difficulties. The general introductory chapter which prefaces the following survey of legal theory is designed to anticipate some problems which are commonly found throughout the whole field. The significance of some observations in this chapter will be immediately apparent. For the rest, the reader may on occasion find it helpful to refer back to these introductory remarks in the course of later chapters. Particularly recurrent problems alluded to are those of definition and of the comparison of differing approaches to the analysis of law.

The text of the first edition has been substantially revised, and two new chapters have been added on subjects which have an obvious claim to the attention of students of legal theory. Chapter 3 deals with some significant practical contributions made by natural law doctrine to the solution of some acute legal and moral problems arising out of the so-called "grudge informer" and allied cases in post-war Germany. Chapter 9 contains an outline of the juristic thought and juridical institutions which originate in Marxist doctrine. Furthermore, existing chapters have been amended so as to take account of some recent assessments of established juristic theories.

Though this book is essentially a primer, it is designed to enable a reader to use it as a self-contained course if his timetable so dictates. Though any study of legal theory will clearly benefit from the ability to draw examples from all aspects of the content of laws, the approach here adopted assumes none but a rudimentary knowledge of legal systems.

The author wishes to repeat his particular gratitude and indebtedness to Emeritus Professor D. R. Seaborne Davies for his advice and encouragement in the preparation of the first edition of this book; and to Mr. C. F. H. Tapper, of Magdalen College, Oxford, who read the original draft and who made many helpful suggestions.

CONTENTS

CHAPTER 1

GENERAL INTRODUCTION

Jurisprudence and legal theory

IT is easier to say what jurisprudence is not, than to say what it is. The definition of any area of study is useful only insofar as it illuminates and does not constrict. It is always tempting to ask for definitions of areas of law or legal study. Attempts to meet the demand may, however, be at best misguided and at worst positively misleading.

Among the many dangers inherent in the search for definitions, two are particularly relevant to the present study. First, definition may precede adequate knowledge of the subject-matter sought to be defined, and misconceptions may be formed at the outset. Second, and just as serious, the definition presented may in turn lead to the imposition on the matter defined of artificial limits not corresponding to practical necessity and reality.

This book does not cover the whole field of jurisprudence. Its concern is with legal theory, with the principal methods which have been used to describe and analyse the essential constituent elements in the phenomenon "law." Nevertheless, the study of legal theory is but one aspect, albeit a major one, of jurisprudence; the introductory remarks in this chapter may therefore be of assistance in other jurisprudential studies which are not within our present compass. A hard-and-fast distinction between jurisprudence in general and legal theory in particular is not truly tenable. Based merely on the verbal connotations of these two terms, it will fail to illuminate their nature. Nor will it be fruitful to attempt to differentiate legal theory from general jurisprudence on account of their respective contents. While jurisprudential study may be made of individual legal concepts such as possession, negligence and corporation, the concern of legal theory is also centred on a legal concept, that is, law itself. Be the analysis of the nature of law as a whole or of particular legal concepts within it, too many features are common to both types of analysis to justify any distinction sought to be drawn between them.

Broadly speaking, legal theory involves a study of the characteristic features essential to law and common to legal systems. Its object is the analysis of the basic elements of law which make it law and distinguish it from other forms of rules and standards, from systems of order which cannot be described as legal systems, and from other social phenomena. It has not proved possible to reach a final and dogmatic answer to the question "What is law?" or to provide exclusive answers to the many questions which have been posed about its essential nature. The claim of a course in legal theory is not that it produces conclusively definitive answers. Its value lies, rather, in a study of the light which juristic work has shed on the distinctive attributes of law. An examination of the relative merits and demerits of some principal expositions of the subject, focussing attention on their points of strength and weakness, is a convenient method of assessing the varying results. Such conclusions as are expounded in the following chapters arise not from any attempts at exclusive definition; they spring, rather, from the juxtaposition and comparison of a variety of legal analyses, differing in nature but often equal in merit.

Some problems of definition

The definition of the area of study entailed by legal theory is but a minor issue when set among the multitude of problems of definition which have confronted jurists in the development of their analyses of law. The variety of contexts in which the term "law" may suitably be employed is too great to allow of one definition of that concept to the exclusion of all others. An exclusive definitive notion of the nature of law may be too restricted to be of use outside the terms of reference of the jurist who adopts it; or else too general a definition may, in an attempt to satisfy everyone, satisfy none.

The conceptual nature of law prevents its susceptibility to forms of definition commonly used in relation to physical objects. When a thing is being defined, the general category to which it belongs may be first outlined, and the particular species to which it belongs within the general category may then be marked off. This form is known as definition *per genus et differentiam*. An elephant, for instance, may be defined by first allocating it to the general category of mammals, and then further specified by a description of its particular characteristics, a trunk, large feet, a tail and so on.

If this form of definition were suitable in the case of law, debates about the essential nature and characteristics of that concept would not have been pursued since time immemorial. Most accounts of the nature of law and legal phenomena consist, not of definitions, but rather of characteristic descriptions. Such is the nature of law that it is impossible first to outline a general category to which it belongs, and then to specify the distinguishing features of law which mark it off and indicate its particular province within this general category. Difficulties of precise definition are further compounded when it is realised that disputants in this field are frequently moved by any number of social or ideological reasons when advancing their suggestions as to the nature of law, and are not concerned only to achieve a logical analysis to the exclusion of relevant human and social values. The term "law" is so wide and can be employed in so many different contexts that jurists will frequently, in reality, be talking about different things. Their opinions may vary according to the objects they have in mind, their background, their education and the social, political and economic climate in which they work.

That it is not always the same thing which is sought to be defined in differing analyses of the nature of law may be far from obvious. The student of legal theory will find it difficult to assimilate approaches which appear as different as chalk and cheese. If one essential distinction is borne in mind, however, much confusion may be avoided. In any comparative study of legal theory, a distinction must be maintained between the character of law and the content of law, or rather of laws. Separate consideration must be given to "law" in a conceptual sense and to "laws" in the sense of individual legal rules. Some analyses of the nature of law are disorientated by want of this distinction. Some criticisms of these analyses have themselves fallen into this very trap. When the same word may be used to refer to aspects of the essential character of law and also to the specific content of a law or legal rule, problems of definition abound.

Classification in legal theory

Not unassociated with the desire to define or delimit the ambit of legal theory and the concept of law itself is the habit of believing that the views of a particular jurist are adequately presented by the device of labelling him under some general description of a class of jurists—classified by some trait or sympathy prominent in their works. Schools of thought and general movements in thought there certainly are; but Mars is hardly described by merely stating that it is a planet in the solar system. Nor is the solar system described by a list, however long, of its major members. Here name-dropping serves no worthwhile purpose. Without a discussion of their context and the reasons which underlie them, a mere list of cases decided by the courts on a particular topic throws no light on the topic itself. Similarly in legal theory, a mere catalogue of the names of jurists who have contributed to the discussion of some particular problem adds little, if anything, to a worthwhile exposition and explanation of the problem itself.

It is true that, for the sake of convenience and easy reference, the major surveys of legal theory adopt general classifications of juristic work. Headings which are frequently encountered include natural law theories, analytical positivism, modern realism, sociological approaches, historical approaches and so on. Students are warned, however, to avoid the pitfall of believing that their task is done by memorising in tabulated or similar form a list of juristic works alongside the titles of general classifications. That should come, if at all, at the end of their studies and not at the beginning For the purpose of fitting in pieces of the jigsaw-puzzle once we have gone some way towards gaining an overall picture of the subject-matter to be examined, such elaborations may be useful to the extent that they are illustrative, but to that extent only. It may well be found that many, if not most, jurists may ultimately be included within a particular category or movement in thought; but to assume that the work of a jurist should display certain features which typify his "classification" would be to do him a disservice. That would be to put the cart before the horse. It is of foremost importance to examine what a jurist has actually written and of minimal significance to know the classifying term which commentators have subsequently attached to his views.

Variations in approach

It is a remarkable fact of legal theory that so many different ideas, so many different forms of expression, have been used to describe what might appear to be one and the same thing. When we commonly refer to law, a readily understandable meaning is usually attached to what is said in typical contexts such as "What is the law on this matter?" or "I am studying law." Why, then, all the discussion about what law is?

The diversity of opinion comes from persons intimately connected with the law amongst whom a degree of consistency might be expected. One explanation of the absence of such consistency lies in the fact that the analysis of law differs from the types of analysis employed in the natural sciences. A principal reason for this difference is to be found in the relationship between methods of investigation and the character of the subject-matter to be investigated. The distinction between prescription and description must be mentioned here, though this distinction will not be examined in detail until the following chapter. The formation of laws is a purposive and prescriptive task. A prohibitory or empowering law is passed by a legislature for a certain reason and with a certain purpose behind it. Furthermore, this regulation of the conduct of people is itself operated by people. The accounts which are given of this enterprise and of the creature, law, which thereby comes into being, are the result of description. Put shortly, the legislator prescribes and the jurist or commentator describes the effect of what the legislature has done, in the course of his wider description of legal phenomena as a whole. The legislator (used here to refer to all organs of a legal system with lawmaking power) is no doubt concerned with past, present and future circumstances which condition the purpose behind his actions. His primary concern is, however, the prescriptive task of saying what shall or ought to happen, the description of circumstances in the background of his laws being of secondary importance only. The legislator may, indeed, be quite unconcerned with anything but the making of a new law, though in practice this will be unlikely.

The methods of investigation adopted by the jurist engaged in the task of describing legal phenomena are necessarily conditioned by the nature of the subject-matter to be examined. With reference to this feature of the analysis of data the task of the jurist or legal theorist differs fundamentally from his opposite number, the expositor or commentator in the field of natural science. Chemistry, for instance, stands for the methods of investigation employed by chemists, and for the principles of matter which are elucidated by these methods. The objects under scrutiny are physical, in one form or another of physical existence as specific entities. Law, on the other hand, is not synonymous with legal science. Nor is law a thing or a physical fact which lends itself to the analytical treatment used in the natural sciences. Its essentially prescriptive character precludes such an approach.

Opinions vary as to the nature of law, the reasons for its existence as a social phenomenon, the characteristics which differentiate it from other forms of regulation and from other institutions of society, as to the place of morality in the law, as to the part which physical force does or ought to play, as to the distinguishing characteristics of those who are or who ought to be legally authoritative, and so on. As mentioned, the term "law" may refer both to the nature of a social phenomenon and also to the actual provisions of a legal system whether generally or individually. This variability in meaning, together with the widely varying backgrounds and purposes of all the writers to have tackled problems associated with the nature of law, has had a considerable influence on the great variety of methods which have been adopted in the analysis of the nature of law. Moreover the connection with each writer has with the operation of a particular legal system, with the creation of laws or with their administration as a practitioner or legal official, or with the teaching of law, or with the study of its nature or of philosophies concerned with law, may exercise some considerable bearing on the type of account which is given. No jurist can conceal his education, his social philosophy, or his ideology forever; nor do many seek to do so.

The ideologies or value-systems underlying some of the theories to be treated in this book will be obvious. The clearest example is Marxist doctrine which has given rise to a concept of law, or of its purposes, directly based on a political philosophy. No less obvious are the values at the base of some major trends in natural law philosophies. The more implicit motive forces behind theories of law were summed up in the memorable phrase of the great American jurist Oliver Wendell Holmes as "inarticulate major premises." The function of law as a means of social regulation inevitably entails a conditioning of legal theory by the values inherent in the structure of any particular society.

Hart has commented on the remarkable number of formulations which have at one time or another been attached to the nature of law.[1] Understood in their context, he says, such formulations can be both illuminating and puzzling. The light thrown by each on

[1] Hart, *The Concept of Law*, Clarendon Press, Oxford, 1961, pp. 1-6.

the object of study may dazzle us so much that other features are simultaneously obscured. Jørgensen[2] takes this observation a stage further when, after having said that "the variants have been innumerable in consequence of the fact that the various authors or schools have emphasised one each of the many perspectives which may be applied to legal phenomena," he continues: "To the legal scientist it may seem natural to consider law as a system or norms, whereas to the politician it may seem reasonable to take law as a means of governing and to look on the rules of law as sanctioned orders or imperatives. No doubt it will seem strange to many at first glance that law has not only none of the firm and closed contents which most people imagine, but has even no constant form. It is, however, the general attitude of probably all sciences today that our perception is sporadic and determined by individual interests, that it is impossible, therefore, to give an exhaustive description of any complex of phenomena observed, but that the description will depend on the interest it is to serve and on the approach accordingly chosen."

Another Scandinavian writer, Professor Karl Olivecrona, sheds further light on the problem of defining something which is certainly not tangible or visible, as is the case with law, and the nature of which is at first relatively unknown.[3] "A difficulty immediately appears when we propose to elucidate the nature of the law. That is how to avoid circularity. The object of inquiry is said to be 'the law' of a modern community. But does not this imply some knowledge of what the law is? How else could any object of inquiry be designated by this expression? But then the inquiry seems to presuppose previous knowledge of its object. We are apparently caught in a dilemma. One seems to be unable to define the object of investigation without clearly already being familiar with it. Not surprisingly, therefore, works on the nature of law often begin with a definition of the concept of law. If a definition of law is not proffered, a concept of law is usually presupposed as a necessary starting point." Where, then, can a starting point be found at which to commence our investigations into the nature of law? Olivecrona continues: "It should be possible here, as well as in other branches of science, to define the object of inquiry without anticipating the result. This means framing the questions

---

[2] Jørgensen, *Law and Society*, Akademisk Boghandel, Aarhus, Denmark, 1973, pp. 4-5.

[3] *Law as Fact*, Stevens and Sons, London, 2nd ed., 1971, pp. 1-6.

without making any assumption concerning the answer.... The common language and the content of the common mind may serve as a starting point for our investigation. We have some immediate knowledge of things just as people had some immediate knowledge of the celestial phenomena from which the study of lightning once began. We therefore have the necessary factual basis from which the inquiry may proceed.

"The course of the inquiry may be set in different directions. One possibility is to study the common mind itself by analysing its notions and tracing their history. This could lead to a more extended knowledge of our ideas concerning 'the law' and the language used to express them. The object of the inquiry could be described as legal ideology. Another possible course is to go beyond the common mind and ask what empirical realities we find where the legal notions are applied. This inquiry is not concerned with ideology but with objective facts.... A third course of inquiry would be to begin with the theories about the nature of 'the law' and try to ascertain the content of their truth.... Of the three courses of inquiry the last one offers certain advantages. It is better to start with the more precise ideas of acute and learned jurists and philosophers than with the more vague notions of the common mind. The point of departure will then be the present position of legal theory."

Though for the moment enlightening, when the variety of approaches to the analysis of the nature of law is being considered, the views of Olivecrona will be examined in Chapter Six to see whether he, too, is not making some unwarranted assumptions.

The problem of the nature of law is rendered even more remarkable when we are reminded that it has provided a source of learned discussion among distinguished lawyers and philosophers for such a very long time—certainly from the early Greeks onwards to the present day. One writer has offered a solution to at least a considerable part of the problem of differences in juristic attitudes.[4] He suggests that variations in approach and some of the major disagreements amongst jurists are attributable to a failure to appreciate the relationship between what can be called "law-concepts," "law ideas" and "law-theories." The basic concept of a writer's jurisprudence or what, for that writer, is law,

---

[4] King, "The Concept, the Idea and the Morality of Law" (1966) 24 C.L.J. 106.

may be called his law concept. Any further explanatory description concerning the nature of that concept of law which cannot be deduced or inferred from the law-concept itself is called that writer's law-theory. A law-idea serves to describe the manner in which a law-concept functions as a practical guide to action: to entertain the law-idea is to accept the guidance to action which it entails. On the basis of these distinctions which may be applied in studying the work of a jurist who is investigating the phenomenon "law," the following proposition is advanced: "It is tentatively suggested that the tendency in jurisprudence is to presuppose one's own law-concept and to assume that every other writer's law-concept expresses a law-theory intended to be applicable to one's own law. Other writers' supposed law-theories are then, on this assumption, readily shown to be defective if not simply false."

While no set formula will be used in the following chapters in the comparison of differing approaches to the analysis of law, it will be valuable to remember that the concept of law explicitly or implicitly adopted by any particular jurist is bound to have a substantial influence on his subsequent exposition. Though the use of an approach of the type just indicated might result in arid study if applied separately to each analysis of law in turn, its employment in the overall comparison of differing juristic attitudes may be fruitful. This particular method of comparative analysis may be beneficial once the reader has become familiar with a considerable number of the salient points contained in the analyses of law which will be discussed in the following chapters.

Differences of opinion in legal theory are not always explicable in terms of set analytical formulae. It is conceivable that a jurist or commentator on legal theory might refuse outright to accept the concepts or explanations of another as being of any value, and base his criticism solely on this ground. One analysis of law might claim superiority over another simply on the basis of a misunderstanding of the other's nature and purpose. A theory of law might contain inconsistencies within itself. A jurist might even set out by posing certain questions and finish with something, albeit in the form of conclusions, not in fact directly related to the questions asked.

No formal approach to the assessment and comparison of contributions to juristic knowledge will be adopted in this book. It would be misguided to formalise the solution of problems and conflicts which the reader will ultimately wish to solve for himself.

As far as is practicable in an introductory text such as this, attention will be paid to both similarities and differences between a number of analyses of the nature of law. If these are considered each to the exclusion of the other there is a danger of missing some notable features of the matter under examination.

A comparative approach to any branch of legal study which both compares and contrasts principles and concepts can lead to a better overall understanding. The exposition of one theory of the nature of law which is set out against that of another can give meaning and life to both. The following chapters compare and contrast the approaches of a number of jurists whose contributions may usefully be considered in relation to one another. A general outline will be given of each legal theory and particular attention will be paid to the various ways in which they are related. Though there are some exceptions, the juristic views to be discussed generally fall into place as a matter of chronological order. The early natural law doctrines probably represent the oldest source of legal theory, and the legal consequences of Marxist doctrine represent one of the most significant major developments in recent legal thinking. On the basis of the developments to be studied, the reader will, it is hoped, be in a position to form a balanced assessment of each of the legal theories to be considered. He may ultimately be enabled to judge whether legal analysis, its concepts and its methods of analysis, have improved, and if so in what ways. It is intended that at the end of this process of juxtaposition of legal theories, the reader will be able to place himself at any stage in the development which will have been traced, and to see what lies behind him and before him in perspective. Once the relationship between one legal theory and another has been appreciated, the reader will be better able to level his own criticism at each one.

The uses of analogy

The study of differing analyses of the nature of law is bound to involve the discussion and comparison of doctrines and concepts which may be far removed from the experience of everyday life, removed even from the everyday experience of the law's operation. The device of analogy is frequently employed by jurists, teachers and students alike in order to expedite the communication of ideas. Analogies may be used in our present field in order to liken an idea or concept which is initially difficult to appreciate, to some other more familiar idea or set of facts. By thus relating one thing or idea to another, or more usually a set of ideas to a set of things or series of events, the initially difficult idea appears to become assimilable to something which seems either obvious or at least more readily understandable. The misuse of analogies is, however, a danger to any discussion. Analogies can be used to great advantage in the clarification of difficult concepts and distinctions. Great comfort may be derived from the discovery of a link between the abstruse abstract and the familiar concrete. But care must be taken. Whatever may be the attraction and apparent usefulness of analogies, they are capable of becoming misconceived in relation to the point to be explained. Even when an analogy is not initially misleading there remains the danger of arguing—perhaps perfectly logically—from one facet of the explanatory device to another in such a way as to distort argument. The point which was originally in need of explanation may be lost sight of. We should beware of extending analogies beyond their often restricted usefulness and, conversely, guard against disbelief in an idea which is being explained by way of analogy merely for the reason that the particular analogy chosen is not apposite to its purpose.

Varieties of criticism

It has been asserted by some who have studied aspects of various theories as to the nature of law that one man's opinion on a particular matter is as good as another's. This may be true, especially in the evaluation of some very different approaches to juristic analysis. But it is true only when the assertion is made subject to two important qualifications: first, the opinions in question should be fully considered and sufficiently reasoned; and second, it is essential that the one should have understood the import of the other's views and is in fact dealing with the same problem. One method of stating the possible causes of confusion has already been mentioned. To assert that criticisms of other's views should be reasoned and considered may state the obvious, but such reservations are ignored only at the cost of confusion.

Those familiar with literary criticism will appreciate the way in which differing standards may be applied when one man treats the writings of another. Two principal methods may be found by which to criticise any piece of writing, whether the critic is addressing his assessment to form, or to content, or to a mixture of the two. The first is to consider whether the project merited treatment at all, or in the particular context in which it appeared. The second is to consider whether it achieved the object intended by its author. When contributions to any field of knowledge, art or literature are criticised out of hand without regard to the object which the author set out to achieve, the second form of criticism is ignored at some cost. When applied to our present field, this latter form of criticism examines whether a jurist has achieved what he set out to do, in his own terms and on his own ground. The former method, on the other hand, inquires whether the object undertaken was justified and worthy of treatment, in terms of the standards and opinions which the critic held even before encountering the work which he is now assessing.

This difference in approach indicates the distinction between subjective and objective analysis. Criticism which is based on an analysis of the degree of success achieved "on his own ground" by an author tends to be much more objective than the other method, which may amount rather to a statement of personal views and inclinations, rather to a dogmatic assertion of a writer's own views, than to a considered assessment of the merit of those of another. The opportunities for objective assessment are clearly greater in the case of legal analyses which have much common ground but which differ in the presence or absence of some further substantial feature, or in the emphasis which each gives to common constituent elements. In the case of legal theories separated by wide differences in ideology, the task of both commentator and student is rendered more complex if the "inarticulate major premises" mentioned above remain inarticulated.

The terminology of legal theory

The language of the law is necessarily precise and contains a substantial terminology which is not part of everyday parlance. The language of legal theory also possesses its own special vocabulary on account of the nature of the phenomena under investigation. No great problem arises for the student in this respect, for he will soon become accustomed to "normative" terminology necessitated by the normative character of law. The concepts of rule, norm, regulation, power, sanction and prescription are commonly encountered in legal theory. The terms applied to methods of juristic investigation, such as "realism" or "analytical positivism" are frequently self-explanatory and will soon become familiar as far as is necessary. Such classifications are, as mentioned, of secondary importance to what each jurist has actually written.

Concepts at first difficult to understand because of the mode in which they are expressed can, by elucidation and exposition, often be reduced to very simple language. But that is not to say that any science or field of knowledge can avoid its own "short-hand" terms. One of the obvious benefits of shorthand terms is the avoidance of lengthy circumlocution. The task of even the newcomer to legal theory will be eased, provided of course that modes of expression adopted to describe legal phenomena are not too cryptic. Once the basic expressions of legal theory are mastered, as they must be, its terminology, whether it be applied to theories about the nature of law in general or to the analysis of particular legal concepts within it, such as negligence, owner-ship or corporation, is no more complicated than that of any other branch of legal study.

However, that is not to say that expositions of jurisprudence or legal theory are universally reducible to lay simplicity. The most complex theory of law might be expounded in apparent simplicity, when in fact over-simplification could result in dis-tortion and misunderstanding. The ability to reason well enough, and with sufficient patience, to grasp the essence of the theory itself must be added to the mastering of individual terms. Some parts of the law are more readily understood than others because they relate to more common experiences of mankind. Legal theory may seem more difficult to comprehend for the very reason that it often relates to matters which are not part of the common currency of everyday life—either of the layman, or the lawyer, or the law student.

Argument in legal theory

The closing remarks of this chapter have a bearing also on the observations, made above, upon definitions in legal theory and upon the terminology involved in its study. Discussion necessitates a starting point. But initial terms of reference must not be treated as definitions. Conclusions on the nature of issues to which they relate should not automatically be deduced from them. They are neither intended nor, of necessity, well adapted for such a purpose.

Nevertheless, since a starting point for discussion is a clear necessity if any exchange of arguments is to gain momentum, the common exhortation to "define one's terms" should be treated with some suspicion. One term must be explained by reference to another, or others, and those will in turn stand in need of "definition." The constant definition of terms would produce an infinite regress. It may be found in the course of a discussion that new terms might suitably be substituted for old. That is not to say, however, that absolute definition in the use of concepts and their attendant terminology must be achieved at the outset of any debate. This may not even be possible, for there will always be those whose attitudes subsequently diverge.

Words are convenient and indeed necessary for the expression of thought, and no concept can be communicated without them. But they are not to be treated as substitutes for thought; they are the servants and not the masters. To take simple example, if an action in tort for negligence is dismissed because "there was no duty of care on the part of the defendant," that merely states a result. It presents none of the essential reasons which led up to that result; there is no magic in the terms themselves.

The allegation is occasionally encountered that the discussion of such and such an issue is "merely verbal," and verbal arguments are sometimes associated with accusations of hairsplitting. In any field in which somewhat complex concepts are examined, a certain accuracy of linguistic usage is required if a satisfactory account is to be given of the subject-matter. However, considerations which have to do with words and linguistic usage are by no means necessarily purely verbal or founded on the quicksand basis of the words in isolation. Language is our means of expression, but the roots of our arguments and analyses lie not in the words themselves but in the notions which await verbal expression.

Despite its title, legal theory relates ultimately to problems of physical existence, though most jurists insist that a study of physical or causal relations is insufficient without the addition of a normative analysis of such relations to account for their specifically legal quality. Legal theory is not concerned with "mere theorising." It might, however, fall into this trap and become an empty form if theory were erected on the inadequate foundation of preconceived and exclusive definition which pre-empts further fruitful discussion. The opinion has been advanced that the question whether or not international law is really law is a merely verbal question and that those who take differing views on its nature are participating in verbal dispute. The question whether that form of law is really law seems to some to have survived only because a trivial question about the meaning of words has been mistaken for a serious question about the nature of things.[5]

A study of the character of international law could indeed be unrewarding if an *a priori* definition of the concept of law had already been constructed which would necessarily exclude that area of regulation. Such a possibility apart, it is very difficult to agree with the proposition that discussion of its nature is merely verbal. Whatever terminology is used, the problem of the nature of international law as compared with that of national or municipal law still remains and deserves explanation. Practical as well as theoretical questions can ensue, just as they can in relation to the question whether a thoroughly iniquitous rule merits the appellation "law." The issue in the latter example is anything but verbal, for acute problems of obedience and punishment may arise for solution. Furthermore, language may be capable of conveying the meaning of the subject-matter to which it refers only if it is examined in the light of such factors as the ideology or social environment of the writer whose views are under discussion. What may appear to be mere niceties of linguistic usage can conceivably affect the meaning to be conveyed.

Since a straightforward and conclusive method of definition is not available in our present field, attention must be directed towards greater accuracy of expression in order to produce a more accurate exposition of the concepts and ideas themselves. The consequent care which must be taken with linguistic usage is anything but merely verbal. Words are indispensable tools for fixing and communicating legal ideas, and even an attack on words must, in the end, be couched in words.

[5] Hart, *The Concept of Law*, O.U.P. 1961, p. 209.

Chapter 2

NATURAL LAW AND POSITIVISM

I

"Our conception of the problem to which our discourse is addressed shapes both" (Roscoe Pound).[1]

THE variety of questions which may be asked about law is wider than meets the eye. The word "law" is used in a great many different contexts, and these contexts are related to each other in an equal variety of ways, some direct, some more complex. Pound's words have a general application to the issues with which this book is concerned. They serve to indicate both that the particular formulation of a question conditions the form and the content of the answer, and also that what we find is inevitably influenced by what we are looking for. It is to be expected that the terms of reference of an answer will be neither much wider, nor much narrower, than those of the question.

The word "law" is ordinarily used to refer to some element of regulation which governs our actions and affairs, and which involves something more than mere reprobation or social censure if we step outside the permitted limits, however liberally these limits may be interpreted. Within this system of regulation there are certain people who are officially permitted or authorised to administer the legal regulations, and sometimes they are under a duty to do so. From such people we are accustomed to expect certain actions which may effect a change in our legal position. In some cases we go out of our way to bring about such changes as, for instance, when entering into a contract. In others, acquiescence in changed legal relations is a matter of necessity, as when a relationship is formed with a utility company for the supply of water, electricity or gas, no real alternative source of supply being available. In others still, a person may be subjected to changes in his legal position or status even though he might have gone out of his way to avoid them, as when a fine or a prison sentence is imposed. The law permits as much as it prohibits. It will be seen

[1] Pound, "Natural Natural Law and Positive Natural Law" (1960) 5 N.L.F. 70.

later that this simple observation can make a substantial difference in the relative abilities of two accounts of the nature of law to explain the general functions of a typical legal system.[2]

When we speak of the law, or rather the laws, to which our behaviour is subject, reference is being made to the specific content of an actual body of legal provisions which have been, and are being, produced largely as a result of the activities of a legislature and a body of law courts; we say, as lawyers or laymen, that "the law on such and such a matter is as follows." Such statements refer to what may be called the "specific content of positive law." From this point of view the law as a whole consists of a great mass of individual legal provisions or laws. When we speak of a legal system, on the other hand, attention is being directed rather more towards its systematic character, and any observations which are made about it will probably be concerned more with the general character than with the particular case. Yet another usage is to be found in such an expression as "the rule of law." In this context the word "law" serves to express a number of ideas, some of them vague, some quite specific, ranging from the judiciary's freedom from political intermeddling to general value judgments as to fairness and equality.

Legal theory deals with questions as to the nature of law. As such, it is more concerned with the character of law or of a legal system than with its content, the specific regulations themselves. Any adequate explanation of the nature of law, however, will obviously have to accommodate the functioning and administration of the particular legal provisions of a system of law. This can be done in a variety of ways, each one stressing one or more particular aspect of the way in which positive laws operate. Some analyses of law give special emphasis to the powers and position of the legislature, some to those of the courts, some to the attitude of the people subject to law, and some to the moral and social values which the laws aim to reflect and foster. In the analysis of elements of law such as these, the methods of approach known generally as "natural law doctrine," "positivism," and "realism" all have something to offer which is worthy of attention and yet they all make competing, sometimes conflicting, claims to approval. Their respective contributions are frequently set against the background of criticisms of one or both of the other methods. The very

[2] See *infra*, Chaps. 4 and 5.

names which have been given to these approaches seem each to convey a claim to superiority or to truth.

One usage of the word "law" so far unmentioned is that which refers to such laws as the laws of gravity or of motion. These are part of the physical laws of matter and of the universe, another term for them being "laws of nature." They refer to and explain the cause and effect relationships which exist between physical things. These relationships are not created by man in the way that the laws of a legal order are created, for all he does is to reach conclusions on the basis of his observation of causal processes and to put forward explanations of what in fact happens. His work may in many instances be prospective or forward-looking, inasmuch as his observations may form the basis of predictions of what will happen in the future. As distinct however from the legislator, who is actually creating laws for the governance and regulation of his fellow men, the natural scientist is engaged in a descriptive and not a prescriptive task. When a natural scientist says that something ought to happen he means that it probably will happen in future, judging from what he has already observed. In the case of a legislator (under which term we may for the moment include judges, who also create or lay down parts of the law) the position is different. It is in a way reversed, for what does happen is a reason for the scientist's statement of what ought to happen as a matter of probability, while in the prescriptive activities of the legislator, the prescription that some course of action or state of affairs ought to result itself furnishes a reason for what may in fact happen as a result of it. In the latter instance moreover the element of probability may be much less straightforward to determine.

A number of important distinctions arise out of this simple comparison of empirical or causal science with the legislative process and legal science. One is the distinction between the descriptive and the prescriptive functions of an investigator. This is a recurrent distinction in any discussion of legal theory. Related to this distinction is the difference between retrospective and prospective elements in analysis. Yet another, even more important distinction, is between causation and what has been called "imputation,"[3] the difference between causal relations and "normative" relations. Whereas the word "ought" may loosely be used in relation to the

[3] Kelsen, *Pure Theory of Law*, Chap. 3, parts 18-22; see *infra*. Chap. 6 generally.

probability of a factual occurrence to express the probable effect of a generally known cause, it has another meaning when applied to law, especially when it comes from the mouth of the legislator. In such a context ought is used to express what *is to* happen, what *should* or *shall* happen. The usage of such terms to express the prescriptive nature of regulation is common to statements of, or about, law and statements of, or about, morals. Clearly the spheres of law and morals do not necessarily coincide, though legal and moral exhortations may coincide in certain cases. Many crimes exist which are generally regarded as offensive to morals. Such is the crime of murder. Similarly one ought not to steal, and stealing is also thought to be immoral, though some cases may be regarded as less immoral than others, and stealing in general may be thought less immoral than murder. Opinions may, however, vary on both counts. Second, there are crimes (of a species proliferating in modern times) which are of a regulatory nature, such as parking offences and penal provisions in statutes of an administrative nature, and which are contrary to legal but not to moral stipulations. But even in relation to such penal offences, it might, however, be thought that any crime, however technical, is immoral—though the reasonableness of such a belief might decrease in the light of the plethora of strict liability offences under our law, the doubt being engendered more by the absence of mental conditions for responsibility than simply by the number of such offences. Thirdly, there are activities widely held to be contraventions of morality but which are not the subject of legal penal prohibitions, the notable example in our own legal system being adultery. In such cases there is no legal ought not[4] though there may be a widespread ought not as a matter of morality.

A justifiable conclusion from these brief remarks on the relationship between legal rules and moral rules is that the legal ought and the moral ought, though they may in fact be to some extent coincident, are separable as a matter of character or nature. In both cases, however, their prescriptive nature is to be distinguised from what happens in practice, from what we may call the "is."

The study of legal theory involves consideration of an Is and three different meanings of Ought.[5] The Is connotes the existence of some fact or set of facts determinable by observation and experiment—by empirical means. The first connotation of Ought

---

[4] Though there is in some of the American States.
[5] Hereafter Is and Ought for easier reading.

concerns factual probability. The second connotes a moral Ought. It expresses what ought, as a matter of morals, to happen. It does not describe what probably will happen. Nevertheless, what has happened in the past will much influence the particular content of each moral Ought. Otherwise, it would be unrelated to man's physical existence, his necessities, his capabilities and limitations.[6] The third Ought is the legal Ought, a normative or prescriptive ought which again will have a probable relationship with what has happened in the past, though it need not have it.[7] This Ought may have moral connotations, though not necessarily so. It will be distinguishable from morals in two respects. First, the positive law content which embodies this Ought is capable of being verified by a relatively direct practical research and may in principle be changed at the will of human beings. Second, as distinct from the moral Ought, this legal Ought is connected in various ways with centrally organised sanctions.

Both the moral and the legal Oughts are concerned with the regulation of human beings but they are concerned with it in different, though complementary, ways and mean different things. Neither is to be identified or regarded as synonymous with the first Ought, the prediction of factual probability—though connections do exist. Our primary concern will be with the normative legal Ought, though the other two types will have to be mentioned from time to time for the sake of comparison and contrast. It is this relationship between the normative Ought of law and the Is of physical existence or statements of fact which has proved to be one of the most perplexing of all the problems of legal theory. It is one which can never be far from our minds, and one which has probably produced the greatest controversy in this field of study. The question of how, if at all, the legal Ought and the moral Ought are to be related is also of the greatest importance and is by no means an easy one to answer. The words of Roscoe Pound which prefaced this chapter ring true in any consideration of the various approaches made by jurists to the relation of the legal Ought to morality and also to fact.

---

[6] For comments on the "positive" morality of a society, see Hart; *Law, Liberty and Morality*, O.U.P. paperback, 1968.

[7] It is said, for instance, that "Parliament can make or unmake any law whatsoever." Legally, it can do this, but the necessities of practical politics will usually require some factual research into the matter to which a new regulation is to be added.

II

The nature of law and the law of nature

The general subject of the nature of law partly involves discussion of "the law of nature." According to the particular ideology behind each of them, various titles have been used for the selfsame subject, such as the law of the universe, the law of God, the eternal law, the law of mankind and the law of reason.

The central claim of a theory of the law of nature is that what naturally is, ought to be. The Is implies the Ought as a necessary consequence of its existence. The law of nature ought to be the governing law for all things, including mankind and human relations. The fundamental hypothesis or assumption behind this theory is that there is a law or a body of laws which governs all things, whether these be gravity, motion, physical and chemical reactions, animal instinct or the actions of man. It might be said that certain actions and reactions are ordained by the law of nature and the corollary might be added that anything which happens to the contrary is happening contrary to nature. If a stone were dropped in normal gravitational conditions, it would be contrary to the laws of gravity if it rose into the air. As it happens, we can be pretty certain it will not. The stone, however, has no reason and possesses no capacity to choose what it will do. Human beings, on the other hand, have these faculties in combination. Unlike the stone, human beings are not practically bound, as a matter of physiological or spiritual necessity, to follow the laws which were supposedly ordained for their relations with each other. The word "ought" might be used in connection with the stone in a statement such as: "This stone ought to fall to the ground if we let go of it." This statement would express a mere probability (though this particular prediction is very well-founded). The Ought in such a statement about an inanimate object could hardly be used in a normative sense. On the other hand, usage of the normative Ought in relation to whatever behaviour is supposed to be naturally ordained for man is apparently much more reasonable. Natural Law theory supposes that there is a law (or set of laws) of nature according to the tenets and principles of which all things, including man himself, ought to behave.

The first premise of natural law doctrine is that what the law of nature is found to be, ought to be followed. Its first problem is how to find what it is. To form a basis for discussion of the nature of the law of nature, a brief outline will be given of the main features of the doctrine's development.[8]

A distinctive feature of this development has been the prominent place given to morality. The part played by morals in formulating theories of the law of nature is sometimes expressly stated, but is more often implicit. Morality has been used in different roles. Sometimes it has been characterised as the product of the prescriptive contents of the law of nature. Sometimes it has been given the dual role of not only being such product but also being the justification, the anchor of conscience, of those prescriptions. In other words, what is, ought to be, and furthermore it ought morally to be so. Thus the Is and the legal and moral aspects of the normative Ought are formed into an amalgam which apparently makes any further questions as to the nature and validity of man-made law unnecessary.

The law of nature must contain guiding principles if it is to have any relevance to the laws which human beings make for the regulation of themselves and others. The wide variations in standards of justice and morality which may be observed at different times, among different peoples and even between different individuals, may lead to the search for one predominant guiding standard; but the variations also serve to indicate the difficulty in determining what the natural principles are to be. *"Honeste vivere, alterum non laedere, suum cuique tribuere"* are the precepts of the law, but the guidance which they offer can only be seen in the application of their attendant principles to particular cases.

A brief historical outline

The history of the law of nature begins, as do many other fields of study, with the Greeks. Greek philosophy on this subject took the form of a search for the absolute, and in particular for absolute standards of right or justice. This search was initially based on a belief in the eternal and immutable, in an absolute supernatural

---

[8] This will be a very brief outline only. For more comprehensive treatment reference should be made to larger textbooks. See *e.g.* Friedmann, *Legal Theory* 5th ed., Chaps. 7-14; Lloyd, *Introduction to Jurisprudence* 3rd ed., Chap. 3.

validity for the laws which men ought to obey. Of course what they
found was in each case influenced—perhaps determined—by what
they were looking for. The first real expression of a natural law
theory in philosophical terms derives from the sixth century B.C.
Human laws were described as having their place in the order of
things by virtue of the power of fate which controls everything. If
indeed this was a philosophy, it was certainly very conservative, not
to say highly reactionary, since its practical function was to provide
a justification of existing institutions by a bare assertion of their
absolute sanctity. The reaction to this movement in thought came
in the following century when the distinction and the possible
conflict between the laws of nature and the laws made by man was
emphasised. This constituted a kind of revolution against the potentially reactionary political implications of the previous ideologies,
which might have been used to justify laws and institutions unjusti-
fiable or even iniquitous by human standards. It is worthy of note
that the relationship between these two contrasting approaches to
the problems of man-made law and legal institutions resembles the
reaction of modern positivism to theories and doctrine concerning
natural law or the law of nature, which took place only two
centuries ago. Bentham showed just such impatience with the
spurious justifications of the status quo expressed by Blackstone.[9]
At this stage, however, a counter revolution took place in Greek
philosophy, and along came Aristotle and Plato to rebuild what
the revolutionaries had been pulling down. To this day it is probably Aristotle who has had the greatest influence on the doctrines
of the law of nature. From this time onwards, it is possible to
trace a more or less continuous development of the search for
absolute values which has remained a major subject of serious
debate until the present day. Aristotle regarded man as a part of
nature, part of matter, but also as being endowed with the distinguishing faculty of reason, which makes man something special
in the general order of things and gives him a particular prominence. This recognition of human reason as both part of nature
and as a capacity for volition, insight and discovery, formed the
basis for the Stoic conception of the law of nature. This was
developed by the Stoic philosophy into an ethical or moral
principle. The Stoics argued that reason governs all the parts of
the universe, and man—a part of this universal nature—is gov-

[9] See section III of this Chapter.

erned by reason; man lives "naturally" if he lives according to his reason. What is more, on the basis of this argument the Stoics held that it was man's moral duty to do this. Thus natural law doctrine reached a stage at which the Is of universal nature leads, via man's exercise of his critical and inquiring reason, directly to the normative Ought of man's behaviour. The normative Ought was considered to be integrally connected with, and supported by, a moral Ought.

Aristotle had given a new found philosophical impetus to the doctrine of the law of nature and had got rid of the magic which had characterised the "pre-revolutionary" doctrines. To this basic framework the Stoics added the element of religion. The way man ought naturally to behave was to be found not in man's individual reason but in divine reason. Under the guiding hand, and no doubt the eloquence, of the celebrated Roman advocate Cicero, the Stoic form of the law of nature took root in the philosophy of the Romans. The *jus naturale* became for the Romans a higher law against which the validity or rightness of human positive law could be measured, and as such it was absolute and unalterable. The principle difference between this Roman philosophy and that of the Greeks was the relatively small interest taken by the Romans in metaphysical and mystical beliefs. They were much more interested in the actual laws which could be seen generally to obtain throughout their growing empire. The *jus naturale* should, strictly speaking, refer to the rules of human conduct which are supposed to be deducible by reason from the general conditions in human society; and the Roman term *jus gentium* was, in the strict sense, limited to those parts of the *jus naturale* which were actually received and observed among all peoples—at least, among all civilised peoples.

The next of the great eras of natural law came with the religious doctrines of Thomas Aquinas. It had not been difficult for early Christian philosophers, if they so desired to give yet another turn to the original Aristotelian doctrine, by particularising the religious element in that doctrine as it was developed by the Stoics. This they did by identifying the God of the Christian religion as the source of the power of divine reason.

One of the most important practical consequences of this new development was the element of revelation which it facilitated. Part at least of the specific content of the divine law could now be found in the revealed scriptures and certain fundamental tenets and sources such as the Ten Commandments. In the particular philosophy of Thomas Aquinas, all things and beings including man, strive to reach their own perfected nature which has been stipulated by divine ordinance. The law of nature thus becomes closer to the law of God, and the normative Ought of the rules of right living, which have been ordained for man, derive further reinforcement from the moral Ought of Christian morality. A distinction was made by the Scholastics (as the followers of Aquinas are called) between the eternal law and the natural law. On one view, these were part and parcel of the same thing, but separable from each other. The natural law constituted so much of the eternal law as could be discovered by man via the exercise of his reason; but in addition certain direct revelations of the divine law have been made to provide the limited reasoning capabilities of man with a more complete picture than he could achieve by himself.[10]

What was to happen in cases of human behaviour and human law which were so particular as to be undiscoverable from any superior source of law? Aristotle was more concerned with natural or absolute justice than with natural law, but his attitude to things which are merely arbitrary or matters of convenience is applicable to both. He merely said, "It is evident which sort of thing, among things capable of being otherwise, is by nature; and which is not but legal and conventional, assuming that both are equally changeable."[11] The attitude of Thomism differed from this treatment of conventionalities by the scope which it provided for laws to change in accordance with human needs and circumstances, as long as such an exercise remained within the ordained or natural sphere. One thing which the Christian philosophy of Aquinas did not do was to lay claim to an ability to deduce from the eternal and absolute principles an answer to every possible concrete question. Its specific content was restricted to the revealed law.

The next major stage in the development of natural law came with its more secularised form, in the time of Grotius and Thomas Hobbes. These seventeenth century philosophers generally refrained from an express rejection of the scholastic conception of the divine will as the supreme source of law. They concentrated

---

[10] Aristotle, *Nichomachean Ethics*.
[11] For the Scholastics the eternal law is the law of God. The Divine law is a partial revelation, direct to man, via the church, and is put on a similar plane to natural law which is a partial discovery of the eternal law by man's application of reason to his natural inclinations.

rather on the rational nature of man, on his capacity to reason
and arrive at reasoned judgments—the feature which had dominated the later Greek philosophy. The emphasis was put by Grotius
not just on reason, but right reason. "Natural law is the dictate of
right reason indicating that any act from its agreement or disagreement with the rational nature of man has in it a moral turpitude or a moral necessity, and consequently that such act is
forbidden or commanded by God, the author of nature."[12] But
although, for Grotius, the law of nature involved a metaphysical
aspect, he gave it a practical function in parts of his pioneering
work in the field now known as International Law. For Hobbes
even the metaphysical aspect disappeared. His formula was as
follows: "The law of nature, that I may define it, is the dictate of
right reason conversant about those things which are either to be
done or omitted for the constant preservation of life and members
as much as in us lies."[13]

Although Hobbes retained the terms "natural law" and "natural
right," he broke with previous tradition and formulated a scale of
values of his own in which the chief principle of natural law was
the natural right of self-preservation. Connected with this was
Hobbes' patently political motive in using natural law to justify
the necessity of an absolute ruler, an overwhelming political power
to protect ordinary people against themselves and against their own
failings. With this stage the doctrine of the law of nature became
stripped of its religious and metaphysical character and, in this
country at least, developed into a movement in political theory,
which had only tenuous connections with its development during
the era of scholasticism. The utilitarian philosophy—the greatest
happiness of the greatest number—in the writings of Hobbes no
doubt exercised an influence on the utilitarianism of Bentham; but
Bentham, as we shall see,[14] called for a total rejection of the
doctrines of the law of nature and of natural rights. Three principal
features of the history of natural law doctrine so far traced may be
summed up as follows: the Greek and Roman philosophers
derived this law from universal nature; mediaeval and modern
theologians have found it in divine nature; and some secular

---

[12] *De Jure Belli ac Pacis.*

[13] *De Cive.* Note, however, that Hobbes regarded natural law principles as devoid of any real power, as compared with the positive law.
He was, in a sense, a positivist.

[14] See *infra*, section III of the present chapter.

philosophers have discovered it in human nature itself.

Some modern attitudes to natural law

The flexibility or vagueness, as the case may be, of natural law doctrines constitutes at once an advantage and a disadvantage. The advantage lies in their purportedly universal applicability, but they are apt to suffer from lack of precision or specific reference to particular problems. Owing partly to this disadvantage, and partly to the manifest increase in the complexity of modern legal systems, modern versions of natural law doctrines have tended to become fragmented as compared with some older traditional versions. They have become either watered-down or broken-down: watered-down in the sense that the old claims to universal and eternal validity are not always urged as strongly, and broken-down in the sense that certain more specific aspects of the nature of laws are given paramount attention, for instance the structure of legislation or the minimum content of laws.

The advent of modern positivism has been the cause of much re-thinking in the natural law camp. Much more than lip-service is often paid by natural lawyers to the claims of positivism. A leading modern advocate of natural law doctrines is Professor d'Entrèves[15] who, with reference to problems of the analysis of the nature of law, says:[16] "The positivist's answer is to sacrifice the *ought* to the *is*; the natural lawyer's to sacrifice the *is* to the *ought*; surely the problem is to express how law can express both an *is* and an *ought*, how it can be both a fact and an ought-proposition. I believe that there is an element of truth on both sides, and that the final word is not so much a matter for legal as for political theory." Having allowed this much, d'Entrèves goes on to put the evaluative and the analytical points of view alongside each other.[17] He asks the question whether the State is to be regarded as a fact or a value, and says: "If the monopoly of power in the modern state is merely a fact, then the whole structure of normative propositions that centre around it is merely a set of hypothetical imperatives, of rules concerning the use of force *if*

---

[15] *Natural Law*, Hutchinson University Library, London, 2nd ed. 1970.
[16] *Ibid* at p. 179.
[17] The terms "evaluative" and "analytical" are used here simply to refer to attitudes to the nature of law which are value-based, *e.g.* on the "goodness" or "badness" of the system, and those which are not.

and *when* the State so disposes. In that case, the 'bad man's' notion of law is correct: laws do not entail any proper sort of obligation. In order that power be binding, in order that laws should be true ought-propositions and not mere descriptions about the use of force, we must add to the mere fact of the existence of the State a value-clause, we must 'invest' its commands with a particular halo and perhaps even conceive the basic norm as a categorical imperative. We must, in other words, be able to speak not only of the power of the State, but of its authority."[18] It should be noticed, however, that the epithets *proper*, in relation to legal obligation, and *true*, in relation to ought-propositions, could well constitute the thin end of the wedge of political ideology and value-judgments, in contradistinction to objectivity in analysis—whether such analysis be legal or political.

Because it is based on some ground such as reason or conscience, a version of natural law doctrine can never aspire to complete objectivity. Nor, given its tenets, would it consider such an approach necessary or indeed worthwhile. But while this much is admitted, many modern advocates of natural law tend to stray away from insistence on the binding quality of natural law and the consequently inferior and derivative quality of positive laws, and emphasize the fact that, without reason and conscience, things just would not continue well and smoothly. The erstwhile grandiose claims of natural law to the general governance of human legal problems have been reduced to the assertion that man must legislate and administer his laws according to reason and conscience if his legal system is to be worthwhile. As d'Entrèves says, perhaps somewhat hopefully: "Old Mother Conscience still does her job well, and surely men never lack a clear knowledge of right and wrong when they are cornered and have to make basic decisions."[19] In a dilemma, or in a corner, the lawmaker's choice may lie not only between good and evil, or even good and good, but also between one form of evil and another. The work of Professor d'Entrèves evidences the fact that natural law doctrine and positivism may have complementary roles to play in the solution of knotty problems bearing on the nature of law. His attention to

[18] *Op. cit.* pp. 183-184.
[19] *Op. cit.* p. 171. The situation in which lawyers have been "cornered" and have had to look to their consciences for a just decision occurred in post-Nazi Germany. For a discussion of the types of case which arose then see Chapter 3, *infra*.

International Law is a good indicator of his attitude. "As for the predicament of the world at large," he says, "let us be perfectly clear that natural law is no cut and dried solution, no infallible cure for all our troubles. Here indeed the problem is not even that of a conflict between natural and positive law, but that of the absence of a legal order altogether. International Law, as things stand today, is a good target for the shafts of the sceptic. But, as Professor Goodhart put it very well, the weakness of international law is not due to the lack of enforcement, but 'to the absence of an international moral sense.' These words can only mean: that what matters is first to 'instaure' or restore the 'international moral sense.' The possibility of agreeing on the 'rules of the game' and abiding by them will follow as a matter of logical consequence. Surely this is where 'natural law' may have a word to say, especially if we take it, as I have tried to, as a minimum of agreement on principles."[20]

Another approach to the reappraisal of natural law doctrine is to fragment the compound of form and content, and to concentrate on specific aspects of each. Professor Fuller's work[21] provides us with a notable example of the attention which may be paid to the form, or the formal structure, of laws in order that they may be judged good, bad, or indifferent. Fuller considers there to be an "inner morality" of law without which undesirable and even iniquitous results may be produced. This so-called "inner morality" takes the form of certain principles of the making and promulgation of laws.

To be good and worthwhile laws should be of general application and should be properly promulgated. In this way, partiality is avoided, and the citizen has a fair opportunity to know what is expected of him. Laws should be prospective, as distinct from retroactive, since this avoids the "brutal absurdity of commanding a man today to do something yesterday."[22] Furthermore, the meaning of laws should be readily comprehensible: "The *desideratum* of clarity represents one of the most essential ingredients of legality."[23] The concept of *legality* is frequently referred to by Fuller, and by it he appears to imply a value judgment with regard

[20] *Op. cit.* p. 172.
[21] *The Morality of Law*, Yale University Press: Revised ed. 1969, Chap. 2.
[22] *Op. cit.* p. 59. For a further discussion of retroactivity in lawmaking, see Chap. 3, *infra*, at p. 67-68.
[23] *Op. cit.* p. 63.

to the "goodness" or "worthwhileness" of the legal system (or part of it) which is under scrutiny. Here as elsewhere, however, it seems that Fuller cannot simply be tied down to the straightforward position that without *desiderata* of the type now being discussed, law should not be acknowledged to exist at all.

Closely related to the obvious requirement of clarity is that of consistency, or the avoidance of contradictions in the laws: "It is rather obvious that avoiding inadvertent contradictions in the law may demand a good deal of painstaking care on the part of the legislator. What is not so obvious is that there can be difficulty in knowing when a contradiction exists, or how in abstract terms one should define a contradiction."[24] Lest it be thought that Fuller is simply stating a truism and that contradictions can be avoided simply by attention to logic in lawmaking, he continues: "It is generally assumed that the problem is simply one of logic. A contradiction is something that violates the law of identity by which A cannot be not-A. This formal principle, however, if it has any value at all, has none whatever in dealing with contradictory laws." In the words of another famous American jurist, Oliver Wendell Holmes, "the life of the law has not been logic, it has been experience."

The lawmaker should also take care to avoid the enactment of laws requiring the impossible. "On the face of it," says Fuller, "a law commanding the impossible seems such an absurdity that one is tempted to suppose that no sane lawmaker, not even the most evil dictator, would have any reason to enact such a law. Unfortunately the facts of life run counter to this assumption." He raises the point that most of the other *desiderata* that make up the "internal morality" of law may also be ultimately concerned with the possibility of obedience. Areas of law involving some of the more extreme examples of strict liability supply us with cases in which the almost impossible, if not the impossible itself, is demanded of the citizen.

A further principle forming part of the "internal morality of law," as Fuller calls his *desiderata* for the legal system, is that of the constancy of laws through time. This principle involves the reasonable claim that the content of laws should not be changed too frequently. The final principle enumerated by Fuller is that

---

[24] *Op. cit.* p. 65.

requiring congruence between official action and declared rule. This principle connotes predictability in the administration of laws. It may also, it is suggested, bear on other requirements of a good legal system, for instance, that the judiciary should be assumed to adopt a prospective (and not retroactive) attitude in the interpretation of statutes. In conclusion, Fuller observes: "It is easy to see that laws should be expressed in general rules that are prospective in effect and made known to the citizen. But to know how, under what circumstances, and in what balance these things should be achieved is no less an undertaking than being a lawgiver."[25]

Finally, with reference to modern attitudes to natural law which concentrate attention on certain specific aspects of its possible content, Hart's views on the "minimum content" of natural law may briefly be considered.[26] After having mentioned some of the traditional attitudes to natural law doctrine, he narrows down their content into a "core of good sense." "There are," he says, "simpler, less philosophical considerations ... which show acceptance of survival as an aim to be necessary, in a sense more directly relevant to the discussion of human law and morals. We are committed to it as something pre-supposed by the terms of the discussion; for our concern is with social arrangements for continued existence, not with those of a suicide club. We wish to know whether, among these social arrangements, there are some which may illuminatingly be ranked as natural laws discoverable by reason, and what their relation is to human law and morality. To raise this or any other question concerning *how* men should live together, we must assume that their aim, generally speaking, is to live."[27] The principle of human survival cannot be considered without any reference to underlying principles, or features, of the human condition. Hart gives five such features, namely: human vulnerability requiring mutual forbearance, evidenced in the simple exhortation "Thou shalt not kill;" approximate equality of human beings, necessitating also mutual forbearance and compromise which is the basis of both legal and moral obligation; limited altruism, since, while the majority of humans are not devils, neither are they angels; limited resources, requiring the institution

---

[25] *Op. cit.* p. 94.
[26] *The Concept of Law*, pp. 189-195.
[27] *Op. cit.* p. 188.

of property; and, finally, limited understanding and strength of will, leading to the requirement of *voluntary* co-operation within a *coercive* system. In summary, Hart says that "we can say, given the setting of natural facts and aims, which make sanctions both possible and necessary in a municipal system, that this is a *natural necessity*; and some such phrase is needed also to convey the status of the minimum forms of protection for persons, property and promises which are similarly indispensable features of municipal law.[28] It is in this form that we should reply to the positivist[29] thesis that 'law may have any content.' For it is a truth of some importance that for the adequate description not only of law but of many other social institutions, a place must be reserved, besides definitions and ordinary statements of fact, for a third category of statements: those the truth of which is contingent on human beings and the world they live in retaining the salient characteristics which they have."

The philosophy of natural law

This very brief account should serve to indicate how very flexible the doctine of the law of nature may be; between some of its features and others there is only a tenuous connection. However praiseworthy some of its features may be considered, we must be careful not to confuse the existence of a belief in something with the existence of the thing itself. The nature of faith, for instance, does not lie in proof. The humility of man may be thought of as a virtue and this humility is certainly very apparent in the desire, which characterises a great part of natural law doctrine, to find or at least conceive of a measure of validity for human laws which is superior to the stamp of positive human authority. In the search for universality, however, the doctrine has found not only its principal strength but also its principal weakness. Its speculative character has placed it at the disposal of people of widely varying political persuasions. As such it can be employed as the vehicle of reform (or even of revolution) or of reaction; it can be used and abused. "Like a harlot," says Ross, "natural law is at the disposal of everyone. The ideology does not exist that cannot be defended by an appeal to the law of nature."[30]

[28] Not necessarily private property. See *infra*, p. 33.
[29] For the meaning of "positivism" see *infra*, p. 40 *et seq.*
[30] Ross, *On Law and Justice*, p. 261.

There are many modern examples of the possibility that great iniquity may be perpetrated in the name of natural law. The fate of Jews in Europe during the Nazi régime, is a notable example of a policy of "natural supremacy." Nor are the widely varying interpretations of natural law or natural principles of society confined to the political sphere. In the economic sphere, too, opposite views can be found. Maritain wrote:[31] "The right to private ownership of material goods pertains to natural law, in so far as mankind is naturally entitled to possess for its own common use the material goods of nature; it pertains to the law of Nations, or *jus gentium*, in so far as reason necessarily concludes in the light of the conditions naturally required for their management and for human work that for the sake of the common good those material goods must be privately owned." With this view may be contrasted some initial provisions of the Constitution, or Basic Law, of the U.S.S.R. While Article 10 preserves a restricted right of private ownership in respect of a house, household and personal articles, income and savings, the fundamental principle of the economy in the soviet states is expressed in Article 4: "The socialist system of economy and socialist ownership of the instruments and means of production established as a result of the liquidation of the capitalist system of economy, the abolition of private ownership of the instruments and means of production, and the annihilation of the exploitation of man by man, shall constitute the economic foundation of the U.S.S.R."[32]

Natural doctrines represent the desire to discover, or at least the readiness to search for, the answer to problems of human law and to questions of its validity; and coupled with this is the belief in the usefulness of such a concept of the absolute. It is, however, paradoxical that the concept of such an absolute should ultimately find itself characterised by the subjective opinions of individual lawmakers and philosophers, with all the relativity that such opinions involve. Much of the doctrine involves the belief in a supernatural force from which the validity or the justification of positive law may be derived, whether such a belief is in magic or in a specific religion. A recurrent feature is the attention given to man's reason, though this was related both to physical conditions and to metaphysical speculation.

---

[31] J. Maritain, *Man and the State*, University of Chicago Press, p. 91.

[32] See *e.g.* Berman and Quigley, *Basic Laws on the Structure of the Soviet State*, Harvard, 1969.

In its references to human, man-made, positive law the doctrine of the law of nature refers to content and also to form (such as a principle of non-retroactivity in matters of legislation), but not really to its character. The Is in this doctrine consists of the law of nature, rather than the laws made by man. The inferiority of what is alternatively called "conventional" law is demonstrated by the derivation of a normative Ought, often a moral normative Ought, from the Is, depending on which particular aspect of the doctrine is being considered. Human laws are to be measured or tested against the supreme, the absolute or the general standard.

The concern of theories of natural law with the content of law leads to one of the principal opportunities for criticising the very nature of the law of nature. Unlike the positive approach to legal analysis, to which the following section of this chapter is devoted, natural law doctrine starts off from certain supposedly self-evident principles, or at least assumptions, of universal validity, and proceeds to reason from them by deduction or inference. Interpretations of the doctrine are, therefore, not limited by any empirically verifiable laws, by any existing man made laws which may be discovered by a process of practical research as distinct from limitless speculation. There is no knowing beforehand what will happen to the content of natural law. A similar remark might be made by an adherent of the modern American realist movement, which emphasises the uncertainty of what will happen in the future to the content of positive, man made law.[33] Both observations relate, however, to the content of each type of law, whereas the character of man-made law still remains a major area of investigation.

If doctrines such as those propounded by Grotius and Hobbes are separated from the main tradition of natural law theory, by placing them in the category of basic political or sociological hypotheses, the rest of the development of the law of nature which has just been outlined can be seen to involve a "dualism." The doctrine presupposes or assumes two orders, a dualism of norms or standards, in the form of the superior law, whatever form it takes, and the inferior man made positive law which is the product of human convention. The doctrine of the higher or superior law is taken for an objective reality. It presupposes the specific existence of supposed facts which lie outside man's limited sphere of

[33] See Chap. 8, section IV, *infra*.

understanding, as distinct from merely speculating upon the possibility of their existence.

A positive law has to pass certain tests if it is to be valid and these tests are provided by the particular legal system of which that law claims to form a part. Its justification or validity as a law is therefore determined by an internal standard. The law of nature, on the other hand, stipulates an external standard except in the case of laws which are held by a particular doctrine to be naturally or ethically "indifferent," in which case the provisions of positive law relating to validity are allowed to come into play. Even here, however, the indifferent human law should not be formulated in any way which might conceivably infringe the presupposed stipulations of the higher order.

From the standpoint of the analysis and criticism of positive law the law of nature requires the measuring of something known against the hypothetical standards of an order which defies empirical verification. Such a philosophy presents the remarkable phenomenon of the rational human mind setting for itself problems which it cannot hope to solve. Even if conjecture based on reason is to be deemed sufficient proof, this can hardly be cause for satisfaction. It is on account of such features that the doctrine of the law of nature has been called "one of the most astonishing features in the annals of human thought."[34]

It is sometimes said that natural law theory bears witness to man's limited imagination. Some of its offshoots, however, illustrate the fertility of man's inventive mind. The "stipulations" of nature have been filled up with numerous ideologies which have, at one time or another, been espoused by legal philosophers. When the assertions in doctrines of the law of nature are reduced to their basic and common elements, we are left with a list—and not a very long one at that—of certain features of society which might reasonably be thought of as necessary for the existence and self-preservation of any social order at all. But even here, apart, perhaps, from the basic factor of the preservation of human life, disagreement is apt to arise. Inroads can be, and often have been, made into the very principle of the sanctity of human life itself. The ancient sacrificial rites of the Aztecs and the Mayas bear witness to this, when seen from a modern standpoint, as also do Eskimo practices with those who were no longer useful (such

[34] Chroust, in an essay in *Interpretations of Modern Legal Philosophies* (1947).

practices having, however, recently been outlawed by the Canadian legislature). The relativity of moral standards might appear to reduce the list to virtually nothing.

III

We move now to the debate at the end of the eighteenth century between Blackstone and Bentham which has much influenced legal theory ever since. Blackstone was the last considerable English natural lawyer. Bentham was the earliest legal positivist trenchantly to criticise it in the foundation of his own view of the nature of law.

Blackstone's definition of municipal law is expressed in the form of a particular kind of law within a general category. For him "Law, in its most general and comprehensive sense, signifies a rule of action; and is applied indiscriminately to all kinds of action, whether animate or inanimate, rational or irrational. Thus we say, the laws of motion, of gravitation, of optics, or mechanics, as well as the laws of nature and of nations. And it is that rule of action which is prescribed by some superior and which the inferior is bound to obey."[35] The type of definition employed by Blackstone is often referred to as one *per genus et differentiam*. It was indicated in the previous chapter that the application of this form of definition to the analysis of law and legal validity is far from straightforward. It is, in fact, doubtful whether any construction of law lends itself to such treatment.

Blackstone's outline of the general category or *genus* to which the term "law" refers may lead to confusion between the descriptive and the prescriptive senses in which the word "law" may be used. The relationship between superior and inferior is thus spread over two types of law which do not have a common substantial connection, and the legally binding character of the prescriptive, normative Ought is consequently obscured. Thus Blackstone's first premise is short and simple and contains the seeds of complex confusion.

In order to differentiate human laws within the general category he says: "But laws, in their more confined sense, and in which

---

[35] Introduction to the *Commentaries on the Laws of England*, Section Two, "Of the Nature of Laws in General." The confusion between character and content is apparent even in these few words.

it is our present business to consider them, denote the rules, not of action in general, but of human action or conduct; that is, the precepts by which man, the noblest of all sublunary beings, a creature endowed with both reason and free will, is commanded to make use of those faculties in the general regulation of his behaviour." Thus Blackstone's notion of positive law attempts at the same time to look back to the governing influences on man's action and forward to his own governing influence on his fellow men—or on the legislator's inferiors. It has been seen, however, that a direct connection cannot be so simply drawn between causal and normative relations. Each of Blackstone's notions of law, and each apparently characteristic term which he uses to describe it, has a double meaning. He attempts to cover far too much and too many aspects of regulation and regularity with his definition.

It has often been alleged that Blackstone's treatment of man made law in its relation to natural law amounted to no more than verbiage. A recent article suggests, however, that such criticisms fail to take account of the philosophical climate in which the *Commentaries* were written, and it is pointed out that, merely because municipal law could be explained in isolation from the immutable principles of nature, this was not sufficient reason for ignoring "questions of rational conscience."[36] Let us, therefore, consider the way in which Blackstone deals with such matters of conscience in his account of law.

The law of nature is, for Blackstone, the will of the Maker. Just as the Maker endowed matter with principles of motion and gravity, so man himself was endowed with "certain immutable laws of human nature." He was also endowed with reason by which to regulate and restrain his free-will and to be able to discover the purport of the laws which were laid down for his governance.[37] Since the fall of man into corruption, some of the laws of the Maker have been revealed to man to assist him in an otherwise impossible task. The laws of nature thus laid down are, for Blackstone, of such authority that no human laws (that is, laws made by man) are of any validity if they purport to contradict them. What is more, the validity even of those which do

[36] J. M. Finnis, "Blackstone's Theoretical Intentions" (1967) 12 *Natural Law Forum*, 163.

[37] It is remarkable how the limited function of discovery which is attached to man's humble position in much naturalist doctrine resembles one of the excesses of legal positivism—the view that all cases can be solved by logical deduction from the general principle in a positive legal rule.

not contradict the laws of nature is derived from them.

Having outlined the respective spheres of operation of natural law and municipal law, Blackstone proceeds to make a consequent distinction relating to matters of human conscience. He makes a distinction between *mala in se* and *mala prohibita*, between actions which are bad in themselves and which ought to be prohibited on this account by human laws, and actions which are prohibited by human laws and classed as *mala* or offences for this reason alone. *Mala in se*, Blackstone says, bind the conscience, while *mala prohibita* do not. The former affect the conscience because the laws laid down in the superior forces of nature were in being before any human laws were even made, let alone transgressed. The latter, on the other hand, annex a penalty to non-compliance on account of the "positive duty" created by human laws and not on account of any pre-existing moral duty to be found in superior natural principles. "Here, conscience is no further concerned, than by directing a submission to the penalty, in case of our breach of those laws," says Blackstone. The prohibitions of man made law which do not derive any element of morality from the principles of nature, cannot themselves turn transgression into moral guilt.

There is something to be said for making a distinction between actions which are bad in themselves and actions which are not, but which may be made offences by human agency. Such a distinction might affect both the content and the scope of criminal legislation and also the scale of punishments to be attached to different types of offence. It could be useful if some kind of test or measure could be found by which to distinguish the two kinds of transgression; but whenever any such distinction has actually been attempted, positive legal systems have achieved only a very limited degree of success. In order to show the way in which even a clear moral transgression will require the intervention of human agency in creating the limits of a criminal offence which embodies it, we may take the prime example of murder. Murder in English law is the unlawful killing of a living human being within the Queen's Peace, when death occurs within a year and a day of the unlawful act. This apparently simple definition of the crime of murder is amplified, as any student of law will know, by a multitude of riders and conditions both in the definition itself and in its necessary interpretation. Even in this clear case of moral turpitude, a *malum in se* depends for its very presence in a positive law system on creative and definitive human agency. Coupled with this so called "relativity of law" is the even more obvious relativity of moral standards among human beings; even where rational conjecture as to absolute principles is made, widely different results may be produced.

Up to now we have considered criticisms which may be made of Blackstone's ideas. Let us take a look at the way in which he uses those ideas, in order to see if even further criticism is possible on this score, and in so doing consider an interesting interpretation of Blackstone's use of his natural law ideas which is given by Hart.[38] The *Commentaries* contain very little defence of laws and existing legal institutions by reference to the supposed provisions of the law of nature, but this possible tool of criticism may have been turned by Blackstone into an indirect means of justification of the laws and the Constitution of this country. This justification is to be understood in terms of the two types of wrong which have just been discussed, in which some matters are classed as morally indifferent. From such indifference, as compared with the positive stipulations of the law of nature as to man's proper conduct, Blackstone appears to conclude that a positive law or legal institution gives rise to no reason for criticism, so long as the law of nature does not have anything to say against it. Any test of moral worthiness, therefore, to which he might appear to submit parts of the positive law turns out in reality to be totally vacuous. The tirade of criticism of Blackstone's ideas and their use, which Bentham later employed in the formulation of his own views on the nature of law and morals, resulted partly from his indignation at the spurious tool of social and legal criticism produced by Blackstone's category of "matters in themselves indifferent."

For Bentham the right relationship between positive law and morality or moral criticism was expressed in the maxim: "Obey punctually, censure freely,"[39] a sentiment which has recently been echoed by a leading Scandinavian jurist.[40] For Bentham the task of the expositor and the task of the censor were separate and not to be confused, and the same applied to the respective subject matters to be investigated by each of them. It is the expositor's job to examine what the law is, and that of the censor to say what

[38] (1956) B.S.A.L.R. 169.
[39] *Fragment on Government*, ed. Harrison; Basil Blackwell, 1960. Preface, p. 10.
[40] See Ross, *On Law and Justice*, p. 32.

it ought to be. An additional reason for Bentham's annoyance at Blackstone's use of the law of nature is explicitly stated in *Fragment on Government*. In the *Commentaries* Blackstone wrote that "no human laws should be *suffered* to contradict" the laws of nature. It is not that no human laws should contradict them, but that none should be *suffered* to do so. This implies not only the absence of a moral duty to obey such a law, but also a moral duty actually to disobey. Blackstone expressly said of an act which is contrary to the laws of nature that "if any human law should allow or enjoin us to commit it, we are bound to transgress that human law, or else we must offend both the natural and the divine."[41] This explicit assertion by Blackstone is regarded by Bentham as something which turns the implications contained in the foregoing statement into a potentially dangerous doctrine. He was clearly aware of the practical and political dangers inherent in a literal interpretation put into practical operation.

So much, then, for the last real gasp of natural law doctrine in the legal writings of this country. With Bentham came the advent of legal positivism and with it the establishment of legal theory as a science of investigation as distinct from the art of rational conjecture. Bentham laid the foundations of this new approach, but, far from containing the solution to problems involving the nature of positive law, his work was only the beginning of a very long and varied series of debates which are still going on today.

IV

The doctrine of the law of nature stands for many principles which are brought together by the search for a common and superior source by which to measure the validity, the justification or the adequacy of man made positive laws. The movement in legal analysis which is generally known as "positivism" includes a wide variety of approaches to legal analysis. Again, however, some unifying characteristics are to be found. The name "positivism" is really applicable to the philosophical movement, and it is only in comparatively recent times that its legal offshoot has emerged as one of the principal portions of legal theory.

"Positivism" in legal theory connotes a method of examining man made law, which has actually been set down by men for

[41] *Commentaries*, Vol. I; Bentham's italics.

men, or "posited."[42] It connotes also the study of law as it is, as distinct from law as it ought to be. Positivist legal theory does not involve a rejection of the Ought in a moral sense as a subject unworthy of study or unrelated to law. It does, however, involve an explicit rejection of the Ought in a metaphysical sense as the direct product of a metaphysical non-positive Is. The Is of legal positivism consists in the existence of human law and its methods of study are strictly confined to this sphere of existence. We also find an Ought in this sphere but it is a non-moral, normative Ought, the Ought of legal as distinct from moral obligation. The search for the most appropriate method of relating this Ought to the Is of positive law has proved to be one of the major problems of the positive approach, and the wide variety of explanations concerning this central problem has led to differences and even vehemently expressed conflicts within the movement as a whole. Some principal aspects of these differences and conflicts will be dealt with in following chapters.

The general philosophy of positivism represented a reaction in favour of a scientific and empirical approach to the analysis of phenomena, against the metaphysical speculation which had preceded its advent. It was Hume who, in this country, dealt the final effective blow to the theoretical basis of natural law doctrine. Hume insisted on the separation of Ought from Is and took the firm line that Ought could not be derived from Is, however else the two could be related. He rejected the existence of natural law on account of its being contrary to empirical and observable truth. The Is of law could thus be brought down to earth. This was not, however, the easiest thing to do and the new type of philosophy with its legal offshoot developed only slowly. The Is was brought down to earth with such a bang that it has taken until now to put all the pieces together again. With the change of attitude in the new legal positivism came the problem of the Ought which is created by man himself, and not out of a supernatural or natural absolute power. This Ought is distinct from the moral or ethical Ought which in practice may or may not possess an ambit coincident with that of the moral Ought of popular human standards.

A common feature which is to be found in natural law doctrines, whatever their particular propositions, is the manner in which the

[42] There is, incidentally, no recognised school of thought known as "negativism," perhaps because in this sense negativism is not the negation of "positivism."

concept of the absolute is forced into moulds created for it by
subjective interpretation. The stipulations of positive law can, on
the other hand, be the object of empirical verification; a fairly
definite picture can be achieved by observation. It is true that
many positive legal rules have "furry edges."[43] Indeed, part of the
benefit which man may derive from legal rules, by which his own
behaviour is regulated, lies in their adaptability and flexibility.
This characteristic of laws is a factor which has influenced some
modern American realist views; the adherents of the modern
American movement demonstrate that sometimes all we can
really do with the specific legal rules constituting positive law is
to use them as the basis for "playing hunches" as to the way in
which judicial interpretation may direct the adaptable parts of
the rules. There is much truth in what these realists say in relation
to the actual legal provisions of a particular legal system.

Writers such as the American realists are looking rather at the
characteristics of the particular case, than at the general concept
of the systematic form of positive law. We can, however, grasp
the idea of man made law as distinct from a non-positive law of
nature without necessarily thinking of any particular legal rules.
Expressions such as "the concept of law" connote just such an
idea. From now on the expression "character of positive law"
will be used to express the idea of a system of man made, positive
regulation; we shall, in other words, be speaking of the character
of the constituent elements of law and legal systems. Distinct
from the term "character," the term "content" will henceforth
be used only when we wish to refer to the aggregate of the specific
and particular legal provisions of the actual legal system of any
state or nation. Such latter references might loosely be described
as references to what the rules say, rather than as descriptions or
analyses of what rules are.

Natural law doctrines are rife with confusions between natural
and normative laws, laws of nature and laws of man, between
laws which are supposed to exist for man and laws which he
prescribes for his own regulation. Versions of legal positivism also
contain confusions of their own. One source of possible confusion
has been the blurring of the distinction between *law* and *laws*.
Both these terms are used in a "positive" sense, but one represents
the concept of law or of a legal system as a whole, and the other

---

[43] See Hart, *The Concept of Law*, pp. 121-132; Dworkin, "Law a System
of Rules," in Summers, *Essays in Legal Philosophy*.

a mass or aggregate of specific legal provisions. It might not appear to make much difference in ordinary, loose usage, whether we speak of "the law of England" or "the laws of England." By these expressions we mean the same thing and, what is more, everybody means the same thing. When, however, we become students of law—or rather of *the* law—we may not mean the same thing by "law" and "laws" even though we think we do, and even though it does not appear to affect our ability to study the subject. In reality, however, we only study "law" in the strictest usage of that term when we come to the field of legal theory. It is only because the general term "law" is tacitly assumed to refer to the particular legal provisions in the system of laws of a state, the institutions and legal practices of which we are studying, that "law" appears to be referable to this specific area of regulation. The laws of France are different in an enormous number of respects from the laws of England, though it is often remarkable how similar if not identical results can be reached in similar situations by very different methods. On the other hand law does not mean something different to a Frenchman from what it means to an Englishman. Theories or analyses of law, it is true, differ among themselves as to the most satisfactory method of accounting for and relating the constituent characteristics of positive law—morals, force, norms and so on. But for a Frenchman and an Englishman who both accept, for instance, the view that law is best explained as consisting chiefly of "rules about force," "law" would convey the same idea.

A variant on this separation of the character of law from the specific content of a system of positive law is the distinction between the conception or idea of the general as the general, and the conception of the general as the aggregate of the particular. For the purposes of legal theory the distinction is one between the concept of law, the conception of a certain type of systematic regulation, and the idea of an aggregate of specific legal provisions. One of its principal consequences is the way in which it leads to a division of theories of law into those which begin with an analysis of the particular case and then simply express it in the plural, thus arriving at an account of what goes on in general, and those which start off from an account of some basic general principles in the character of law and then proceed to an examination of how the general characteristic is manifested in particular cases. Examples of the former method are Austin's theory of law as the commands of a sovereign and Gray's account in terms of judicial pronouncements. Of the second method the most obvious example is Kelsen's account of the way in which the general stipulation of law is "concretised" in various stages until it reaches an individual case. When each of these explanations of law comes to be considered it will be useful to bear in mind these suggested distinctions in order to separate the general notion of authority from its concrete products in particular cases. In natural law doctrine both the character and the content of human law were determined by a rationally conceived but nonetheless metaphysical absolute. Accounts of positive law which concentrate on its particular content as much as natural law theories concentrated on the valid and justifiable content of the laws of man, tend to become as disorientated as would theories of natural law in the absence of their hypothetical absolute. Such relativity can be avoided by positivist accounts of the nature of law, if they turn their attention to the character of law, and particularly if they do this by reasoning from the general concept to the particular concrete case. Unless positive accounts do this they may become at best parochial and at worst inaccurate.

The separation made by legal positivism between consideration of what law is, and of what the law ought to be, seems necessarily to involve the view that even an immoral Ought would count as law if it satisfied a formal test of legal validity—in other words, if it counted as law in a legal system. Positivism also considers it a matter of indifference, for the purposes of legal analysis, whether the legal system as a whole is virtuous or iniquitous. In addition to the consequent ability of a moral Ought to serve as a separate and extrinsic standard, by which to criticise the nonmoral normative Ought of the law, the separation provides for the identification of law at any given moment. This approach also affords a more suitable context for processes of reasoning in which law is being proved, applied or distinguished.[44]

There seems, however, to be an even more cogent reason for the distinction made by legal positivism between what law is and what law ought to be. Whilst freely admitting that the content of law, the specific content of a positive legal system, ought

[44] See Dias, "The Value of a Value-Study of Law" (1965) 28 M.L.R. 397. See also, the same author's article "Temporal Approach toward a New Natural Law," (1970) 28 C.L.J. 75, in which he argues that the concept of law adopted by a jurist will depend to a very great extent on the "time-frame" in which that concept figures.

morally to embody certain principles of fairness and human justice, it can be said with all consistency that *the law*, the content of positive law, need not match up to such standards in order to qualify as *law*. The admission which has just been made, incorporating a value-judgment as to the content of law, is quite consistent with a view of the character of law expressed solely in terms of what is. Before the advent of legal positivism the attention of legal theorists was so concentrated on examining whether human laws matched up, in respect of their particular content and form, to the general tenets of presupposed natural principles that the question of the character of positive law remained in the background. Positivism, in order to support its claims to furnish an objective and universal account of the character of law, must make a temporary exclusion of the varying content of laws from its province of examination. It is on account of their apparent refusal to accept this separation that some typical criticisms of the positivist approach are difficult to follow, for within the same anti-positivist view it is possible to find "law" and "the law" being used to mean the same thing. If the non-positivist view amounts to asserting that an analysis of the character of law or the nature of law ought to provide for the exclusion from the province of legality of all laws which do not comply with certain moral standards, it gets dangerously near to a verbal definition of law, which would claim to rule out certain considerations from the material to be investigated before we even begin. If that view required the exclusion of unjust or immoral potentialities in the character of law itself, it would simply be contrary to human experience. If the criterion to be used in identifying legal validity is to require a minimum moral standard, then the non-legal Ought would seem to lay claim not only to the characterisation of the legal Ought but also to that of the legal Is.

CHAPTER 3

THE DICHOTOMY IN PRACTICE

I

A BRIEF survey has been given in the previous Chapter of the bases and competing claims of natural law doctrine and positivism. In ensuing Chapters, discussion will centre on various interpretations of a positivist approach to legal analysis which have been adopted by writers of differing persuasions. For the moment, however, attention will be turned in the direction of a sizeable and acute practical problem which confronted the internal courts of post-war Germany after the collapse of the Nazi régime and the defeat of Germany in the Second World War. Lest it ever be thought that divisions of opinion between natural lawyers and positivists are bound to remain academic, the briefest reference to the reasoning of post-war German courts and the nature of the problems which came before them will dispel any such suspicion.

The strongly rational and scientific approach to the analysis of all social phenomena, including law, came not least from Germany, whence the well-known positivist axiom *"Gesetz als Gesetz."*[1] Such a sentiment had a considerable appeal for the legislators and the people, for it represented a straightforward, analytical and unromantic approach to the solution of some equally unromantic and immediate problems of subsistence. Respect for law, if not for legality[2], was maintained even by Adolf Hitler and his National Socialist Party in their eventual assumption of power during the early 1930's. It has been said, indeed, that Hitler came to power on the coat-tails of legality. Despite the manifest and iniquitous excesses which he later perpetrated, Hitler nevertheless took care to preserve the letter of some fundamental legislation. Two principal examples, which we shall refer to again shortly, were the Weimar Constitution of 1926 and the Criminal Code of 1871, factors were later to provide positivists with somewhat "legalistic"

---

[1] Law (duly enacted) is law—an anti-metaphysical assertion used by positivists to demonstrate the finality of a correct procedural origin of a law.

[2] "Legality" is frequently used to express an additional value-judgment as to the quality or goodness of laws. It is used, *inter alia*, by Fuller, to express his anti-positivism.

solutions to post-war legal problems. These are but two of the many features of the Nazi régime which enable us to say that Germany under Hitler was certainly not in a state of anarchy, though the extent to which the principle of legality was pursued may be a matter of argument.

The problems which are to be examined in this Chapter are characterised by the fact that iniquity may be perpetrated in the name of law. The cases are often dubbed "grudge-informer" cases, for many concerned post-war charges against informers who had acted according to the letter of Nazi statutes but who were primarily motivated by malice and an intention to harm or even eliminate the subject of the information. The iniquity of laws which permitted or even encouraged informers often lay in the apparently disproportionate penalties attaching to complaints about the régime and suchlike by those who were informed upon. As the régime became increasingly desperate as it approached collapse, so the penalties for certain complaints became increasingly disproportionate. Under one law, the penalty might be anything from one day's imprisonment to execution, according to "circumstances." Since it is clear that no circumstances could differ so drastically as to warrant such an extreme variation in penalties, the example is one of the possible iniquity of a duly enacted law. The "grudge-informer" situation arises when a charge is later brought, in the courts of the succeeding régime, in relation to actions of the informer which were within the letter of enacted law when they were done. Professor Fuller[3] puts the problem and some possible solutions, in the context of an imaginary series of events which, it is not difficult to see, are generally very similar to those in Nazi Germany. We shall consider his alternative solutions and then proceed to examine a variety of cases which actually came before the post-Nazi courts for decision. Finally, the jurisprudential and philosophical questions arising out of these cases will be discussed in general terms.

II

Some solutions in theory

Professor Fuller asks his readers to suppose themselves Minister

[3] *The Morality of Law*, revised ed., Yale U.P., 1969, appendix.

of Justice of a nation of some twenty million inhabitants, and that they are confronted at the outset of their term of office by a serious problem.

In national election attended by much disorder the Headman of a political party or society calling themselves the Purple Shirts is elected President of the Republic and his party obtains a majority of the seats in the General Assembly. The party was successful at the polls because of its campaign of reckless promises and ingenious falsifications, and because of the physical intimidation of the night-riding Purple Shirts who frightened many away from the polls who might have voted against the party. "When the Purple Shirts arrived in power they took no steps to repeal the ancient Constitution or any of its provisions. They also left intact the Civil and Criminal Codes, and the Code of Procedure. No official action was taken to dismiss any government official or to remove any judge from the bench. Elections continued to be held at intervals and ballots were counted with apparent honesty. Nevertheless, the country lived under a reign of terror." [4]

Fuller goes on to paint his colourful picture of the iniquitous Purple Shirt régime, including the mysterious disapperance of unco-operative officials, nights of terror, arbitrary seizure of property and the retrospective ratification of such gangsterism by secretly-passed statutes. "During the Purple Shirt régime a great many people worked off grudges by reporting their enemies to the party or to the government authorities. The activities reported were such things as the private expression of views critical of the government, listening to foreign radio broadcasts, associating with well-known wreckers and hooligans, hoarding more than the permitted amount of dried eggs, failing to report a loss of identification papers within five days, *etc.* As things then stood with the administration of justice, any of these acts, if proved, could lead to a sentence of death. In some cases this sentence was authorised by 'emergency' statutes; in others it was imposed without statutory warrant, though by judges duly appointed to their offices." After the collapse of the Purple Shirt régime a demand arises that these grudge-informers be punished. It is the problem confronting the reader, as a new Minister of Justice, to decide upon a course of action. Five deputies are called to give advice, and five alternative courses of action, together with justifications, are produced.

[4] *Op. cit.* p. 246.

The advice of the first deputy is simply to do nothing, since the acts which the informers reported were unlawful according to the rules of the régime then in actual control. Though the principles of law then obtaining differed from those of the present régime in ways which may be considered detestable, they were nevertheless then the law of the land. To condemn some of the Purple Shirt laws but to condone others would lead to arbitrariness and lack of certainty. "If we now seek to unscramble the acts of the Purple Shirt régime, declaring this judgment invalid, that statute void, this sentence excessive, we shall be doing exactly the thing we most condemn in them."[5]

The second adviser reaches the same conclusion, but by exactly the opposite route: "A legal system presupposes laws that are known, or can be known, by those subject to them. It presupposes some uniformity of action and that like cases will be given like treatment.... In my opinion law in any ordinary sense of the word ceased to exist when the Purple Shirts came to power.... We must put this whole dark, lawless chapter of our history behind us like a bad dream.... Let us do nothing about the so-called grudge-informers. What they did was neither lawful nor contrary to law, for they lived, not under a régime of law, but under one of anarchy and terror." On the other hand, Fuller's third deputy declares himself suspicious of any reasoning which smacks of "either-or" alternatives, and considers it wrong to assume either that the Purple Shirt régime was in some way outside the realm of law or that all its doings should be regarded as being entitled to full credence as the acts of a lawful government. He regards the conclusion reached by his two colleagues as both ethically and politically impossible. He therefore suggests: "If we must condemn the criminal acts of the party and its members, it would seem absurd to uphold every act which happened to be canalized through the apparatus of a government that had become, in effect, the *alter ego* of the Purple Shirt party. We must, therefore, in this situation, as in most human affairs, discriminate. Where the Purple Shirt philosophy intruded itself and perverted the administration of justice from its normal aims and uses, there we must interfere." The fourth deputy rejects this method of treatment completely, saying that the proposal to pick and choose among the acts of the deposed régime is thoroughly objectionable. "It is," he says, "Purple

---

[5] *Cf.* the surprising but unassailable reasoning of Lord Reid in D.P.P. v. Knuller (Publishing, Printing and Promotions Ltd.) (1972) 2 All E.R. 898.

Shirtism itself, pure and simple. There is only one way of dealing with this problem that is compatible with our philosophy of law and government and that is to deal with it by duly enacted law, I mean, by a special statute directed towards it. Let us study this whole problem of the grudge-informer, get all the relevant facts, and draft a comprehensive law dealing with it." He is not unaware of the many difficulties involved in such a course, not least of the problem of defining the.acts to be the objects of retroactive condemnation, and of the ethical difficulties raised by retroactive criminality in any form. Nevertheless, the choice between evils should be squarely faced.

The final piece of advice, from the fifth deputy, is a remarkable one but perhaps not unacceptable. He notes the irony of condemning the "criminal" aspects of Purple Shirtism by retroactive legislation, describing such a method as a resort to one of the most iniquitous devices of the deposed régime. He suggests a very rough compromise: "This matter of the grudge-informer is already in the process of straightening itself out. . . . The people are quietly handling this thing themselves in their own way and if we leave them alone, and instruct our public prosecutors to do the same, there will soon be no problem left for us to solve. There will be some disorders, of course, and a few innocent heads will be broken. But our government and our legal system will not be involved in the affair and we shall not find ourselves hopelessly bogged down in an attempt to unscramble all the deeds and misdeeds of the Purple Shirts." It is true that such a recourse to gun-law might avoid some of the practical or ethical difficulties involved in the other four courses of action suggested by his colleagues. Nevertheless, it would from a legal and ethical point of view create more problems than it would solve, or at least avoid. After all, one of the most fundamental aims of any legal system is to secure physical order and safety and the protection of individuals and their property against random attacks.

Needless to say, these five alternative approaches to the solution of this knotty problem do not cover all the possibilities, but they do serve as very useful indicators of the typical and major approaches which might be made. Two involve doing something and three involve doing nothing. None specifically mentions either natural law or positivist justifications, though it is possible to read between the lines and to detect evidence of one or other of these persuasions. Let us now turn to the decisions in some actual cases in order to discover evidence of natural law or positivism.

III

Some solutions in practice

One of the most celebrated of recent jurisprudential debates concerning a practical dilemma is that between Professor Hart and Professor Fuller.[6] The controversy between these two distinguished disputants arose out of a report in the *Harvard Law Review* of the decision of a provincial court of appeal in post-war Germany which determined the fate of a grudge-informer.[7] In 1944 the defendant, wishing to be rid of her husband, reported to the authorities derogatory remarks he made about Hitler while home on leave from the German army. The defendant wife (the defendant in the post-war charge) having testified against him, the husband was sentenced to death by a military tribunal apparently pursuant to statutes making it illegal to assert or repeat any statements inimical to the welfare of the Third Reich. After having served some time in prison, and at a time when the German military could not afford to kill its own personnel, the husband was sent to the Eastern Front. He survived the war, and afterwards began an indictment against his wife for the crime of unlawful deprivation of liberty under paragraph 239 of the German Criminal Code of 1871. As in the case of Fuller's hypothetical example[8] this fundamental piece of legislation had continued in force throughout the period of the Nazi régime. The end result of the issue in the provincial appeal court was that the sentencing judge (who had also been indicted for the alleged offence on account of his having passed sentence and so operated as a direct cause in the series of events) was acquitted of all liability. It was no doubt politic and prudent to do this, for in such a situation there is ample support for a plea of duress.[9] The wife, however, was convicted of the

---

[6] (1958) 71 Harv. L.R. 593-629; 630-672. See Lloyd, *Introduction to Jurisprudence* (3rd ed.) pp. 240-248 for essential extracts. For a survey of the debate, see Section IV of the present Chapter.

[7] (1951) 64 Harv. L.R. 1005-1007.

[8] *Supra.* p. 48.

[9] If the accused in such a case was liable to the death sentence, it would no doubt have been folly for judges deliberately to flout the régime even if they had wished to do so. But see, further, below as to the decision.

offence on the grounds that she utilised the Nazi law out of her own free choice, a law which was "contrary to the sound conscience and sense of justice of all decent human beings" to bring about the death of her husband.

In an article commenting on this report in the Harvard Law Review upon which Hart and Fuller based their discussion, Pappe[10] notes that the provincial court of appeal, in setting aside the earlier acquittal of the accused wife, did not hold the Nazi legislation in question to be invalid. Although the court considered it to be highly iniquitous and to have been regarded as "terror law" by most of the German people, it did not violate natural law. The military court had therefore acted within its legal competency and the actions of its judges could not, therefore, be impugned. The decision of the provincial court of appeal was, however, inconsistent in some measure, since one of its reasons for holding the wife's actions to be criminal was that they were "contrary to the sound conscience and sense of justice of all decent human beings." It is extremely difficult to see how such reasoning can stand consistently beside a refusal to hold the relevant legislation to be in violation of the principles of natural law. The nature of these principles would, after all, be expressed in the same type of language which is used to describe natural law.

This much-criticised decision is not representative of later approaches to the problem in issue. There was, however, for a time, a paucity of the informative decisions in the type of case immediately in question here, owing to the fact that in the first years following the war, such cases were adjudicated under the Allied Control Commission laws and directives. Article 1 of *Military Government Law No. 1: Abrogation of Nazi Law* expressly abrogated certain laws of the Nazi period, and Article II provided: "No German law, however enacted or enunciated, shall be applied judicially or administratively within the occupied territory in any instance where such application would cause injustice or inequality, either (a) by favouring any person because of his connection with the National Socialist Party, its formations or affiliated or supervised organisations or (b) by discriminating against any person by reason of his race, nationality, religious beliefs or opposition to the National Socialist Party or its doctrines." Within the Legal Division of the Control Division there was some doubt as to the

---

[10] (1960) 23 M.L.R. 260: "On the Validity of Judicial Decisions in the Nazi Era."

exact effect of Article II, in particular as to whether it involved the express abrogation of laws of the type which it described (as in Article I), or whether it merely gave the Allied Control Commission the right to publish further lists so as to add to the content of Article I. This doubt was, however, part of a rather different problem from the one under discussion; for the Allied Control Commission could be regarded as having imposed its own wishes and values, as it were, *ab extra*. The post-war German courts themselves were faced with the acute problem of determining the status of laws which had formed part of the continuing legal system[11] of which they themselves were now officers.

A more informative case, with almost identical facts, was decided at a higher level in 1952. The Federal Supreme Court was faced with the following situation. The husband of the accused served with the German army from 1940 onwards, while his wife led an adulterous life at home. After an unsuccessful attempt had been made on Hitler's life on July 20, 1944, he wrote to his wife, saying: "If Hitler had been done in, this dirty mess would be all over." The accused handed this and other letters to the local party leader, and after being found by her husband at home with another soldier, and the ensuing acrimony, she again denounced her husband to the Nazi party. He was subsequently arrested and tried by a court-martial. The presiding officer told the wife that she was under no obligation to give evidence under oath; that the accused husband lay under threat of capital punishment; and that, without her sworn evidence, proof of the charge against the husband was likely to be insufficient.[12] The wife nevertheless insisted on giving evidence under oath, with the result that her husband was sentenced to death. He was not, however, executed but kept under arrest and finally returned to his army unit in April, 1945, and survived to bring a charge against the wife.

In 1951 a court of first instance acquitted her of any criminal liability, saying that the court-martial which had passed sentence on her husband was lawfully constituted and had acted within the law; and that, while a highly educated person would have acted unlawfully in denouncing another in the circumstances of the time, the accused, being an ordinary member of the public,

---

[11] Since the rise to power of the National Socialist Party and of its officers was as a result rather of infiltration than of revolution.

[12] The justice meted out to the accused husband was not, therefore, completely arbitrary, though the degree of punishment was iniquitous.

had acted without the criminal intent necessary to support the charge. The Federal Supreme Court, however, sent the case back. The judgment was strong and clear, but there was nevertheless no reference to natural law or to supra-positive norms of a higher order. Its judgment was, in fact, wholly positivistic, relying as it did for authority on the established rules and principles of the German criminal law and of the Weimar Constitution. The Federal Supreme Court held[13] that, even on the assumption that the statute was legally valid, there was insufficient justification, in the circumstances of the case, for a condemnation. The sentence passed by the court-martial was arrived at without due consideration being given to the Nazi statute and to the established principles of the German criminal law.

The Nazi statute required the incriminating remarks to be made in public, whereas they were actually made solely within the most intimate and private relationship, namely marriage. No special circumstances were adduced to rebut the privacy implied by this relationship. The assumption of guilt on the part of the court-martial was therefore derived from an arbitrary and unlawful interpretation of the law. If the death sentence had actually been carried out, the execution would have been a case of criminal homicide according to the provisions of the Criminal Code. Furthermore, one of the immemorial unwritten principles of German criminal law prohibits cruel and excessively hard penalties.[14] The statute was designed, purportedly, to protect the military morale of the German people, but the injury to that interest in the present case was minimal. Applying its long-standing principles of interpretation, some of which arose out of legislation which had continued in force throughout the Nazi period, the Federal Supreme Court held that the sentence passed by the court-martial was pronounced, not in the course of applying the law, but as a matter of arbitrary abuse of judicial authority.

If what was done was thus to be held to constitute the crimes of unlawful deprivation of liberty and attempted murder, some distinction had to be found between the criminality of the wife's actions and the process of the court-martial if its judges were not to be adjudged accessory to these crimes. It was held to be no

---

[13] 1 ST R 123/51; BGHST 3, 110-129 (1952).

[14] *Cf.* The Constitution of the United States of America, Eighth Amendment, about which there has been controversy in relation to the constitutionality of the death penalty.

defence to the wife that she claimed to have trusted in the legality of the court-martial procedure. It was held that there was, despite the warped ideas and values of many people in Nazi Germany, an awareness that the legal process could be abused for purposes of intimidation and suppression. The Federal Supreme Court held it to be a matter of common knowledge that the popular sense of right and wrong, far from being stifled during the Nazi period, was in fact heightened. The accused did not act to reveal crime, but merely sought a means of getting rid of her husband so that she could continue her adulterous life. Her malicious motive thus negated what might, to a person with a *bona fide* belief in the legality of the statute, process and sentence, have been a defence. The reasoning was peculiar to this case, the merits of which were considered to dictate the result that she was guilty of crime. No generalisations as to the breach of natural or supra-positive norms were delivered. Furthermore, the judges of the court-martial, though they were not acting lawfully in the execution of public justice, had the defence of intimidation. Indeed, a judge or official who refused to obey orders was in danger of his life.

The result of this case is satisfying for the legal positivist who, despite his acceptance of the position that law is valid so long as it emanates from sources recognised as conferring legal validity, nevertheless abhors the particular content of such laws as the one in question. The decision of the Federal Supreme Court indicates that the legislators—perhaps, rather, the political pressure groups within the party—were hoist by their own petard. As is frequent in the case of a dictatorship, the Nazi leaders and policy-makers were driven to perverting procedure as distinct from the substantive law. It was on procedural grounds that the judgment of the Federal Supreme Court was based, and not on any natural law-orientated rejection of the content of the Nazi legislation in question.

This decision is *ad hoc* and does not contain the seeds of any general approach to the grudge-informer situation and allied problems. It is possible for both positivists and natural lawyers to derive some satisfaction from the case. The positivist will note that the solution was reached without any express invocation of supra-positive law, while the natural lawyer will no doubt rejoice in the result and also look favourably on the method by which the legal position of the court-martial judges was differentiated from that of the accused wife. It is possible to find many elements of compromise in the Federal Supreme Court decision, and the case may be seen to represent a middle way between competing principles and methods of solving the problem.

There are, however, many post-Nazi decisions which rely heavily if not completely on natural law doctrine or the invocation of supra-positive norms to counter the Nazi injustices. A strong antipositivistic trend began in a judgment of a district court[15] at Wiesbaden in 1945. The plaintiff's parents, who were Jews, were deported in 1942 and their property was confiscated. A few years later they died in a concentration camp. The defendants in this civil action for restitution subsequently acquired the said property from the Finance Office, but were ordered to restore it in this post-war judgment. "According to the doctrine of natural law," said the court, "there exist certain rights which the state cannot abolish by legislative act. These are rights which are so deeply rooted in the nature and essential characteristics of human beings that their abrogation would destroy the nature of man as a spiritual and moral being." The laws by which the property of Jews was authorised to be confiscated were held to contravene natural law and were therefore held to be null and void.

A blanket condemnation and nullification of all Nazi laws simply on account of their pedigree would, of course, have been as impolitic as it would have been impractical. An interesting case arose in 1947 before the Supreme Regional Court at Kiel, in which a distinction was drawn between "absolutely immoral laws beyond the power of any government" and valid military measures taken in the course of what was, admittedly, considered to have been an illegal, aggressive war. The court was of opinion that a decree of Hitler ordering the extermination of certain inmates of a concentration camp, on the pretext that they were no longer able to work, was such a severe violation of the idea of justice that it should be regarded as void *ab initio*. On the other hand, a Nazi law imposing the death penalty for deserting from the Army during the Second World War was held valid and enforceable despite the fact that this war had been judged to be an illegal

---

[15] The Bundesverfassungsgericht, or Federal Constitutional Court, is a special court established by the Fundamental Law of 1945. The civil and criminal courts are the Bundesgerichtshof (Federal Supreme Court), the Oberlandesgerichte (Courts of Appeals), Landgerichte (District Courts) and Amtsgerichte (Local Courts). This decision is therefore at a low level.

war of aggression by the decision of the International Military Tribunal at Nuremberg. The court in this case affirmed the decision of a lower court which had convicted an army deserter who had killed a policeman who tried to arrest him. Evidence which indicated that the deserter was acting out of motives of implacable opposition to the Hitler regime was held to be irrelevant.[16]

Not all decisions arrived at on the basis of admittedly objectionable statutes were held, in the post-war cases, to be objectionable *per se*, while many decisions based on pre-Nazi decisions were held to be so. "Neither a purely legislative nor a purely judicial review of the legal Nazi legacy could offer a comprehensive solution. The Federal Constitutional Court ... therefore developed and applied sociological theory of law with a view to a compromise solution; *i.e.* a solution which permits the courts to weed out the unwholesome, while preserving such legal relationships as, though based on Nazi enactments, require preservation in the interest of legal continuity and order."[17] Let us now consider the result of the application of some of the more broadly-based principles which the constitutional courts have, by reason of the nature of the problems arising for solution, been able to apply.

The *Grundgesetz*, or fundamental law, of the West German Federal State of May, 1949, declares[18] that the German people *acknowledge*[19] inviolable and inalienable human rights as the basis of every human community. It speaks of these rights as *guaranteed*, a term which indicates that they are not themselves to be considered as the product of the constituent power or legislature. This and subsequently enumerated rights are declared to be immediately binding on the legislature, executive and judiciary, and it is further provided that in no case may the legislature violate the essential content of a fundamental right.[20] Furthermore, in most cases the Constitutional Court of the individual *Land* or province has the ultimate decision concerning the application of

[16] For further decisions of the immediate post-war period, see Bodenheimer: "Significant Developments in German Legal Philosophy since 1945," (1954) 3 Am. Jol. Comp. Law, 379.

[17] Pappe: "On the Validity of Judicial Decisions in the Nazi Era," (1960) 23 M.L.R. 260.

[18] Article 1.

[19] Italics supplied, to emphasize the declaratory, as distinct from creative, effect.

[20] Articles 6 and 19; for a full discussion, see Rommen, (1959) 4 Nat. Law Forum 1: "Natural Law in the Decisions of the Federal Supreme Court and of the Constitutional Courts in Germany."

the provisions of the provincial constitutions which, in effect, establish within the constitution itself a gradated system of rules and values. "The general revival of natural law, the universal abhorrence of the misdeeds of a régime that 'made injustice a system,' and this distinction of rank among the provisions of constitutions produced as a necessary consequence the explicit establishment of judicial review."[21] As Rommen indicates,[22] it was a peculiarity of continental legal thinking that this review was reserved to special constitutional courts.

A gradation or hierarchy among constitutional principles is created in the *Grundgesetz* and in the constitutions of most of the individual *Länder*. Lest doubt be cast on the fact that some provisions are more "fundamental" than others, and that one or a small group of articles is regarded as the final authority, it should be pointed out that the principles which find expression therein transcend all positive law, even positive constitutional law. However, "to avoid the continual threat of turning fundamental rights into merely relative values, they are given explicit and solemn acknowledgment by the constitutions."[23] The *Bundesverfassungsgericht*, or Federal Constitutional Court has held[24] that these fundamental principles are limitations on the original constituent power itself. With reference to the first nineteen articles of the Federal Constitution, the Federal Supreme Court has said: "They are referred to in the *Grundgesetz* as inviolable and inalienable human rights; not as granted by the Constitution, but as existing before it and independently of it.... Not even anterior law can be applied if it violates them...."[25] The *Grundgesetz* obliges every judge to acknowledge the suprapositive rank of the genuine fundamental rights. That compels him to the juridical conclusion that these rights were valid always even *before* the *Grundgesetz* was formally ordained; they were thus juridically valid also during the rule of the Nazi régime."[26]

The Federal Supreme Court and the Federal Constitutional Court have even, following some decisions of provincial Constitutional Courts, accepted that it is not a contradiction in terms to

[21] *Ibid.* p. 7.

[22] *Ibid.* p. 8.

[23] *Ibid.* p. 17.

[24] 2 B Verf G 51.

[25] An interesting assertion to set against the strongly positivist nature of Kelsen's concept of the basic norm; see further, Chapter 6, *infra*.

[26] Advisory opinion 11 BGHZ 81 with regard to 6 BGHZ 208.

declare that a constitution may itself contain unconstitutional norms. This position is justified by the doctrine that the Constitution contains positive norms of lower and higher rank, and that the norms of the highest rank, or the most fundamental of rights, are recognised as suprapositive norms which are not created but merely recognised by the Constitution. The Federal Supreme Court made an obvious reference to the Nazi régime when it held[27] that a "denial of suprapositive *Recht*[28] binding upon the constituent power would make a constitution-maker *rechtmässig*, as if he intended only to legalise an arbitrary and tyrannical régime and thus make it binding on the judiciary."

The Federal Constitutional Court set the seal on the fate of many Nazi laws when it said:[29] "The idea that the original constituent power may ordain anything according to mere will would be a relapse into the spirit of a value-free legal positivism which has been overcome in recent juridical science and practice. Experience under the Nazi régime has taught that even the legislator may posit injustice, and that, consequently, the ordinary administration of justice should be armed against a possible development of similar régimes so that, in the extreme case, it may be able to give effect to the principle of substantive justice in preference to the principles of the security and certainty of the legal order."

IV

The jurisprudential debate

Enough has been said already about the possible solutions in theory to the grudge informer situation and allied problems, and about the *dicta* and decisions in decided cases in this area, to show that any natural law—positivist controversy based on such a situation will not easily resolve itself into two clearly-defined opposing positions. However, the debate alluded to earlier[30] between Hart

[27] 11 BGHZ 2, advisory opinion according to para. 80, BVGG—the fundamental norms of the Constitution.

[28] The term *Recht* connotes both *law* and *justice*; it is possibly due to the strength of positivism in England for such a time that we do not have an equivalent term. See Salmond, (1895) 11 L.Q.R. 121.

[29] 3 B Verf. G 231.

[30] Hart, "Positivism and the Separation of Law and Morals," (1958) 71 Harv. L.R. 593-629; Fuller, "Positivism and Fidelity to Law," *ibid*. pp. 630-672.

and Fuller is an excellent example of the manner in which positivist and antipositivist may do battle. Their debate arose out of the report of a relatively early and unauthoritative post-war decision of the new German legal system, but its implications for jurisprudence reach very much further than the confines of that particular case.

One German legal philosopher of note who shared the pre-war positivist attitude to the nature of law was Gustav Radbruch. He held that any resistance to an evil or ill-thought-of law should remain a matter for the personal conscience. It should, he thought, be worked out by the individual as a moral problem, and the validity of a law could not be impugned by showing that its requirements were morally evil or even by knowing that the effect of compliance with the offending law would be even worse than the effect of disobedience.

Austin, one of the early positivists, refuted the view that laws which conflict with fundamental principles of morality thereby cease to be laws. Indeed, he went further and described such a conviction as "stark nonsense."[31] However, Austin and Bentham were also of opinion that, though law should be accounted for in strictly positivist terms, nevertheless if laws reached a certain intolerable degree of iniquity then there would be a plain *moral* obligation to resist them and disobey.

With reference to legal analysis itself, as distinct[32] from the question of obedience to laws, it has been said that "legal theorists are engaged in a form either of cartography or of ideological warfare."[33] During the Nazi period, Radbruch's views changed dramatically, and the ideology which moved Radbruch to change his role from that of a cartographer was a pressing one. He "concluded from the ease with which the Nazi régime had exploited subservience to mere law—or expressed, as he thought, in the 'positivist' slogan 'law as law' (*Gesetz als Gesetz*) and from the failure of the German legal profession to protest against the enormities which they were required to perpetrate in the name of law, that 'positivism' (meaning here the insistence on the separation of law as it is from law as it ought to be) had powerfully con-

---

[31] John Austin, Lectures on Jurisprudence (ed. Campbell) I, p. 215.
[32] According to some views about to be discussed, such a distinction would serve only to beg the question.
[33] Honoré: Groups, Laws and Obedience: in *Oxford Essays in Jurisprudence*, Second Series, ed. A. W. B. Simpson, O.U.P. 1973; p. 1.

tributed to the horrors. His considered reflections led him to adopt the doctrine that the fundamental principles of humanitarian morality were part of the very concept of *Recht* or legality and that no positive enactment or statute, however clearly it was expressed and however clearly it conformed with the formal criteria of validity of a given legal system, could be valid if it contravened basic principles of morality."[34]

Hart looks with sympathy on the motivation behind Radbruch's *volte face* but nevertheless describes it as naïve. A more fundamental question, equally germane to the Nazi situation, is as to why emphasis on the slogan "law is law," and the distinction between law and morals, acquired a sinister character in Germany, but elsewhere, as with the Utilitarians themselves, went along with the most enlightened[35] liberal attitudes. In contradistinction to Radbruch's reaction to the Nazi tyranny, perpetrated in many cases in the very name of the law, Hart says: "Surely the truly liberal answer to any sinister use of the slogan 'law is law' or of the distinction between law and morals is, 'Very well, but that does not conclude the question. Law is not morality; do not let it supplant morality."

The result of the prosecution of one grudge informer, and the decision of the regional court at Bamberg in 1949 have been discussed.[36] Hart says of this case: "The unqualified satisfaction with this result seems to me to be hysteria. Many of us might applaud the objective—that of punishing a woman for an outrageously immoral act.... There were, of course, two other choices. One was to let the woman go unpunished; one can sympathise with and endorse the view that this might have been a bad thing to do. The other was to face the fact that if the woman were to be punished it must be pursuant to the introduction of a frankly retrospective law and with a full consciousness of what was sacrificed in securing her punishment in this way. Odious as retrospective criminal legislation and punishment may be, to have pursued it openly in this case would at least have had the merits of candour. It would have made plain that in punishing the woman a choice had to be made between two evils, that of leaving her unpunished and that of sacrificing a very precious

---

[34] (1958) 71 Harv. L.R. at p. 617.
[35] Hart's sympathy with the Utilitarians is clear elsewhere in his writings, *e.g. Law, Liberty and Morality*, O.U.P., 1962.
[36] *Supra*, p. 51.

principle of morality endorsed by most legal systems."[37]

Professor Fuller's divergent opinion on this issue is summed up in these words: "Most of the issues raised by Professor Hart's essay can be restated in terms of the distinction between order and good order. Law may be said to represent order *simpliciter*.[38] Good order is law that corresponds to the demands of justice, or morality, or men's notions of what ought to be."[39] In his book *The Morality of Law*[40] he argues that, in addition to the claims to respect and obedience which make up the *external* morality of the law, there exist certain other criteria (such as identifiability and non-retroactivity) which constitute law's *internal* morality.[41] He criticises the incompleteness of a strictly positivist account of law in saying: "There is a twofold sense in which it is true that law cannot be built on law. First of all, the authority to make law must be supported by moral attitudes that accord to it the competency it claims. Here we are dealing with a morality external to law, which makes law possible.[42] But this alone is not enough. We may stipulate that in our monarchy[43] the accepted 'basic norm' designates the monarch himself as the only possible source of law. We still cannot have law until our monarch is ready to accept the internal morality of law itself."[44] Fuller adds that these external and internal moralities of law reciprocally influence one another; a deterioration of the one will almost inevitably produce a deterioration in the other.

Professor Hart, he says, neglects almost completely what Fuller calls the "internal morality of law." "In this," says Fuller, "I believe he is profoundly mistaken. It is his neglect to analyse the demands

[37] *Op. cit.* at p. 619. It may be noted that both Radbruch and Fuller would have preferred retrospective legislation. For further remarks on retroactivity in lawmaking, see later in this Chapter.

[38] A notable admission.

[39] (1958) 71 Harv. L.R. at p. 644. It was a fellow countryman of Professor Fuller who said that you cannot please all of the people all of the time.

[40] Yale U.P., 1969, revised edition.

[41] Not, it is suggested, a term of art, but a term of reference, to Fuller's own concept of law. Hart's use of "internal" and "external" in relation to the nature of rules has different connotations. See Chapter 5, *infra*.

[42] The last phase contains, it is submitted a preconceived concept of law which it is Fuller's object to analyse. It appears to imply that obedience to law is synonymous with its existence.

[43] Fuller uses, for the sake of argument, the simple picture of a single monarch.

[44] *Op. cit.* p. 645.

of a morality of order that leads him ... to treat law as a datum projecting itself into human experience and not as an object of human striving. When we realise that order itself is something that must be worked for, it becomes apparent that the existence of a legal system, even a bad or evil legal system, is always a matter of degree.[45] When we recognise this simple fact of everyday legal experience, it becomes impossible to discuss the problems presented by the Nazi régime with a simple assertion: 'Under the Nazis there was law, even if it was bad law.' We have instead to inquire how much of a legal system survived the general debasement and perversion of all forms of social order that occurred under the Nazi rule, and what moral implications this mutilated system had for the conscientious citizen forced to live under it."[46]

Hart is critical of Radbruch's changed view and says that only confusion can arise from his approach. "For if we adopt Radbruch's view, and with him and the German courts[47] make our protest against evil law in the form of an assertion that certain rules cannot be law because of their moral iniquity, we confuse one of the most powerful, because it is the simplest, forms of moral criticism. If with the Utilitarians we speak plainly, we say that laws may be law but too evil to be obeyed. This is a moral condemnation which everyone can understand and it makes an immediate and obvious claim to moral attention. If, on the other hand, we formulate our objection as an assertion that these evil things are not law, here is an assertion which many people do not believe, and if they are disposed to consider it at all, it would seem to raise a whole host of philosophical issues before it can be accepted."[48]

Paradoxically, however, it is Fuller's contention that Hart's approach itself opens the way to confusion. "So far as the courts are concerned, matters certainly would not have been helped if, instead of saying, 'This is not the law,' they had said, 'This is law but it is so evil we will refuse to apply it.' Surely moral confusion reaches its height when a court refuses to apply something it admits to be law...."[49] Professor Hart, he indicates, would

[45] It is difficult to see how this view bears out any inadequacy in Hart's analysis. Hart's view, and that of Utilitarians in general, can readily accommodate the notion of an admitted law which is nevertheless undesirable, owing to content or method of promulgation or implementation.

[46] *Op cit.* p. 646.

[47] Not all of them, or in all cases, as has been discussed above.

[48] *Op. cit.* p. 620.

[49] *Op. cit.* p. 655.

not in fact advocate such an approach to the grudge-informer situation and allied problems. Oddly enough, Hart's preference for the retroactive statute is one which he shares with Radbruch, but Fuller adds: "The informer problem was a pressing one, and if legal institutions were to be rehabilitated in Germany it would not do to allow the people to begin taking the law into their own hands, as might have occurred while the courts were waiting for a statute."[50] Fuller's conclusion represents something of a compromise, though it is still of an antipositivistic bent. "While I would not subscribe to all of Radbruch's post-war views—especially those relating to 'higher law' I think he saw, much more clearly than does Professor Hart, the true nature of the dilemma confronted by Germany in seeking to rebuild her shattered legal institutions. Germany had to restore both respect for law and respect for justice. Though neither of these could be restored without the other, painful antinomies were encountered in attempting to restore both at once, as Radbruch saw all too clearly. Essentially Radbruch saw the dilemma as that of meeting the demands of order, on the one hand, and those of good order, on the other. Of course no pat formula can be derived from this phrasing of the problem. But, unlike legal positivism, it does not present us with opposing demands that have no living contact with one another, that simply shout their contradictions across a vacuum. As we seek order, we can meaningfully remind ourselves that order itself will do us no good unless it is good for something. As we seek to make our order good, we can remind ourselves that justice itself is impossible without order, and that we must not lose order itself in the attempt to make it good."[51]

Positivism and justice

In *The Concept of Law* Hart prefaces his discussion of justice and morality with St. Augustine's rhetorical question: "What are states but robber-bands enlarged?"[52] The quotation is particularly apposite to describe some of the cases mentioned in the foregoing discussion. If states are something more, however, than robber-bands enlarged,[53] and if law is to be analysed otherwise than in

---

[50] *Op. cit.* p. 655; retroactivity in lawmaking is discussed later; *infra.* pp. 67-68.

[51] *Op. cit.* p. 657.

[52] Confessions, iv, quoted in *The Concept of Law*, Chap. 8 p. 152.

[53] *Cf.* Hart's description of Austin's analysis as the "gunman situation writ large": *The Concept of Law*, Chap. 2, p. 19 *et seq.*

terms of *formal* validity alone, what further features are necessary and how are they to be described and measured? Hart indicates the relativity of the concept of justice, and the consequent difficulty of isolating material factors in legal validity, when he says: "A tall child may be the same height as a short man, a warm winter the same temperature as a cold summer, and a fake diamond may be a genuine antique. But justice is far more complicated than these notions because the shifting standard of relevant resemblance between different cases incorporated in it not only varies with the type of subject to which it is applied, but may often be open to challenge even in relation to a single type of subject."[54]

Hans Kelsen who, as will be seen in a later chapter,[55] advocates a stricter and more formal positivism than Hart, goes even further in emphasising the relativity of value-judgments: "If the history of human thought proves anything, it is the futility of the attempt to establish, in the way of rational considerations, an absolutely correct standard of human behaviour, and that means a standard of human behaviour as the only just one, excluding the possibility of considering the opposite standard to be just too. If we may learn anything from the intellectual experiences of the past, it is the fact that only relative values are accessible to human reason; and that means that the judgment to the effect that something is just cannot be made with the claim of excluding the possibility of a contrary judgment of value. Absolute justice is an irrational ideal or, what amounts to the same, an illusion—one of the eternal illusions of mankind."[56]

The internal courts of post-war Germany were certainly not concerned to formulate any concept of absolute justice; they were confronted with a variety of puzzling cases, all of which demanded a solution which was at once rapid, conscionable and practical. But though a positivist would deny that the search for justice in these difficult cases was based on any natural law foundation, even as strict a positivist as Kelsen would not deny the weighing of factors as a worthwhile *moral* exercise. "The view that moral principles constitute only relative values does not mean that they constitute no value at all; it means that there is not one moral system, but that there are several different ones, and that, con-

---

[54] *The Concept of Law*, Chap. 8, p. 156
[55] *Infra*. Chap. 6, on the Pure Theory of Law.
[56] Kelsen, *What is Justice?*, Univ. of California Press, 1971, Chap. 1, p. 21.

sequently, a choice must be made among them. Thus, relativism imposes upon the individual the difficult tasks of deciding for himself what is right and what is wrong. This, of course, implies a very serious responsibility, the most serious moral responsibility a man can assume. If men are too weak to bear this responsibility, they shift it to an authority above them, and, in the last instance, to God."[57]

German attitudes themselves

The views of Radbruch have been briefly considered. Professor Wieacker wrote in 1952[58] that the perversions of an "illegitimate" positivism, which sanctioned the most hideous cruelties and atrocities committed by the rulers so long as they were clothed in the outward forms of the law, led to a strong revulsion and furnished one of the chief causes for the revival of a value-orientated theory of justice.[59] "The shortcomings of an undiluted positivism will remain undetected only in those peaceful and saturated periods of legal history in which disjunctions between the positive law and the prevailing ideas of justice are rare and unusual. In times of crisis, social stress, or tyrannical government, any complacent belief in the ethical neutralism of the law will inevitably be shattered."

Though many of the decisions of the post-war internal German courts are more than sufficient to dispel any such complacent belief, even the relatively few cases which have been considered here are enough to show that "undiluted positivism" is by no means as powerless to deal with acute legal and moral problems as might have been imagined. Even among German writers themselves there has been some reaction against such views as those of Radbruch. Engisch, for instance, seeks to steer a middle course between what he calls the "normativistic" and the "naturalistic" falsifications of the law. In his opinion the natural sphere of things and the normative sphere are intertwined and cannot be torn apart in any scientific theory of law. Engisch consequently rejects the approaches of both Radbruch and Kelsen.

Professor Schmidt also repudiates a natural law revival when

[57] *Ibid.* p. 22.
[58] Privatrechtsgeschichte der Neuzeit, pp. 327-8, 348 *et. seq*; 356-7, as digested by Bodenheimer, *op. cit.*
[59] Such a value-orientation relates, of course, not just to the concept of justice but to the concept of law itself.

he says that there exist no self-evident legal principles[60] of a "supreme" character, and that all attempts to work out an ethical system of universal validity must be regarded as having failed. He goes on to say, however, that we do not have to embrace a resigned positivism. A monstrous injustice prescribed by formally valid sources cannot be held to bind the judge. But this does not follow from any concept of "natural law" or "universal moral law" but is a consequence of what he calls our "living morality."[61] It is submitted that such middle courses as have been suggested by these and other German positivists can equally well be dubbed versions of a Utilitarian approach such as that adopted by Hart.

A postscript: retroactive lawmaking

In a limited sense, all law is retroactive insofar as it is applied after and as a result of an event or combination of events. However, the general norm or rule, albeit not always the particular manifestation of that norm or rule in a given case, is usually prospective in nature. That is, it sets down a rule for guidance, and provides a measure against which future conduct may roughly be assessed for its legality.

A retroactive law, particularly a statute claiming retroactive application, is an anomaly, since it can be said to guide conduct only in a very artificial way. Those who act in the belief that their conduct is not unlawful, or at least without ever adverting to its legality or illegality, may be guided to the courtroom and thence to prison, but this is the only guidance they will receive. Fuller has described the injustice of a retroactive criminal statute by dubbing it "the brutal absurdity of commanding a man today to do something yesterday."[62] It would be going much too far to say that *any* statute or law having retroactive effect is, *eo ipso*, undesirable. The laws of most, if not all, systems of any complexity need the rectifying device of retroactivity in many areas of the non-criminal law. "Like every other human undertaking, the effort to meet the often complex demands of the internal morality of law may suffer various kinds of shipwreck. It is when things go wrong that the retroactive statute often becomes indispensable as a curative measure; though the proper movement of law is

---

[60] Note the implied refutation, therefore, of the preamble to the Constitution of the United States of America.

[61] Schmidt, *Gesetz und Richter: Vom Wert und Unvert des Positivismus*, quoted by Bodenheimer, *op. cit.*

[62] *The Morality of Law*, Yale U.P. 1969, p. 59.

forward in time, we sometimes have to stop and turn about to pick up the pieces."[63] As Fuller points out,[64] the literature of jurisprudence pays surprisingly little attention to retroactive laws. Austin is one of the few jurists to have considered the problem in any detail from the point of view of legal theory: "Injury or wrong supposes unlawful *intention*, or one of those modes of unlawful *inadvertance* which are styled negligence, heedlessness and rashness. For unless the party knew that he was violating his duty, or unless he *might* have known that he was violating his duty, the sanction could not operate, at the moment of the wrong, to the end of impelling him" to obey the command.[65]

Fuller considers retroactive laws in the context of a whole system when he puts the practical aspect in its strongest form: "Taken by itself, and in abstraction from its possible function in a system of laws that are largely prospective, a retroactive law is truly a monstrosity. Law has to do with the governance of human conduct by rules. To speak of governing or directing conduct today by rules that will be enacted tomorrow is to talk in blank prose. To ask how we should appraise an imaginary legal system consisting exclusively of laws that are retroactive, and retroactive only, is like asking how much air pressure there is in a perfect vacuum."[66]

The device of a retroactive statute to solve the difficulties of the grudge-informer cases and allied problems has been criticised for the amount of research and consequent time that a comprehensive statute would necessitate.[67] This further element of injustice which is pointed out in the nature of a retroactive statute serves only to emphasise yet again how many varied and often conflicting interests and values are in issue. The Utilitarian approach, weighing good and bad, justice and injustice in a quantitative balance is but one possible approach to a solution.

A footnote

The hypothetical and practical examples which have been con-

[63] *Ibid.* p. 53.

[64] *Ibid.* pp. 52-3.

[65] John Austin, *Lectures on Jurisprudence*, 4th ed. (1879) p. 485. Note Austin's attention to the fact of obedience to laws, or at least to the behaviouristic aspect of attitudes to the legal command and sanction. See, further, Chap. 4, *infra*.

[66] *The Morality of Law*, Yale U.P. 1969, p. 53.

[67] *Supra*, p. 50.

sidered in this chapter remind us that jurisprudence and legal theory may not be able to supply exclusive and definitive answers, but they do have the virtue of raising many, if not most, of the questions which must be posed before ever a solution is attempted. With the utmost respect to the natural law solutions to the type of problem which has been outlined in this chapter, to insist on such finality as some versions of a natural law approach clearly do is to pre-empt any further discussion. Such further discussion, and its implications for both legal theory and for the practical outcome, is well illustrated by the Positivist and Utilitarian standpoints. In such a pressing practical problem, some sort of satisfactory outcome had to be reached in every case. It is possible that even a strict positivist might ultimately reach a conclusion which coincided in form, if not in substance, with that arrived at by his natural law antagonist. It is submitted, however, that one or other version of a positivist approach to the grudge informer situation and allied problems may often be advantageous if only because it can better facilitate the discussion of a great variety of different questions, unhampered by preconceptions of an ideal solution.

CHAPTER 4

BENTHAM AND AUSTIN

I

JEREMY BENTHAM had such a low opinion of natural law doctrine that he condemned it as "this formidable non-entity the law of nature." At the early age of fifteen, Bentham attended a course of lectures given in the winter of 1763-64 by Sir William Blackstone, and even then showed profound disagreement with much of what he heard. The transition from the peculiar brand of natural law doctrine in the work of Blackstone to the rigorous positivism of Bentham represents one of the major developments in the history of modern legal theory.

Bentham the legal positivist

An outline has already been given of some of the competing claims of naturalism and positivism. A positivist approach to legal analysis, so far from rejecting any consideration of the ways in which the content of existing law may be improved, and so far from refusing to consider moral questions in relation to law, can be of greater assistance in the improvement of existing law than much natural law doctrine. The particular advantage which positivism may claim here is that, in the very posing of questions concerning legal reform and evaluation, the scope and the subject matter of such questions can be positively delineated. A prime example of just such a claim is found in the legal writings of Bentham.[1] He insisted on the separation of matters analytical and matters evaluative—on the distinction between "exposition" and "censure" in jurisprudence. At the same time he was responsible, directly or indirectly, for one of the greatest contributions to legal reform in this country ever to come from the mind of one man. "Bentham's work shows clearly that a positivist definition of law goes together with the most emphatic awareness of the difference between good

---

[1] Bentham's total literary output was enormous. It has been said, with regard to legal theory, that Austin took over from Bentham and made into the basis of his own theory what Bentham had expressed almost as *obiter dictum* in the course of his examination of much wider themes.

and bad, and with a strong legal philosophy."[2] Indeed, the reactionary implications of Blackstone's own brand of natural law
doctrine, and the blurring of distinctions vital to a positivist
approach to the analysis of law, are principal targets of Bentham's
criticism.[3]

The combined contribution

Bentham and Austin are dealt with together in this chapter because
they may be considered jointly responsible for formulating an
analysis of law now commonly known as the Imperative Theory.
The analysis has attracted this name on account of the part played
in it by the "commands" (or imperatives) issued by a "sovereign"
or sovereign body. Characteristic statements of this theory of law[4]
have attracted much criticism, and among those who have pointed
to the deficiencies in this account of law are jurists who differ
fundamentally among themselves as to the proper analysis of the
nature of law.[5] Yet those very jurists emphasise the significance of
some kind of imperative element in law. Various ways of formulating this imperative element are apt to obscure its nature rather than
clarify it. In this respect, Austin's formulation has attracted more
trenchant criticism than that of Bentham. It should not, however,
be forgotten that these two jurists played a very large part in providing an introduction to much of the juristic work which has
come after them. In comparison with some of the recent products
of a positivist approach to legal analysis, the expositions of law
given by Bentham and Austin contain many inadequacies—some
of them major ones—in respect both of the theory and of the
practical administration of law. But the step represented in their
writings, from the preceding natural law thought to early forms

[2] Friedmann (1948) L.Q.R. 341, at p. 343.
[3] Bentham's concentration of attention on the nature and ambit of positive law, divorced from conjectural assertions about metaphysical, non-
positive legal standards, and Kelsen's elimination from legal analysis of
non-legal considerations including justice and morality, can be compared
in respect of the advance which each writer's work represents on the type
of work which preceded it; see, further, Chap. 6.
[4] Notable differences exist between Bentham's account and Austin's
account. It should be noted, moreover, that Hart's criticism of the Imperative
Theory presents a "typical model" stripped of peripheral detail. See Hart:
The Concept of Law, Chap. 2.
[5] Both Kelsen and Olivecrona, for example, whose explanations of the
nature of law are at variance, nevertheless share in criticising Austin's
account. See *infra*, p. 114; and Chap. 6, pp. 130-135.

of legal positivism, nevertheless remains of the greatest significance.

A major part of Austin's contribution to legal analysis is to be found in *The Province of Jurisprudence Determined* which was published in 1832, the year of Bentham's death. At the time of its publication it attracted but little attention. It was not until 1945 that the influence of Bentham's ideas upon Austin's account of law in terms of "sovereign commands" was fully appreciated. Austin's debt to Bentham was revealed on the discovery in the archives of University College, London, of an unpublished work by Bentham, completed in 1782, which was originally intended to form part of *The Principles of Morals and Legislation*, published in 1790.[6]

Merit and demerit

The general proposition of positivism is that the nature of law is to be examined in relation to what is found to exist as a product of human action. Emphasis is laid on creation rather than upon the emulation of a superior or higher law. The Imperative Theory, as one of the earliest forms of positivism, gives particular emphasis to the human creative element in law. This emphasis represents both the merit and the demerit of positivism's earliest expressions. The law-creating act is a prominent feature of almost all accounts of the nature of law in general. But if the legal or prescriptive significance of the acts and events which figure in the creation and perpetuation of a legal system is described in terms of its identity with the physical acts themselves, the essentially prescriptive character of law is liable to be obscured.[7] The making or laying down of legal rules is given particular attention by both Austin and Bentham. The very name positivism relates to "law as it is laid down," or posited. A concentration on the circumstances which surround the laying down of such rules is readily understandable. But the occurrence of this process in the form of physical and observable events is, as will be seen, only part of the whole story.

---

[6] Bentham and Austin were, for a time, in contact with each other in London.

[7] The relationship between law and fact, and between the validity and the efficacy of law, will be one of the principal matters arising in Chap. 6. It is there suggested that in their shift of attention from the conjectural to the specifically positive, early positivists over-corrected in their concern with the facts of man made law.

II

Law and sovereignty

The basis of Bentham's account consists in the assertion that law is made up of the orders issued by a sovereign power. The relationship between sovereign and subject is one between superior and inferior, a relationship of power and subjection. Bentham's notion of government is expressed in the following passage from his political treatise *Fragment on Government*: "When a number of persons (whom we may style *subjects*) are supposed to be in the habit of paying obedience to a person, or an assemblage of persons, of a known and certain description (whom we may call *governor* or *governors*) such persons altogether (*subjects* and *governors*) are said to be in a state of political society."[8]

In the first chapter of his recently discovered work, now published under the title *Of Laws in General* Bentham writes: "A law may be defined as an assemblage of signs declarative of a volition conceived or adopted by the sovereign in a state, concerning the conduct to be observed in a certain case by a certain person or class of persons, who in the case in question are or are supposed to be subject to his power; such volition trusting for its accomplishment to the expectation of certain events which it is intended such declaration should, upon occasion, be a means of bringing to pass, and the prospect of which it is intended should act as a motive upon those whose conduct is in question."[9] In Chapter Two he throws more light on his notion of sovereignty, saying: "Now by a sovereign I mean any person or assemblage of persons to whose will a whole political community are (no matter on what account) supposed to be in a disposition to pay obedience; and that in preference to the will of any other person."[10]

The elements of certainty in the description of the sovereign body and of the sovereign's superior position are even further emphasised by Austin. A feature reminiscent of Bentham's initial definitions of law and sovereignty is found in Austin's composite definition of both the notion of sovereignty and what he calls an

[8] Chap. 1, para. 10—Bentham's italics.
[9] Bentham, *Of Laws in General*, ed. Hart; Athlone Press, 1970, Chap. 1, p. 1.
[10] *Ibid.*, Chap. 2, p. 18.

"independent political society." "If a determinate human superior, not in the habit of obedience to a like superior, receive habitual obedience from the bulk of a given society, that determinate superior is sovereign in that society, and the society (including the superior) is a society political and independent."[11] This relationship is further described as one of sovereignty and subjection.

Austin insisted that a true sovereign should attract the obedience of political inferiors and should not render obedience to any superior. He stressed the requirement that the sovereign or sovereign body within a state should be *determinate*, and this feature, together with the necessary absence of limits on the sovereign power, contributes to the essence of Austin's central notion of legal authority and also to its chief weakness as a general explanation of legal power. His restrictive definition (for a definition it purports to be), requires that habitual obedience should be rendered to one and the same determinate person or body of persons. A principal reason for his insistence on such a monolithic form of legal superiority may be found in Austin's fifth lecture, in which he states that "no indeterminate party can command expressly or tacitly, or can receive obedience or submission." The personal and direct notion of a command, central to Austin's exposition, seems thus to have influenced one of the very characteristics of the legal authority from which it issues.

Austin insists on both indivisibility and illimitability as necessary characteristics of a sovereign power. Bentham insists on neither. "It may happen," says Bentham, "that one person or set of persons shall be sovereign in some cases, while another is as completely so in other cases." In admitting this simple fact of life relating to legal authority, Bentham shows an awareness of the necessity to adapt legal concepts to the theoretical and practical ends which they are designed to serve. Such, however, is the inflexible nature of Austin's definition of sovereignty which results from his elliptical account of notions which depend on both legal and political, as well as sociological, considerations that a false dilemma is presented. This dilemma takes the form of a choice between a determinate person or body and a split into more than one "independent political society." The terminology which Austin uses and the ideas which it expresses make it difficult, if not impossible, for us to find any satisfactory account of, say, the federal

[11] Austin, *Province of Jurisprudence Determined*, ed. Hart (Weidenfeld and Nicolson), Lecture VI, p. 194.

system of legal authority which operates in the United States of America.

While, however, criticising Austin's inflexible concept of sovereignty, Raz[12] insists that we should nevertheless be careful not to attribute to Bentham more than he actually wrote. Of Bentham's original notion of sovereignty, Raz writes: "He did not have an explanation of divided sovereignty. He suggested no way of deciding whether a certain legal power is part of a sovereign power, and, if so, of which. Nor did he explain what are the relations, if any, between the various powers constituting one sovereign power. Similarly, he did not explain satisfactorily how sovereignty can be legally limited. He was aware of certain legal phenomena which he could not reconcile with the doctrine that in every legal system there is one undivided and unlimited sovereign, and consequently he declined to subscribe to that theory."

The shortcomings of Austin's account which have so far been mentioned appear to stem from a confusion of legal superiority and political superiority. At another point at which this confusion becomes apparent, the width of Austin's notion is as remarkable as the narrowing effect of the restrictions of indivisibility and illimitability. In his final lecture in *The Province of Jurisprudence Determined*, Austin asserts that in a democracy the electorate constitutes a part of the sovereign body. This tendency to make propositions about law and about politics in the same breath might be interpreted as a sign of realism in his approach. But this virtue is apt to become a vice in legal analysis, especially when characteristic structure and sociological function are considered jointly. In addition to its being rather difficult to conceive of this particular aspect of Austin's notion of sovereignty alongside some of the restrictive characteristics which were mentioned earlier, it is fairly clear even at this stage of a course of study in legal theory that investigations will have to be made which are of a rather different type from those so far encountered if a satisfactory account is to be given of the notion of legal authority. It is also clear that something more will be necessary than the mere enumeration of the outwardly observable characteristics of a system of law. On this basis we may be induced later to describe the nature of Austin's approach as observation, not explanation. Particular attention will be given in the following Chapter to the attitude to authoritative

[12] Joseph Raz, *Concept of a Legal System*; O.U.P. 1970, p. 10.

rules of those subject to them. Such a consideration is conspicuous by its absence from the work of Austin.

Law and sanctions

Bentham's definition of "a law" has been given. The notion of a sanction attaching to behaviour which is contrary to law is apparently no more than an addition to the basic definition. For Austin the sanction is a vital part of the idea of law. He lays great emphasis on the close interrelation of three elements in law, namely, "command," "duty" and "sanction": "... command, duty and sanction are inseparably connected terms: each embraces the same idea as the others,[13] though each denotes those ideas in a peculiar order or series. A wish conceived by one, with an evil to be inflicted and incurred in case the wish be disregarded, are signified directly and indirectly by each of the three expressions. Each is the name of the same complex notion."[14] Austin asserts that every law or rule is a command, or that laws and legal rules are a "species of commands." Law as a whole is therefore the aggregate of these individual laws or commands. "A law" is to be regarded as a typical model for law in general. The element of sanction which is contained in such a model is further described by Austin in these terms: "The evil which will probably be incurred in case a command be disobeyed or (to use an equivalent expression) in case a duty be broken, is frequently called a sanction, or an enforcement of obedience. Or (varying the phrase) the command or the duty is said to be sanctioned or enforced by the chance of incurring the evil."[15]

It is clear that only a small number of laws in a legal system relate directly to the application of sanctions, especially if the notion of a sanction is to be defined, with Austin, as a chance or threat of some evil or harm. The type of legal rule which most nearly approximates to Austin's model is a rule of criminal law which requires that a certain physical or material sanction be

[13] Despite this assertion, one of the major defects of Austin's account of law stems from his examination of the legal sanction, in relation to the *breach* or negation of law, and not to law itself. His explanation thus attracts strong criticism of the type levelled by Kelsen; see *infra*, Chap. 6. See also, however, Raz, *op. cit.*, Chaps. 1 and 2.

[14] *Province of Jurisprudence Determined*, pp. 17-18.

[15] *Ibid.* p. 15.

annexed to certain behaviour. Even then, however, the other essential elements in Austin's notion of law render his account inadequate as a proper explanation of both theory and practice. There are large and important areas of the law in which the definition in terms of sanctioned commands breaks down entirely,[16] since many legal rules are designed to perform an altogether different social function. The rules which provide facilities to act in certain ways in order that a certain action can produce legal consequences cannot find a proper place in Austin's account.

The name given by Hart to such rules is "power-conferring" rules. These may confer either public or private powers—for instance, the power or authority to legislate, and the power to make a will, provided that in each case a certain procedure is followed or a certain special form adopted. In order to point out the inadequacy of Austin's account of legal sanctions, Hart discusses the example of a failure to comply with the provisions of section 9 of the Wills Act 1837, which requires a certain number of attesting witnesses for the formation of a valid will. It is a distortion to think of a failure to comply with that provision as a "breach of duty," still less as an "offence."[17] It might be objected that it does not really matter whether the word sanction is extended to cover legal invalidity, nullity or inconvenience, or not. The answer to that is to stress the importance of examining what Austin did say, as distinct from discussing what his views might be moulded into.[18]

The device of forcing the bulk of non-criminal laws into Austin's scheme of commands and sanctions by extending the idea of sanction to include the nullity of an invalid act of the civil law is rejected by Hart. "In the case of a rule of criminal law we can identify and distinguish two things: a certain type of conduct which the rule prohibits, and a sanction intended to discourage it. But how could we consider in this light such desirable social activities as men making each other promises which do not satisfy

[16] Austin's idea of law as the aggregate of sanctioned commands would not, according to Hart, exclude the notion of "orders backed by threats." It is on this basis that Hart criticises Austin's explanation; see *The Concept of Law*, Chap. 3, pp. 27-33.

[17] For Hart's criticism of Austin on this point, see *The Concept of Law*, Chap. 3

[18] *The Concept of Law*, Chap. 3, pp. 33-35. He also discusses an alternative method of accommodating sanctions, which consists of narrowing the term "law." This method, which is in effect that adopted by Kelsen, is the subject of Chap. 6, *infra*.

legal requirements as to form? This is not like the conduct discouraged by the criminal law, something which the legal rules stipulating legal forms for contracts are designed to suppress. The rules merely withhold legal recognition from them. Even more absurd is it to regard as a sanction the fact that a legislative measure, if it does not obtain the required majority, fails to attain the status of a law. To assimilate this fact to the sanctions of the criminal law would be like thinking of the scoring rules of a game as designed to eliminate all moves except the kicking of goals or the making of runs. This, if successful, would be the end of all games; yet only if we think of power-conferring rules as designed to make people behave in certain ways and as adding 'nullity' as a motive for obedience, can we assimilate such rules to orders backed by threats."[19]

Bentham's account admits both punishments and rewards, which he calls respectively "coercive motives" and "alluring motives." Austin, however, refuses to allow the term "sanction" to be extended to cover rewards: "I think that this extension of the term is pregnant with confusion and perplexity."[20] The difference of opinion between these two jurists is attributable, not to a difference in interpretation of the term "sanction" itself, but rather to the relative lack of concern shown by Bentham with the element of sanction in his concept of law. Bentham pays more attention, however, to sanctions when discussing methods of enforcement of laws at a later stage in his work. Austin attempts to cover more ground with his initial definitions, but his attempts were directed along unsuitable lines.

Questions as to the identificatory mark of law, and questions as to the motives for which people obey law, are separable and should be kept separate in legal analysis. Both Bentham and Austin are concerned with the former question rather than with the latter. Austin, however, speaks of the "chance" or "likelihood" of the application of a sanction, and also at times of the "fear" of sanctions. Bentham, too, uses expressions which imply a factual cause and effect relationship between the issuing of a law and the securing of obedience to it, notwithstanding that his introductory definitions are framed in terms of an "expectation" on the part of those subject to laws and of the purpose or "intention" behind

---

[19] Hart, *The Concept of Law*, Chap. 3, p. 34.
[20] *Province of Jurisprudence Determined*, Lecture I, p. 16.

the imperative stipulation. In a chapter entitled "Force of a Law" there is a brief discussion of the motives upon which reliance is placed by the law in order for it to produce the effects at which it aims. "Motives of some sort or other to trust to it evidently must have: for without a cause, no such thing as an effect: without a motive, no such thing as an action."[21] Whenever motives and causal relationships are introduced into legal analysis the danger arises of obscuring the essentially prescriptive character of law.[22] Both Bentham and Austin invite such a confusion. But, again, their relative merit is to be assessed in the light of the relationship drawn by each between law and sanctions. In such a comparison, Bentham attracts less criticism than Austin.

Sovereignty in action

The initial definitions by Bentham and Austin of their notions of sovereignty have been given. This section examines that notion in action, considering the use to which the idea is put. Criticism of the essential features of this idea are left to section III of this chapter. Here again, the claims of Bentham's explanation to be a satisfactory analysis of law seem stronger than those of Austin's theory. Attention will accordingly be paid to Bentham's elaboration of the notion of sovereignty in such a way as to anticipate at least some of the criticisms which versions of the Imperative theory have attracted.

At the very beginning of the first chapter of his work *Of Laws in General* Bentham gives his initial definition of a law.[23] He continues: "Taking this definition for the standard, it matters not whether the expression of will in question, so as it have but the authority of the sovereign to back it, were by his immediate conception, or only by adoption." To this he later adds: "A will or mandate may be said to belong to a sovereign in the way of conception when it was he himself who issued it and who first issued it, in the words or other signs in which it stands expressed: it may be said to belong to him by adoption when the person from whom it immediately emanes is not the sovereign himself (meaning the sovereign for the time being) but some other person:

---

[21] *Of Laws in General*, ed. Hart, 1970, Chap. XI, p. 133. Note that this chapter is placed well apart from those containing the initial definitions.

[22] See *supra*, Chap. 2, generally.

[23] See p. 73, *supra*.

insomuch that all the concern which he to whom it belongs by adoption has in the matter is the being known to entertain a will that in case such or such another person should have expressed or should come to have expressed a will concerning the act or sort of act in question such will should be observed and looked upon as his.... The mandate which the sovereign in question is *supposed*[24] to adopt may be either already issued, or not: in the former case it may be said to be his by susception; in the latter by pre-adoption."[25]

Bentham was clearly aware of the artificial and unrealistic results which would ensue if the sovereign or sovereign body were said specifically to produce and promulgate all the "commands" or "orders" of which the content of the positive law of a state is made up. His exposition therefore includes the idea that the sovereign, though directly responsible for originating some of the positive law, also takes over or adopts orders given by others. In particular, the notion of "pre-adoption" is one perhaps rather unrefined way of expressing the forward-looking or purposive aspect of legal authority.

The notion of the sovereign's adoption of orders issued by political subordinates produces some remarkable results. It will be remembered that Bentham's definition specifically relates to "a law," and therefore to the law in general via the definition of each individual part within the aggregate whole. His account is thus to be regarded as being of an "atomic" nature.[26] The basic definition is further elaborated thus: "Under the term 'law' ... we must include a judicial order, a military or any other kind of executive order, or even the most trivial and momentary order of the domestic kind, so it be not illegal."[27] The notion of adoption of the orders of others is neither more nor less realistic than the notions of susception and pre-adoption. They all represent an attempt to account for the way in which valid legal acts acquire their authoritative character. Since the sovereign is described as occupying the highest place in the hierarchy of the legal system, the idea of the "authoritative backing" of the sovereign is used.

[24] Italics supplied. For a similar use of "supposed," see *supra*, p. 73.
[25] *Of Laws in General*, Chap. II, p. 21.
[26] Such a concept of law should be contrasted with the type which takes its starting point in the general notion of legal authority as distinct from the particular manifestation in the form of a positive legal rule. Of the more general approach, Kelsen's analysis is a good example.
[27] *Of Laws in General*, Chap. I, p. 3.

Bentham continues: "The mandates of the master, the father, the husband, the guardian, are all of them the mandates of the sovereign: if not, then neither are those of the general nor of the judge. Not a cook is bid to dress a dinner, a nurse to feed a child, an usher to whip a schoolboy, an executioner to hang a thief, an officer to drive the enemy away from a post, but it is by his orders. If anyone should find a difficulty in conceiving this, he has only to suppose the several mandates in question to meet with resistance: in one case as well as in another, the business of enforcing them must rest ultimately with the sovereign."[28]

The remarkable variety of orders to which Bentham's concept of "a law" refers stands in need of explanation. Such an explanation is difficult to give without knowing the purpose which the author had in mind—if, indeed, the wide ambit of the term "law" is anything but a necessary result of Bentham's initial definitions.[29]

It might appear that Bentham fails to distinguish between an order which is given on the basis, or in the form, of a specific rule of law, and an order which in general terms is lawful, that is, not illegal. Anything in the form of an order capable of being "adopted" by the sovereign and which is not contrary to law becomes, in Bentham's view, law. It might be that this involves the omission of an important alternative, namely, that such an order may constitute law (or *a* law) but need not necessarily do so. It should, however, be noted that laws and mandates for Bentham include permissions as well as commands or orders. An Act which is capable of making law, via the relationship described by Bentham between subject and governor, can thus be accommodated in Bentham's concept of "a law" by means of his remarkably wide construction of an imperative or mandate. Viewed in this light, Bentham's theory may be seen to be much more flexible than the rigid formulae set out by Austin in his restrictive and sometimes even *a priori* definitions.

Austin's theory, too, contains the notion of adoption of orders

---

[28] *Of Laws in General*, Chap. II, pp. 22-23.

[29] Friedmann sees in Bentham's concept of law an anticipation of Kelsen's theory of "concretisation," from the general proposition about law to the particular case. For this theory, see Chap. 6, *infra*. For Friedmann's view, see *Jeremy Bentham and the Law*, 1948. Despite some basic differences between their respective accounts, their theories may be compared on account of the provision for the "filling-in" of gaps in general mandates or imperatives to cover all cases. The very different ways in which Bentham and Kelsen arrive at this result should, however, be noted. For the concept "basic norm," see *infra*, pp. 120-124.

issued by others, or "tacit commands."[30] When, for instance, custom is elevated to the status of a legal rule by the decisions of courts of law the legal rules which emerge are classed by Austin as tacit commands of the sovereign legislature. "The State, which is able to abolish, permits its ministers to enforce them: and it, therefore, signifies its pleasure, by that its voluntary acquiescence 'that they shall serve as a law to the governed'." Despite the ingenuity[31] of this device, the notion of a "tacit command" remains, on one construction, a contradiction in terms. A "command" is appropriate to stand for the express issuing of an imperative, and the term is usually employed to describe the action of a person who does this. The addition of the adjective "tacit" detracts from the ordinary meaning of the very word to which it relates.

III

This section is devoted to some of the principal criticisms which versions of the Imperative theory have attracted. It will be remembered that four essential elements are to be found in Austin's account. These are: sovereignty, defined in terms of a "habit of obedience" on the part of political inferiors; commands; the duty created by sovereign commands, and the legal sanction consisting in a penalty to non-compliance with the legal duty. With the arguable exception of sanctions, these elements are also, in one form or another, essential to Bentham's account. Objections to these ideas and to their particular use will now be considered.

Sovereignty and "habit of obedience"

Both Bentham and Austin use the expression "habit of obedience" in their characterisation of sovereignty. The authority of the sovereign is inferred from observations as to the habitual obedience which is rendered by the bulk of a given society. Bentham's expression "disposition to pay obedience" appears in this context to mean the same thing as "habit." Both notions are themselves characterised by the way in which they are suited to describe the results of practical observation.

The idea of a "habit of obedience" has been severely criticised

---

[30] See *Province of Jurisprudence Determined*, Lecture 1, pp. 30-33.
[31] Some might say ingenuousness.

for its inability to furnish an adequate explanation of legal authority and of the authority-based relationships of which a legal system is composed.[32] In particular, "habit" is appropriate for a statement of factual conclusions based on observation of physical events. It is not at all satisfactory, however, when the task at hand is to explain the *reason* for which observable regularities may be said to occur in the field under examination, and not merely to describe what those regularities are. Any examination which does not do this is likely to produce observations, not explanations.[33] Law concerns far more than mere coincidence, and legal authority is not well described merely in terms of a set of observable regularities.

Hart's criticism of the Imperative theory must eventually be considered in the light of his own concept of legal rules and of a system made up of such rules.[34] Suffice it here to say that Hart gives an account—which Austin, in particular, does not—not just of what happens in fact, but of the reason for which it happens. The idea of a "habit of obedience" represents a weakness in the accounts of both Bentham and Austin. Its relation to a particular sovereign at a particular time leads to its inadequacy as an explanation of the continuous nature of legal authority during the peaceful internal stability of a social order, represented by a number of consecutive government régimes.

The abilities, or powers, and disabilities of the sovereign body as they exist during the régime of that body are necessary considerations in an analysis of the meaning of sovereignty, at any time and in any conditions. The same applies to the rules of succession which have, in the first place, endowed the sovereign or sovereign body with legal authority. Austin fails to give an

[32] See especially the *Concept of Law*, Chap. 4, pp. 50-60, in which Hart indicates the essential differences between habits and rules. It should be noted that such criticisms of the accounts given by Bentham and Austin concern much more than a mere choice of words. The expression "habit of obedience" describes an idea, and it is this idea which has been said to be unsuitable in an account of the related notions of obligation, authority and the "binding force" of law as they are used to describe features of a legal system.

[33] Explanations, that is, which relate to the nature and structure of law, as distinct from explanations of why people obey law, which no theory of law can hope to answer.

[34] The inadequacies of the Imperative Theory which bring into relief the concept of law as a system of rules are discussed by Hart in *The Concept of Law*, Chap. 4; see also Hart's introduction to *The Province of Jurisprudence Determined*, pp. xi-xii.

adequate explanation of either of these essential features; in his fifth lecture he speaks simply of a person or body with habitual obedience and a "generic title" to succeed. This abstraction is as near as Austin gets to accounts of the nature of legal authority which have been put forward more recently. Does Bentham's account fare any better?

It might at first seem that the functional aspects of Bentham's "sovereign" go some way towards guarding his explanation against typical criticisms of Austin's theory. In particular, the notions of adoption, pre-adoption and susception of orders issued by others appear better to account for the continuous nature of a legal system, in as much as a political superior looks back to the commands or orders of his predecessors and forward to those of his successors. The point at which this device becomes inadequate is that at which it is necessary to explain, not only what can be observed to be happening in a legal system, but also the reasons for which it is happening in this way.

As to the continuity of legal and law-making authority into the future, Hart says that "it is characteristic of a legal system, even in an absolute monarchy, to secure the uninterrupted continuity of law-making power by rules which bridge the transition from one law-giver to another; these regulate the succession in advance, naming or specifying in general terms the qualifications of and mode of determining the law giver. . . . In explaining the continuity of law-making power through a changing succession of individual legislators, it is natural to use the expressions 'rule of succession,' 'title,' 'right to succeed,' and 'right to make law.' It is plain, however, that with these expressions we have introduced a new set of elements, of which no account can be given in terms of habits of obedience to general orders."[35]

Although they are to a very limited extent descriptive of some aspects of the factual events and circumstances surrounding the legislative process, the notions of adoption, pre-adoption, and susception of orders issued by others are neither in all cases necessary nor in any case sufficient, to account for the nature of legal authority.

Definition of sovereignty

The very idea of sovereignty may be defined in such a way as to

[35] *The Concept of Law*, Chap. 4, p. 53.

produce a wholly vacuous formula. The principal way in which to do this is to formulate an *a priori* definition of sovereignty and then to exclude from the ambit of the term anything which does not fall within the prescribed limits. The difficulties in the way of arriving at a definition of law were indicated earlier. The same difficulties are encountered in the analysis of individual concepts within that of law itself. Sovereignty is such a concept. For Dicey, the "sovereignty of Parliament" meant an absence of fetters on legislative power. The converse proposition, that if Parliament was subject to any legal limit it would not be "sovereign," follows naturally from the first premise. The major fault in such a notion lies in the assumption that "Parliament" is sufficiently described by calling it by that name. The word can be, and indeed usually is, used to refer to the visible manifestations and workings of an institution concerned with certain meetings and procedures and with its personnel at any particular time. In a stricter and more accurate sense, however, "Parliament" stands for a complex legal concept which connotes, *inter alia*, a whole mass of powers, duties, liberties, liabilities, disabilities and so on. Furthermore, absolute accuracy requires the description of these features at a particular time, for they are themselves subject to amendment and rearrangement. The label "Parliament" is finally attached to such a description. On this view the very idea of "Parliament" must be described in such a way as to accommodate any intrinsic limitations or disabilities which it possesses for any particular purposes or matters.

It might still be argued that the descriptions, or rather definitions, of sovereignty given by Bentham and Austin at least reflect one aspect of the positive constitutional position in this country at the time at which they were writing. But however attractive it might at first sight appear to be to imbue a theory as to the nature of law with a "realistic" aspect, by means of a concentration on the observable features of the legal process in a particular system, such an approach is doomed to failure as a general analysis of the nature of positive law. The notion of a sovereign or sovereign body is, in particular, lacking in certain fundamental respects as the basis of an explanation of legal authority. For the purposes of legal analysis, the specific existence of a legal institution should not be identified with its own functional legal significance. Even more care must be taken to avoid this identification in the case of the specific existence of legal institutions which possess functional

and geographical restrictions such as, for instance, the comparatively hierarchical system of legal authority prevailing in this
country.

Sovereignty, command and sanction

The close interrelation of these three notions is clear from Austin's
initial definitions. The one comes to be defined in terms of the
others. The potential ambit of each is curtailed by the assumption
that the others may be outlined by set formulae. It has been seen[36]
that the idea of a "command" influences the characteristic features
of the sovereign body from which it is supposed to issue. The
relationship of sovereignty and subjection is carried to the length
of defining the sovereign command in terms of a coercive sanction.
The restrictions which such an approach produces far outweigh
any apparent clarity or elucidation which it might offer. Such an
attempt at clarity of definition may in fact result in obscurity.[37]

Despite Austin's assertion, in relation to the ideas of command,
duty and sanction, that "each is the name of the same complex
notion,"[38] his doctrine, as Raz points out, excludes the possibility
of any internal relation between laws constituting a necessary
element in a legal system. By "internal relation between laws"
Raz means the "relation between laws one or more of which refer
to or presuppose the existence of the others." "Austin's theory of
legal system is virtually a by-product of his definition of 'a law.'
Both the theory and the definition revolve around and pre-suppose
the applicability of one concept—the concept of sovereignty."[39]

Command, imperative and obligation

Austin describes what he means by a "command" in this way: "If
you express or intimate a wish that I shall do or forbear from some
act, and if you will visit me with an evil in case I comply not with
your wish, the expression or intimation of your wish is a command. A command is distinguished from other significations of
desire, not by style in which the desire is signified, but by the

[36] See p. 74, supra.
[37] Some criticism has already been given of Austin's use of the notion of
"sanction": see p. 76, supra. Further criticism will be found in the introduction to Kelsen's account of the nature of law; see Chap. 6, pp. 114-117,
infra.
[38] See p. 76, supra.
[39] Raz, op. cit., p. 6.

power and the purpose of the party commanding to inflict an evil or pain in case the desire be disregarded."[40] Thus, for Austin, a "signification of desire" or an expression of will is characterised by the annexation of an "evil" in the event of non-compliance. If a harm is neither threatened nor willed in the event of disobedience, the expression of will does not amount to a command, even if such expression of will happens to be phrased in imperative terms. Austin noticed that law (or *a* law) had something to do with what is prescribed to happen, with what shall happen, such prescription being the import of the expression or act of will in question. But in order to make it a legal act, something has to be added. For this reason the person or body of persons from whom the command is supposed to emanate is called a sovereign, invested with the characteristics outlined earlier in this chapter. To account for the element of coercion in law, the sanction is connected in a very simple way with the non-compliance with such a command. When the explanation of law given by Kelsen comes to be considered later, it will be seen that the same basic elements—act of will and sanction—may be treated in a very different way so as to avoid the shortcomings of Austin's theory. It is interesting to note that two of the foremost critics of Austin's "command" theory are fundamentally at variance with each other. Kelsen and Olivecrona base their accounts of the nature of law on some kind of imperative element, but they differ very much in their basic conceptions of law and as to the way in which the basic elements of law are to be arranged and explained in order to produce an adequate account of its nature.

The inadequacy represented by the over-personalised and inflexible nature of Austin's sovereign, is similar in its implications to the equally unsatisfactory role which the notion of a command is made to play in the imperative theory of law. The notion of determinate sovereignty and that of the issuing from that source of commands are both aspects of the same vain search—the desire to find the source of law in terms of a factual description, to explain elements of a legal system in terms of cause and effect in relation to specific institutions of positive law.

[40] *Province of Jurisprudence Determined*, pp. 13-14. The formulation may be compared and contrasted with the approach of Olivecrona, who both criticises the notion of a command as constituting law, and also lays stress on the particular forms which are observed during the making and promulgation of legislation, in order that it may have the required psychological effect. See *Law as Fact* (1st ed., 1939), The Binding Force of Law.

The product of the command of the sovereign or political superior is the legal duty. But for Austin this duty is not of a truly stipulative, purposive or prescriptive kind. The binding force in his notion of duty consists in the occurrence (or the factual probability) of actual compulsion, not in legal obligation. For Austin, the subject of the legal system is "obliged" by the command of the sovereign.[41] This explanation is not essentially different from that in which a bank robber threatens a cashier with a gun, saying or implying that the gun will be used in case the cashier does not comply with the demand. Coercive orders of this kind, when multiplied and blown up into a whole mass of orders backed by threats, are supposed to represent the whole of the law of a state. It is true that a coercive order connotes both an imperative element in law together with an appreciation of the coercive nature of legal, as distinct from other types of rules. Austin is to be given credit for emphasising just this. However, a clear example is to be seen here of the over-correction from the conjecture and metaphysical speculations of natural law, to a down-to-earth positivist approach based squarely on factual observations and assertions. The condition of "being obliged" consists in the fact of certain compulsion having its desired effect. It can be expressed as an observable fact that A has been coerced or compelled by B to do or refrain from doing something; we can make the statement of factual result, of cause and effect, that A has been *obliged* by B to take such a course of action. On the other hand, the statement that A is under a legal obligation towards B does not lend itself to this type of factual description. A statement of legal obligation is made on the basis of an accepted proposition to do with what *ought* to be the case, what *ought* to happen. It is a statement based on the prescriptive nature of law. A person can be obliged to do something without being under an obligation to do it; indeed, these two states will coincide only on the actual application of a legal sanction, and even in that case the notion of "being obliged" to perform the legal duty itself becomes strained, sometimes even totally distorted. The application of the legal sanction is itself conditioned by the legal norm which directs it. On the other hand, a person can be under an obligation to do something without ever in fact being obliged to do it. Something more subtle is therefore needed to

---

[41] For a lucid explanation of the distinction between "being obliged" and "being under an obligation" see Hart, *The Concept of Law*, pp. 80-88; see also *infra*. Chap. 5, p. 97.

account for legal obligation—something not identical with the cause and effect consideration of the breach of legal duty and the probable application of legal sanction.

Olivecrona[42] takes as his object of criticism a theory which maintains that the law consists of the commands of the state, and which represents law as the will of the state. He emphasises that a "command" is something more than a mere declaration of will. "A command is an act through which one person seeks to influence the will of another." He says of the Imperative Theory of law that it is "tenable as an explanation of the law only if it can be shown that the rules of law are the commands of some person, or persons, belonging to the State organisation.... The State is an organisation. But an organisation cannot, as such, be said to command."

An atomic view of the law

A final observation which must be made in relation to any form of an imperative theory of law relates to its atomic nature. Both Austin and Bentham concern themselves with "the law" and with the definition and characteristics of the individual laws. As such, their accounts lay claim to an explanation of law in terms of the aggregate of a mass of particular cases, each of which is supposed to possess the features which they define. This aspect of their theories must be borne in mind when they are set against analyses which conceive of "law" initially in general terms and which proceed to an account of particular cases only after the general concept has been fully elucidated.[43]

It is, in a way, paradoxical that these first attempts to arrive at a satisfactory explanation of law by means of a positivist approach should have come to be seen as inadequate as a general and universal account of the positive laws upon which they concentrate.

---

[42] *Law as Fact, op. cit.*, Chap. 1, pp. 30-49. See also Hart, *The Concept of Law*, Chap. 2, "Laws, Commands and Orders."

[43] See further, Raz, *op. cit.*, Chap. 2; also Chap. 3.

CHAPTER 5

LAW AS A SYSTEM OF RULES

I

Introductory

THE opinions held by Sir William Blackstone on the subject of natural law can be criticised in two ways: one concerns the way in which he expresses his ideas, and the other their essential nature. A similar approach can be taken to the assessment of the juristic writings of Bentham and Austin, whose ideas possess deficiencies in respect both of their detailed expression and of their original conception. Those two early positivists are to be given credit, however, for the substantial advance which their work represented and for the attention given by them to certain ideas which, though more recently developed, and in different ways, have had an undoubted influence on legal theory.

It would, however, be a pity to detract from the originality of some prominent modern theories of law by reading into the earlier theories more than is really there. Though interpretation of a writer's views is rewarding, and in some cases necessary, the policy of reading between the lines can be taken too far.[1]

The feature with which we can justifiably find fault in the work of these two writers, especially in that of Austin, is the way in which the detailed expression of their analysis of law brings their ideas to a stage beyond which they cannot go, and to a situation in which their theories cannot satisfactorily explain a number of elements which are of central importance to the nature of law. The basic fault—the fault in the conception of the analysis itself— is one which inevitably conditions the detailed exposition. But that exposition, it is suggested, goes even further in its effects to impose final and fatal limitations on an original concept of law which, if treated in a different and more adequate manner, might possibly

---

[1] For a remarkable defence of Austin's use of the notion of "habit of obedience" see Manning, in an article in *Modern Theories of Law*, expressing the view that Austin had already said what Kelsen has more recently expounded, though in different terms. Note also, in this connection Hart's *caveat*: *The Concept of Law*, Chap. 4, p. 65. See, however, Raz, *The Concept of a Legal System*, O.U.P. 1970, Introduction, p. 4.

have been expressed in such a way as to avoid some of the many criticisms which have been levelled at it by modern jurists.

We have already considered some aspects of the detailed scrutiny of a typical model of the Imperative Theory made by Hart. A central part of that criticism relies on his concept of legal rules which, he says, is absent from the analysis of law which he is criticising. The faults to which the flaw in the basic concept could lead have also been outlined at various points in our discussion of the writings of Bentham and Austin. These faults included, principally, the failure to characterise the nature of legal acts and institutions in a way which distinguished this aspect from their physical existence and occurrence; the over-simplification inherent in the hierarchical account of legal power and subjection; and the failure to explain the continuity of legal authority and its products.

Before embarking on a summary of Hart's positive contentions one point must be emphasised. It will be clear from the outset that his analysis of a legal system, and especially of its inherent element of legal authority, is noticeably different from other explanations of law which we have considered and from others which are still to be considered. The explanations given by Bentham and Austin are based on the description—even the definition—of a sovereign or a political superior. To such superior is given the role of issuing commands which somehow bind political inferiors, the subjects of the system. Put in this way the whole matter of the binding force or obligatory quality of legal authority is to be considered, as it were, from the sovereign downwards to those subject to the law thus produced. Even when the attitudes of those subjects themselves are mentioned it is only by way of emphasising the power which flows from the sovereign's position and permeats the whole hierarchy. Bentham, too, in a discussion of the motives for compliance with the will of the sovereign, provides an outline of the particular ways in which the orders of the sovereign or sovereign body may be expected to become viable propositions.

The essence of a major part of Hart's approach is strikingly different. This lies in the predominance he gives to the attitude to the rules of the legal system of those who are subject to it, especially its officials, and whose actions and dealings are conditioned by the rules and the regulations of which that system is composed. This does not, it should be added, amount to an investigation or evaluation of motives for obedience in causal terms such as those employed by Bentham. Indeed, an explanation of law in terms of motives for obedience is expressly criticised by Hart; for if it consists merely in an enumeration of factors which *will* or *probably will*[2] result in the subject's compliance with the stipulations of the law, no adequate separation can be made of the practical effectiveness of law from its own inherent validity.

The problem of having to make a separation between the prescriptive or stipulative element in positive law, and the descriptive consideration of the mechanics of the practical administration of a legal system in terms of physical causes and effects is one which has already been introduced in outline in Chapter 2. When Kelsen's approach to legal analysis comes to be considered it will be seen that it has been thought necessary to go to some lengths in order to arrive at some kind of formula by which both to relate and to distinguish the factual manifestations or physical circumstances of the context of a legal order, and the legal significance to be attributed to them. Nothing could be more obvious and clear than the proposition that law is connected with fact. On many views it is equally clear that a legal situation—one in which law or certain legal concepts are to be seen at work— cannot adequately be assessed in terms of their identity with factual events. A goal in the game of football has, for example, a meaningful significance which is connected with, indeed based on, the observable event of a piece of inflated leather of a certain size and shape directed by a player into a net. But the goal has certain consequences which have a special significance when, and only when, it is described in the context of the system of rules which surround the game. Surrounding facts, such as the strength of the wind, or the reactions of the spectators, neither add to nor detract from the "goal-ful" quality of that event. And even in this simple example of the non-identity of fact with its rule-orientated significance, we have to look further and consider the rules which concern and regulate such things as the size and material of the ball, the size of the net, the offside rules, and the circumstances in which the ball is considered or ruled, out of play.

It is apparent from some of the analogies to be found in *The*

---

[2] See Austin, *Province of Jurisprudence Determined*, Lecture I, p. 16; criticised by Kelsen: see *infra*, Chap. 6, pp. 115–117. See also Hart, *The Concept of Law*, Chap. 5, p. 81.

Concept of Law, that Hart is fond of comparing rules of law with the rules of certain games. Such analogies can be of considerable illustrative usefulness, and his book shows them to be so.[3] It should always be remembered, of course, that there are limits to the use to which any analogy can be put. Analogies have many limitations and their use can end in abuse. The role which they play in Hart's analysis of law is in line with the characteristics of much of the rest of his approach to jurisprudential questions. His analogies are used in order to illustrate and to exemplify, to provide an inquiring and illustrative approach to legal analysis. To be specific in relation to his analogies between law and games, Hart does not mean that *because* there are likenesses to be seen, *therefore* the two types of rule are to be regarded as being of the same nature. His aim is, rather, to provide a starting point in the appreciation of more or less familiar everyday affairs, which can then usefully serve as a basis for understanding different but related and readily comparable elements in the nature of law. The purpose of such an exercise is to illustrate likenesses and not to seek for any identification of parts of the subject matter of the comparison, still less the whole of it, with the phenomenon under examination. Above all, the purpose of this exercise is certainly not to provide a definition of one in terms of the other.

The inquiring and open-ended nature of Hart's approach to legal analysis becomes apparent at many points in his book, and a similar view can be taken of his method of examining and analysing legal concepts. In his article "Definition and Theory in Jurisprudence,"[4] the recommendation is made that legal concepts such as right, duty, and corporation should be examined in typical contexts. The scope for research into the meaning and functions of a particular legal concept is limited only by the number of uses in all possible contexts to which the term of reference denoting the legal concept can be put. The mere fact that it can be said, with all justification, that a "right" exists in such and such circumstances, does not mean that whenever the term "right" is used it always means the same thing. In fact, the self-same term may be employed to refer to factual situations and physical events which have very little in common with each other. An

---

[3] Though all analogies possess their own inherent limitations, this is not to say that the initial choice of analogy cannot have a bearing on the adequacy of the consequent discussion; See *supra*, Chap. 1. p. 11.
[4] (1954) 70 L.Q.R. 37.

appreciation of this illustrative and distinguishing character of Hart's method of analysis can be of considerable assistance in understanding the way in which his approach may be defended against some criticisms which have been levelled at it.

II

Rules, habits and obligations

The proposition in *The Concept of Law* is that law is a system of rules, and that such a system can best be regarded as a union or combination of what Hart calls *primary* and *secondary* rules. We shall first consider what is involved in his notion of a rule, distinguishing it especially from the idea of a habit, and then go on to examine the nature of the union of two types of rule which he separates according to their character, such union producing the legal quality of the rules within a systematic and coherent whole.

Hart begins with a reminder that jurists who have favoured an analysis of law in terms of an idea of "orders backed by threats" and also those who have investigated law in its relation to morality or justice speak alike of law as containing, if not consisting largely of, rules. It will be seen in a later chapter that even those writers who go so far as to deny that the expression "binding force of law" has any real meaning, resort to the notion of a rule in their analysis of a legal system.[5] It therefore appears to be quite justifiable to make a start in an examination of these accounts by inquiring into the nature of rules, especially if this notion, properly characterised, can furnish the missing link in the theories so far considered.

It will be remembered that in the accounts given by Bentham and Austin, the central notion of authority, or at least legal superiority, was expressed in terms of a "habit of obedience". This habit could apparently be observed generally as a matter of fact. One point of similarity between social rules and habits is noted by Hart. In both cases, the behaviour in question must be general, though not necessarily invariable. He gives the ex-

[5] See esp. Olivecrona, *Law as Fact*, Chap. 4, p. 134, in which he says that "Law consists chiefly of rules about force": see also Chap. 7, p. 139, *infra*.

ample of taking one's hat off in church, such a practice being something which, as a matter of common parlance, happens "as a rule." The use of such an expression might, however, conceal three notable differences between a habit and a rule in the field of the regulation of human conduct.

First, if a social group is to be said to have a habit, it will be enough that behaviour in fact converges. But even if the behaviour of the group is convergent, even if the behaviour of its members is in fact identical, this is not sufficient to constitute the existence of a rule which stipulates that behaviour. Second, where social rules exist requiring certain behaviour, any deviation from the standard thus set will be a reason for criticism. The reader might well inquire at this stage as to how far the members of the group must accept the rule as a standard of behaviour and of criticism of contrary conduct. Hart asserts that such a question need not worry us more than the question as to the number of hairs a man may have and still be bald. The matter might be expressed in terms of a majority, albeit a majority with wide variations.[6]

The third distinguishing feature is the most important from the point of view of an understanding of Hart's concept of law. This is the element of the internal aspect of rules. A habit can be attributed to a social group on the basis of the observable behaviour of the majority of that group. No member of the group need think about the habitual behaviour; indeed, less consciousness is likely to exist of a general social habit than of a social rule. Still less, says Hart, need the members of the group strive to reach or intend to maintain it. "It is enough that *each for his part* behaves in the way that others also in fact do. By contrast if a social rule is to exist some at least must look upon the behaviour in question as a general standard to be followed by the group as a whole. A social rule has an internal aspect, in addition to the external aspect which it shares with a social habit and which consists in the regular uniform behaviour which an observer could record."[7]

Hart notes that the internal aspect of rules is often misrepresented as a matter of feeling in contrast to the externally observable

---

[6] A similar problem can be found in the establishment of physical conditions which are suitable for the use of Kelsen's concept of the "basic norm" in connection with them. See Chap. 6, pp. 120-121, *infra*.

[7] *The Concept of Law*, Chap. 4, p. 55; italics supplied.

characteristics of physical behaviour.[8] Such feelings, he says, are neither necessary nor sufficient for the existence of "binding rules." In his view, there is no contradiction in saying that people accept certain rules but experience no feelings of compulsion. "What is necessary is that there should be a critical reflective attitude to certain patterns of behaviour as a common standard, and that this should display itself in criticism (including self-criticism), demands for conformity, and in acknowledgements that such criticism and demands are justified, all of which find their characteristic expression in the normative terminology of 'ought,' 'must,' and 'should,' 'right' and 'wrong'."[9] It would, for example, be understandable to refer to behaviour contrary to any legal rule as "wrong" even in an entirely non-moral sense, whereas it would be inappropriate to condemn as "wrong" behaviour which diverged from what happened to be a social habit.

It can be seen, therefore, that a purely external or disinterestedly descriptive approach is inadequate as an account of the nature of a social rule, and that only an examination of the *internal* aspect of such a rule can furnish an explanation of the reason for its acceptance. Before going on to consider the way in which, according to Hart, a system of rules can become a legal system, we must take a look at his important account of the idea of obligation and of the way in which it is to be distinguished from the state of being obliged.

A person may be under an obligation to do something while not being necessarily forced, compelled or obliged to do anything. Conversely a bank clerk who is obliged or forced to hand over money to a gunman is under no obligation whatsoever to take this action. One of the faults in Austin's account of law is his definition of obligation in terms of the chance or likelihood that the person subject to it will suffer punishment or incur a sanction in the event of disobedience to the rule which imposes the obligation.[10] Hart points out that "it is crucial for the understanding of the idea of obligation to see that in individual cases the statement that a person has an obligation under some rule and the prediction that he is likely to suffer for disobedience may diverge."[11] It

[8] See Chap. 8, p. 160, *infra*, for the analysis of legal obligation in terms of feelings put forward by Ross.
[9] Hart, *op. cit.*, Chap. 4, p. 56.
[10] See Chap. 6, p. 115, *infra*.
[11] *The Concept of Law*, Chap. 5, p. 82.

should be clear from the example of the gunman situation that the notions of being obliged, and being under an obligation, refer to very different physical situations. Each furnishes the key to the understanding of a very different event. For those who are subject to the controlling influence of a system of rules, or who are at least within that system, even if they do not always actually obey, the violation of a rule is not only a basis for predicting a hostile reaction but also the *reason* for such reaction. In this way Hart distinguishes between normative terminology and the terminology of causation. The statement that a rule or an obligation exists concerns something more than the mere relationship of cause and effect between one event and another.

The legal system

It now remains to consider the way in which rules take on a legal quality and become parts of a legal system. Up to this point we have considered a view of social rules, distinct from mere social habits, which has the potential of acting as the basis of an explanation of the regulatory element in law. We have at our disposal the distinction between the internal and external aspects of law and the distinction between *being obliged* as a matter of fact, and *being under an obligation*, a condition which involves in most instances a statement of what should or ought to happen on the basis of a generally accepted norm or standard. It now remains to consider the way in which this potential becomes realised and to examine the way in which Hart describes the change from the "pre-legal" to the "legal" world. Hart's method is to make an initial distinction between two types of rule. "Under rules of the one type, which may well be considered the basic or primary type, human beings are required to do or abstain from certain actions, whether they wish to or not. Rules of the other type are in a sense parasitic upon or secondary to the first; for they provide that human beings may by doing or saying certain things introduce new rules of the primary type, extinguish or modify old ones, or in other ways determine their incidence or control their operations. Rules of the first type impose duties; rules of the second type confer powers, public or private. Rules of the first type concern actions involving physical movement or changes; rules of the second type provide for operations which lead not merely to physical movement or change, but to the creation or variation of duties or obligations."[12]

It is most important to note that Hart expressly denies any claim that such a combination of primary and secondary rules will be found wherever the word law is properly used.[13] His proposition is that "most of the features of law which have proved most perplexing and have both provoked and eluded the search for definition can best be rendered clear, if these two types of rule and the interplay between them are understood."

Hart begins with a picture of a community in which only primary rules exist, of a society without a legislature, courts or officials of any kind. Such a group is living in what he calls a pre-legal state. Some leading sociologists have contended that even the most primitive societies, if they have merited the appellation "society" at all, have possessed some form of recognised or centralised authority. It is, however, possible to make use of the idea of a pre-legal state of affairs in the context of an analytical account of the make-up of a legal system, as distinct from that of a specifically chronological development of a social group or community. In any but the simplest of communities a form of social control based on unofficial rules would be defective and would, according to Hart, require three principal modifications.

First, doubt or uncertainty would ultimately be bound to arise in the group as to what the rules are, or as to the scope of admitted and accepted rules. Second, the rules would have a static character; there would be no recognised forms of procedure by which old rules could be superseded by new ones, or adapted to new circumstances. To do this, rules would be needed of a different type from the primary rules which are sought to be created, modified or extinguished. Among other things, rules would be required which could provide for the release or transfer of obligations. The third defect of a régime based on unofficial, primary rules alone would be, in Hart's words, "the inefficiency of the diffuse social pressure by

[12] *The Concept of Law*, Chap. 5, pp. 78–79. Note that no claim is made to specify the chronology of any actual change from a community's "pre-legal" to its "legal" state. Note also that the division between duty-imposing and power-conferring rules is not *coincident* with that between primary and secondary rules. The latter may often, for instance, incidentally impose duties. See Raz, "On the Functions of Law," essay in *Oxford Essays in Jurisprudence* (2nd series) ed. Simpson; O.U.P., 1973, p. 278 *et seq.*

[13] Note and compare the way in which Ross avoids the question of definition of the term law by confining his attentions to the characteristics of a "national legal system."

which the rules are maintained." There would be an absence of a final and authoritative means of determining disputes about the rules, their incidence and their violations. Furthermore the régime would lack the very important social tool of a regular and standardised system of punishment or sanctions. An unregulated and inefficient form of personal retribution would have to do its work.

"The remedy for each of these three main defects in this simplest form of social structure consists in supplementing the *primary* rules of obligation with *secondary* rules which are rules of a different kind. The introduction of the remedy for each defect might, in itself, be considered a step from the pre-legal into the legal world; since each remedy brings with it many elements that permeate law: certainly all three remedies together are enough to convert the régime of primary rules into what is indisputably a legal system."[14] There are differences between the secondary rules themselves; but they share the characteristic of being on a different level or plane from primary rules in so far as they are about those primary rules or parasitic on them.

The remedy for the first-mentioned defect of the régime of primary rules is the introduction of what Hart calls *rules of recognition.* By the acceptance and employment of such a rule the members of the community to which it refers will be able to tell whether a supposed rule is in fact a rule of that community, to be supported by the social pressure which it exerts. It will provide for the authoritative acknowledgement that such and such is a legal rule of the group, to be followed and enforced within the group. The remedy for the defect of the static quality of the primary rules is the introduction of *rules of change.* These rules give power to introduce new rules relating to the conduct of the members of the group and to eliminate old rules. The expression "rules of change" also covers the power which is conferred on private individuals in certain circumstances to carry out such transactions as the formation of a contract or the making of a will. To remedy the inefficiency of the régime of primary rules and the consequences which flow from that inefficiency, secondary *rules of adjudication* are introduced, under which power is given to certain individuals to make authoritative pronouncements as to the incidence or breach of primary rules. Such rules will identify the individuals who have the authority to adjudicate and will specify the procedure to be followed

[14] *The Concept of Law*, Chap. 5, p. 91.

during the course of adjudication. The secondary rules provide also for the authoritative and centralised sanctions of the system.

Some previous faults rectified

We are now in an even better position to form an assessment of the theories of Bentham and Austin. The Imperative Theory, though a good start in the development of positivism as we have come to know it, suffered from a double deficiency. It contained neither the concept of a rule as it is elucidated by Hart nor, consequently, the important dual classification of such rules. The result of the first fault was the description of the attitude of the people subject to a legal system, as consisting merely in a habit of obedience. The outcome of the second was the over-direct and highly personalised characterisation of legal authority with its accompanying crude account or the consequences of the violation of a sovereign command.

Let us look a little further into Hart's concept of the "rule of recognition" as it is used to characterise legal authority within a legal system, together with the dependent notion of legal validity.

When a rule of recognition of the legal authorities exists within a community and contributes towards its legal system, both private individuals and officials of the system are provided with authoritative criteria for identifying primary rules of obligation. Such criteria may, for instance, specify the enactments of the legislature, custom and judicial decisions. Where, as in the type of modern legal system with which we are familiar, a variety of authoritative sources exists, any possible conflict is provided for "by ranking these criteria in an order of relative subordination and primacy."[15] The ranking is not as rules of recognition, but as rules of change; in other words, equally ultimate rules of recognition may give rise to superior and subordinate rules of change.

We are here again reminded of Hart's emphasis on the acceptance of rules by those who are subject to them. This approach is to be distinguished from one which is based on the notion of imposition or enforcement of legal authority from the highest point. With the former approach, the position of custom in the complex pattern of authoritative sources of law can be described more adequately and realistically than as the product of some kind of tacit legislative

[15] The proposition has been criticised by Ross: see infra, p. 107.

acquiescence. A concentration on the finality or predominance of any one of the many possible sources of law is likely to produce an unbalanced picture of what is really going on within the legal system. Such a fault is common to both the Imperative Theory of law, in which law is represented as the commands of the sovereign or sovereign body (with us, the legislature), and to an American approach to law, typified by Gray,[16] in which the constitutive or creative character of the judicial decision is given prominence in legal analysis, at the expense of other equally important elements of law.

The acceptance of rules

There are similarities between primary rules and secondary rules. They both constitute standards by which actions may be critically appraised, and each connotes the acceptance of standards which form the basis of specific rules. But herein lies a possible difference between primary and secondary rules. Hart tells us that the existence of a union of such rules is not all that is needed to describe the relationships to law which are involved in a legal system. "It must be supplemented by a description of the relevant relationship of the officials of the system, to the secondary rules which concern them as officials. Here what is crucial is that there should be a unified or shared official acceptance of the rule of recognition containing the system's criteria of validity."[17] Whereas a general obedience to the rules of behaviour which are valid according to the legal system's ultimate criteria of validity, is the only condition which the mass of private individuals need to satisfy in order for us to speak of the existence of a legal system, the rules of recognition, of change and of adjudication must be accepted as *common public standards of official behaviour* by the officials of the system. While private individuals may, as Hart puts it, obey "each for his part only" and for any motive whatever, the officials of the system must regard the rules of recognition, change and adjudication as "common standards of official behaviour and appraise critically their own and each other's deviations as lapses."[18] The term obedience is sufficient to describe the attitude or relationship to law of individuals as far as primary rules are concerned, but

[16] See *infra*, Chap. 8, pp. 168-173.
[17] *The Concept of Law*, Chap. 6, p. 111.
[18] *Ibid*. Chap. 6, p. 113.

inadequate and misleading when applied to the attitude of officials of the system to the secondary rules which they employ. It is this consideration which leads Hart to say: "The assertion that a legal system exists is therefore a Janus-faced statement looking both towards obedience by ordinary citizens and to the acceptance by officials of secondary rules as critical common standards of official behaviour."[19] One notable consequence of this potential difference in attitudes within a legal system is the possibility of a community in which only the officials accept and act according to the system's criteria of legal validity, one in which the mass of the populace just follow like sheep. There is, as Hart says, little reason for thinking that a society living according to such a system could not exist, or for denying it the title of a legal system. In other words, the shared official attitude, adopted critically, is a necessary characteristic of a legal system, while it is sufficient that private individuals should obey or acquiese in the legal rules.

Acceptance, however, of whatever kind, is the basis of the supreme criterion of legal validity within a system—the rule of recognition. Though particular attention will have to be paid to the attitude of officials as judges and policemen and to institutions such as the legislature and the courts, the general conduct of the community will have to be considered in order to form the basis of a definite assertion about or description of the rule of recognition or of the complex rules which make it up. On the basis of what can be concluded from observations of the system of law, statements can be made which are of a different kind from mere assertions of fact. These are statements about legal validity, statements of what Hart calls an *internal* nature, on account of their significance to people who employ them in relation to legal phenomena under examination, and who use and accept them as guiding standards for their behaviour. In relation to law and legal obligations we make use of what is called normative terminology, comprising terms such as "ought," "should" and "obligation." This terminology is of a different kind from the language of causation which directly concerns the relationship of one fact or physical event to another. For Hart, the internal aspect of the validity of law can be better understood if the use of an accepted rule of recognition in making internal statements is properly appreciated and distinguished from an external statement of fact that the rule is accepted. He says that "the word 'valid' is frequ-

[19] *Ibid.* p. 113.

ently, though not always, used, in just such internal statements, applying to a particular rule of a legal system, an unstated but accepted rule of recognition. To say that a given rule is valid is to recognise it as passing all the tests provided by the rule of recognition and so as a rule of the system."[20]

III

Criticisms of Hart's analysis of law

Some of the principal criticisms of Hart's approach to legal analysis amount to more than mere criticisms of his own particular account of law in terms of a union of primary and secondary rules. They go further and express doubts concerning the very nature of legal positivism. Two such criticisms will be considered in this section.[21] The third criticism to be examined is of a narrower kind and comes from the Scandinavian jurist Ross, whose own positive[22] contentions will be considered in Chapter 8.

Fuller's view

Fuller regards law as a purposive system, its particular purpose being that of subjecting human conduct to the guidance and control of general legal rules. The view which he criticises sees the reality of law in the fact of an established lawmaking authority; and what this authority determines to be law is law. "There is in this determination no question of degree; one cannot apply to it the adjectives 'successful' or 'unsuccessful'."[23] Fuller criticises Hart's concept of the rule of recognition as it is used to account for the persistence of law, and also its incidence during a particular legal régime. To take the latter first, he objects to the way in which Hart appears to read into his characterisation of the rule of recognition the notion that it cannot contain any express or tacit provision that the authority which it confers can be withdrawn for abuses of it. Fuller expresses regret at what he considers to

[20] *The Concept of Law*, Chap. 6, p. 101.
[21] Both, significantly, come from American writers who have themselves made a substantial contribution to Anglo-American (especially to American) jurisprudence.
[22] Not necessarily in a technical sense.
[23] Fuller, *The Morality of Law*, 2nd ed. Yale University Press, 1969, Chap. 3.

be the absence of any element of "tacit reciprocity" in the rule of recognition. "Every step in the analysis seems almost as if it were designed to exclude the notion that there could be any rightful expectation on the part of the citizen that could be violated by the law-giver."[24]

The possible responses to Fuller's objection vary according to whether we regard it as subjective or objective. If it is subjective, then the differences in attitude might be put down to a basic difference between the concepts from which each jurist proceeds at the very beginning of his analysis of law. If it is objective, then it may be suggested in reply that an important element of social reciprocity is inherent in the very idea of the acceptance of a rule, still more of a system of rules; and it is on the general and the official acceptance of such rules that the rule of recognition ultimately depends. Admittedly, the use of the word "acceptance" in relation to a malevolent dictatorship would be strained if the people within that system were in a state of subjection amounting to suppression. Nevertheless it would appear that Fuller's personal predilections are based rather on his own value-judgments and on his approach to the legal authorities in the light of their "degree of success" than on an analytical approach to these phenomena.

According to this critic, the basic error which permeates Hart's treatment of the rule of recognition is that he is attempting to give "neat juristic answers to questions that are essentially questions of sociological fact." Yet is it not equally arguable that Hart's analysis, though based of course on the sociological fact of the very existence of a society with a legal system, is more concerned, and justifiably so, with the legal or juristic implications which arise from sociological observations? This answer gains support from Hart's concern with the separation between the terminology of facts and events and normative terminology, which is necessarily involved in the descriptions of legal situations and relationships. Fuller's criticism would appear to stem from his unwillingness to accept that law can be described in terms of a non-moral "ought" which is a necessary step in an account of the factors which lie behind those sociological facts.

Fuller is of the opinion that this basic error is most apparent in Hart's treatment of the problem of the persistence of law. The example is given of a non-ideological *coup d'état*, which is a

---

[24] *Ibid.* p. 140.

clear model of a change in the rule of recognition and yet probably constitutes the least threat to the persistence of the law which governs such areas of the law as property, contract and marriage. He alleges that the result which is demanded by Hart's analysis is that such rules lose their force and that this result "violates the experience of history." Yet can it not be said that, despite a usurpation of the accepted rules of succession, the numerous rules which do not concern this aspect of legal regulation will probably continue to be accepted and acted upon as a matter at least of convenience?[25] If a new rule of recognition, based on the claims of the usurper, does not come into being owing to a general lack of acceptance, then it is unlikely that any state of affairs would come into being to which the expression "legal system" could at any stage usefully be applied. When matters of sociological fact are sufficiently developed, then a juristic statement can be made about them. To demand anything more from a method of juristic analysis is to make a vain attempt at forcing it into a task for which it was never intended.

Dworkin's view

A similar dissatisfaction with the limitations of legal positivism appears to lie behind Dworkin's criticism.[26] Is law, he asks, a system of rules? Hart, by his description of rules as having an "open texture," recognises that they have furry edges; he accounts for troublesome cases by saying that the judges have and exercise a discretion to decide cases by a kind of judicial legislation. The difference between this view of law and that of Dworkin is that the latter considers that much more attention should be paid to the elements of a legal system which do not really function as rules. Dworkin says that "when lawyers reason or dispute about legal rights and obligations, particularly in these hard cases when our problems with those concepts seem most acute, they make use of standards that do not function as rules, but operate differently as principles, policies and other sorts of standards."[27] Indeed, his criticism is a very wide one, for he says: "Positivism ... is a model of and for a system of rules, and its central notion of a

---

[25] See Kelsen, *Pure Theory of Law*, pp. 208-211.
[26] See Summers, *Essays in Legal Philosophy*, Basil Blackwell, 1968, p. 25 *et. seq.*
[27] *Op. cit.* p. 39.

single fundamental test for law forces us to miss the important roles of these standards that are not rules." The distinction between rules and such other standards is, says Dworkin, a logical one. Rules are applicable in an "all-or-nothing" fashion and are either valid or invalid. This is not however the way in which principles, policies and other sorts of standards operate. The latter have a dimension of weight or importance, a quality which rules do not possess. It is characteristic of conflicting principles that their relative weight of importance will have to be assessed before coming to a practical conclusion based on them. If, however, two rules conflict then one of them will not be a valid rule. Sometimes, says Dworkin, a legal provision may function logically as a rule and substantially as a principle as, for example, in the case of a dispute in respect of unreasonable restraint of trade.

The general allegation emerges from criticism which is designed to point out the shortcomings of a positivist approach that positivism "stops short of just those puzzling, hard cases that send us to look for theories of law. When we reach these cases, the positivist remits us to a doctrine of discretion that leads nowhere and tells nothing."[28]

Hart himself does not claim to cover all aspects of a legal system by his theory. What he does, and it is a considerable task, is to outline a way in which some of the major perplexities in legal analysis may be better understood. He does not claim an explanation of every element in the practical administration of a system of legal rules. The description of a legal system as a union of two different types of rule is aimed at a truly satisfactory account of the essence of such a system. On the basis of the rule of recognition—itself the product of sociological observation— an analysis can be made of the legal system as a systematic, coherent whole. Given this basis, the ancillary aspects of law can be better explained in their relation to it, and the operation of the principles and policies, as they reflect changes and conflicts within and between various social interests, understood in its light. Hart uses the expression "rule-governed operation"[29] in relation to the business of the courts. This expression can in the broadest sense be used to represent the operation of law in society. If a community has a legal system then it is useful to inquire into the nature of that system. The coherence and unity which it possesses

[28] *Op. cit.* p. 60.
[29] *The Concept of Law*, Chap 7, p. 150.

must be described in terms of the most basic elements on which it depends. Once this basis is accounted for, the no less important, but characteristically different, matters which arise in connection with the rule governed operations may be described. The word discretion may not, indeed, be a completely satisfactory description of all situations which involve the administration of principles and policies. But it is one which is understandably encountered at the point of convergence of two types of inquiry: the analysis of the character of a system of legal rules, and the investigation of operation of the content, the actual stipulations involved in these rules.

Discretion is indicative of the relative freedom of action which is permitted to the courts within the rules which govern them, to carry out their "rule governed operations." It refers to an objective analytical approach to subjective notions. The description of the operation of "principles and policies" and their "weighing" relates, it is suggested, rather to an account of the ways in which the specific content of legal rules is dealt with by official organs of the legal system.

The approach of Ross

Hart's view of the component parts of the rule of recognition assumes that, when a plurality of sources is recognised, they will be ranked in an order of relative subordination and primacy. According to Ross[30] it is because of this hierarchical structure that it becomes possible to consider the various rules of recognition as being integrated logically in one rule. "In this way" says Ross, "the logical unity of the system is guaranteed." But this much cherished unity is, he says, more in the nature of a fiction or a postulate than a reality. Ross prefers to regard the various sources of law, not as a logical hierarchy, but as a set of co-operating factors.

His other principal criticism is of a more subjective kind. The view which Ross takes of a distinction between the internal and external aspects of legal rules is more or less reducible to the distinction between facts and feelings.[31] In consequence he holds Hart's use of the word acceptance to depict the "internalisation" of the rule to be misleading, since it seems to point too much in

[30] See 71 (2) *Yale Law Journal*, 1185 *et seq.*
[31] See *infra*, Chap. 8, section II.

the direction of a deliberate decision. It may, says Ross, happen that, in extraordinary situations such as revolutions, an attitude of allegiance to the legal authorities is the outcome of a deliberate decision. Most people will, however, feel themselves bound by the social norms of their group without ever being conscious of any choice or decision. For Ross, a social rule presupposes an observable regularity and also the fact that the rule must be felt as socially binding by the people who follow its stipulations. The point which Ross thereby precludes himself from taking is that a description of the nature of a rule, in particular a legal rule, in terms of its internal aspect is something different from a one-dimensional description of the existence of an attitude, whatever name we give to it, it is something more than this. For Hart, the distinction between internal and external is not one which divides physical behaviour and feelings—though that distinction may certainly be drawn. It is, rather, one which divides "two radically different types of statement for which an opportunity is afforded whenever a social group conducts its affairs by rules."[32] Thus the criticism levelled by Ross at Hart's discussion of a "critical reflective attitude" appears to be based primarily on Ross's own desire to describe law in terms of distinction between fact and feeling, without accepting the specific use to which Hart puts his own version of the distinction between the internal and external aspects of a legal rule.

IV

Law and legal concepts

The nature of Hart's approach to the analysis of law in general is reflected also in his treatment of the analysis of individual legal concepts which play a part within the legal system as a whole.[33]

One of his most important propositions is that "though theory is to be welcomed, the growth of theory on the back of definition is not." Theories which are founded on a supposed definition of the terms which label them, cannot hope to arrive at an elucidating description; they are hedged about with limitations right from

[32] See Hart's review of Ross, "On Law and Justice," in (1959) 17 C.L.J. 233.
[33] See especially "Definition and Theory in Jurisprudence" (1954) 70 L.Q.R. 37.

the start. One such limitation is likely to be a failure to take sufficient account of the specialised way in which legal language is used. Hart suggests, therefore, that we should take words such as right, duty, and corporation, not alone but in typical contexts in which these words are made to perform a particular kind of task. The employment of a legal concept will involve a statement of legal conclusion concerning its factual context. Its application to a group of facts involves something essentially different from a mere description of the relationship between one physical fact and another. The statement, for instance, that someone has a legal right or is under an obligation, concerns an idea by nature distinguishable from one expressed directly in terms of causation. Nor does such a proposition actually state the rule of law from which the conclusion is drawn; it is the conclusion drawn from the unstated interaction of the facts to which the rule is applicable, and the rule itself. To use the analogy with a game, as Hart so often does, the difference between the statement "He is out" and the statement "The ball has hit the wicket," is readily apparent, though the purely factual result is common to both statements.

Simpson[34] has criticised the use of this last analogy on the grounds that, just as the state of "being out" is rule defined, the same applies to "ball" and "wicket," since they are regulated by the laws of the game. It is suggested, however, that the former statement is different from the latter, since it is not readily intelligible except in the form of a conclusion from an existing but unstated rule. The physical existence of a group of pieces of wood could, on the other hand, be pointed out to an external observer possessing no understanding of the rules of the game, whatever name he was told to give to these things. The criticism appears to concern the analogy rather than the theory behind it.

The same critic also asserts that it is futile to attempt to "prise apart" legal linguistic usage from non-legal; such usages are related in such complex ways that deliberate separation will distort both. It would appear, however, that Hart is not concerned to prise apart such usages, but rather to emphasise that statements involving legal concepts represent something more than the mere relation of one ("non-legal") fact to another. We can agree that legal and extra-legal usages should not be prised apart, while also admitting that the usage involved in describing the operation of

[34] 80 L.Q.R. 535, "The Analysis of Legal Concepts."

a legal concept implies a special and all important background which is not otherwise present. A basic element in this background is, of course, the very existence of a legal system.

The legal significance of statements which employ legal concepts is to be understood from two essential elements in Hart's treatment, and both these elements are closely related to his approach to the analysis of the concept of law itself.

First, the meaning of such concepts is to be examined in typical contexts in which they are used in order to account for the result of applying unstated rules to factual situations. When this process is carried to any length, conclusions may be drawn as to its meaning, in terms of the way in which the concept functions for those who use it. The resulting conclusion as to the "meaning in context" displays the outcome of Hart's openly illustrative approach and bears witness to his avoidance of a restrictive and definitive analysis. It is also reminiscent of the internal aspect of legal rules, for it serves to account for the specifically legal significance of certain specially related events and situations to the people who are involved in them.

Furthermore, the manner in which people are able to employ a particular concept in order to perform a particular task in statements about their legal relations has, as one of its principal elements, the assumption of the existence of a legal system. This treatment of legal concepts may thus be regarded as a further and more detailed step in an analysis of law. In both the positive suggestions which Hart makes, and in the characteristics of his approach to analysis, we can detect connections with his treatment of the wider problem of the nature of law.

CHAPTER 6

KELSEN AND THE GREAT MYSTERY

I

Introductory

A DISTINCTION must be made between law or laws in a descriptive sense and law or laws in a prescriptive sense. If the distinction is not made, then the imperative or prescriptive nature of man-made, positive law is likely to be mis-stated or even ignored. Another, rather different distinction, necessary in a comparative assessment of legal theories, consists in the distinction between propositions about law framed in descriptive terms and those framed in prescriptive terms. Even if the essential difference between, for instance, laws of nature and laws of man, or positive law, is perceived, it still remains possible to frame an analysis of the latter in a mixture of terms, some of which deal with what "ought to happen" and others with what "does happen" or "will happen" in practice. Such a mixture of statements is to be found in Austin's legal analysis. In the course of the present chapter yet a third distinction is made, again of a similar kind though rather different in conception; this consists in the separation, insisted on by Kelsen, of legal rules or norms in a prescriptive sense and the same terms used in descriptive statements about the law.

It is an example of the operation of the laws of gravity that a stone will fall to the ground if we drop it, but this is not to say anything about what "is to be the case" or about what "shall happen." The statement means only that we can, on the basis of what happens in certain conditions in the world of cause and effect, make an informed prediction of what will continue to be the case. Although laws or rules in this descriptive sense can form the basis of such predictions of what will happen in the future in similar circumstances, and thus can be to a limited extent forward-looking, the forward-looking nature of the prescriptive rules of positive law consists of their being used as guides for, or stipulations relating to, the physical actions and events with which they are connected. A law or rule in the legal sense is linked only indirectly with what has happened in past circumstances. Subject to an important qualification[1] it can be said that, although a legal rule will no doubt be connected with a background of factual conditions, the reason for which it is to be called a law or a legal rule lies in its having a proper place within a legal system.[2] The reason is not to be found in its ability to serve as a comprehensive explanation of what has been observed to happen in practice. If a factual or practical contradiction is found with regard to what is put forward as a law in the descriptive sense, then the simple and unavoidable conclusion is that the supposed law has been incorrectly formulated. If, on the other hand, a law or legal rule in the prescriptive sense is occasionally disobeyed in practice, this will not indicate the existence of any fault in the formulation of that particular legal rule.[3] In other words, the efficacy or effectiveness in practice of a legal rule is to be distinguished from its own inherent validity.

This distinction between validity and efficacy is one which is applicable to a variety of problems relating to the structure and operation of a legal system, and more than one view may be taken of the relationship between them. An argument can be put forward which defines one in terms of the other.[4] Accepting, however, for the moment, that opposite arguments are tenable, it is useful to be aware of some different problems to which the distinction between validity and efficacy may relate. First, there are clearly degrees of efficacy of a legal provision in securing its aims; if a law had to be efficacious in this sense in order to be valid, one of the primary objects of having laws at all would be confused, since the only valid laws would be those which the majority of people chose to observe. Second, there is the question of the effectiveness of a law when considered in the light of its application by legal officials, especially by the courts. This question has given rise to notable differences of opinion. In an analysis of law which accommodates its prescriptive character and highlights the normative significance of a legal provision in such a way as to indicate, without necessarily describing, the element of purpose behind the making of positive law, statements can be made about the validity

[1] See *infra*, p. 129; also p. 122.
[2] Even the "pure" analysis of law put forward by Kelsen has its roots in fact-based considerations. Such a point of connection must exist in any examination of positive law.
[3] Widespread inefficacy of the legal norm or of the legal order as a whole necessitates different considerations. See *infra*, p. 127.
[4] See *infra*, Chap. 8, section II.

of a law before the question of its effectiveness in operation can even arise.

Until midway through the eighteenth century the confusion of the first type outlined above, between these two different senses of law, was still noticeable in the juristic thought of this country. When early manifestations appeared of analytical positivism, in the shape of the legal theories of Bentham and Austin, this fault was observed and to a considerable extent corrected. Juristic concentration shifted to the examination of the character of the man-made rules of positive law. But this corrective process was not developed in the most suitable way. In particular, the explanations given by Bentham and Austin of the notion of sovereignty and the central importance of the sovereign's position in a legal system were still too much based on propositions which were limited in their scope, being relevant only to some aspects of the notions of law and legal systems, and being particularly inadequate as explanations of the nature of rules and of the continuity and range of application of legal authority. It might, perhaps, seem remarkable that such explanations, framed as they were in accordance with purportedly observable factual conditions, should become the less adequate for an account of the nature of legal phenomena. In one very real sense, the nearer they moved to practical considerations of the type used by the proponents of the Imperative Theory, the further they became from an analysis of law which could serve as a general and comprehensive explanation of its nature.

The inadequacy lay in a transition in juristic thought from hypothesis and assumption—it might even be called the conjecture in much natural law thinking—to the description in apparently factual terms of a concept which does not lend itself to the type of positive delineation attempted by Austin and Bentham. The movement away from the frequently metaphysical doctrine of much natural law doctrine involved, for these early positivists, an analysis framed in terms of observable fact, of observations as to what goes on in the practice of a positive legal system. But in this very attitude lay the basis of the movement's insufficiency. One of the principal faults in the Imperative Theory of law was its inability to give a satisfactory account of the nature of a legal rule. Bentham and Austin both used the expression "habit of obedience" in their discussion of the relative positions of sovereign and subject. Although such a notion as habit can suitably be employed in describing the attitude of an external observer, who is giving an objective account of what can de deduced to be happening (or rather to have *happened*) in the system he has come upon, it is insufficient to explain the significance of a legal rule or the nature and meaning of legal authority from the standpoint of one who is subject to the legal system of which those elements form part.

In spite of the deficiencies of the explanations given by Bentham and Austin, their theories did highlight some kind of imperative or directory element in law. Hart's preference for a description of the nature of legal obligation and of the coherence of a legal system in terms of an "internal" attitude to the acceptance of rules has been stated. We may now examine the legal theories of Kelsen and Olivecrona, noticing in particular the way in which an imperative element in the concept of law is described by them.

The legal theories of both these two jurists are considered here because they seem, in many respects, so diametrically opposed to one another in approach and in their original conception, and yet exhibit some remarkable similarities of expression. When the divergent treatments by these two jurists of the notions of legal authority, laws and physical force—all of which elements are found in one form or another in the Imperative Theory—are compared even against the common background of a positivist approach to law, the difference in explanation will be seen to be such that Olivecrona was moved to refer to Kelsen's central thesis as "The Great Mystery."[5]

II

Law and sanctions

One of the principal deficiencies of a theory of law founded on the orders or commands of a sovereign, supported for their effectiveness by the threat of application of a sanction, is its failure to account for the situation in which an organ or official of the legal system either omits or refuses to execute the sanction attaching to breach of the legal duty imposed by the command of the sovereign. Who brings a sanction to bear on such an official? This will surely have to be done by another official. But if the

[5] Olivecrona, *Law and Fact*, 1st ed., 1939, Einaar Munksgaard, Introduction, p. 21.

same question is then repeated, such an explanation leads to an infinite regression. The inclusion of the element of physical coercion in the form of a sanction annexed to the breach of a legal duty is at first sight realistic. However, the manner of its inclusion involves the description of something attached to the breach of law and, therefore, of something separate from the legal rule or legal duty created by the command of the sovereign.

Kelsen's method of avoiding this regression is bound up with his explanation of the way in which the validity and efficacy of law are related. For him, too, the notion of a sanction connotes some element of coercion, but in Kelsen's theory the sanction forms a part of his very concept of law. He says: "Law is the primary norm, which stipulates the sanction."[6]

Before proceeding to an explanation of Kelsen's own theory of law, let it be noted first of all that the inclusion of the element of sanction in the formulation of his concept of law, as opposed to its separation from that concept and inclusion in the description of the consequences of breach of the legal duty, enables him to avoid the logical defect under discussion. Since the sanction is something which is stipulated by law itself, the theory is able to account for the possibility of disobedience of those subject to legal duties without entering into the practical consequences of a supposed "negation" of law which we find in the Imperative Theory. That theory's inadequacy in this respect lay in one of the very confusions which its proponents might have concerned themselves to avoid, namely, the confusion of prescriptive and descriptive elements in the common term "law." In the course of his discussion of the meaning of a sanction, Austin said "The evil which *will probably be* incurred in case a command be disobeyed . . . is frequently called a sanction, or an enforcement of obedience. Or . . . the command or the duty is said to be sanctioned or *enforced* by the *chance* of incurring the evil."[7] It is in the blurring of the distinction between what *will* happen and what *shall* or *ought* to happen, that the Imperative Theory of law contains one of its major defects. It is in its purity and freedom from the relativistic character of considerations of the social effectiveness of particular legal rules that Kelsen's theory of law has its principal merit as a comprehensive and universally

[6] Kelsen, *General Theory of Law and State*, Harvard Univ. Press, 1945, p. 61.

[7] *The Province of Jurisprudence Determined*, Lecture I, p. 15, italics supplied.

valid explanation of the concept of law. The way in which Kelsen describes the fault under discussion is as follows: If it were necessary to guarantee the efficacy of a norm prescribing certain behaviour by the use of another norm providing for a sanction in case the first norm was not obeyed, a never ending series of sanctions would be inevitable. Such a necessity would produce what Kelsen calls a *regressus ad infinitum*.[8] Kelsen maintains that the distinguishing characteristic of a legal rule is not that it is a rule the efficacy of which is brought about by a further rule which provides for a sanction; it is, rather, the fact that the legal rule provides for a sanction. It stipulates that the sanction shall be applied. Approached in this way, the question of coercion or constraint ceases to be one which concerns the way in which legal rules can be made effective and becomes one which relates to the content of the rules themselves.[9] Kelsen's account of the nature of law thus considers the legal rule and the sanction as part and parcel of the same thing, instead of separating them and considering first one and then the other. The fact that no guarantee can be given that all legal rules will be effective in practice does not mean to say that a theory of law cannot describe the nature of law by reference to sanctions. It simply means that a better method will have to be found than the examination of the rule and the sanction as separate elements of law. Kelsen sums up: "All the norms[10] of a legal order are coercive norms, that is, norms providing for sanctions; but among these norms there are norms the efficacy of which is not secured by other coercive norms. Norm n, for example, runs as follows: If an individual steals, another individual, an organ of the community, shall punish him. The efficacy of this norm is secured by the norm $n+1$: If the organ does not punish the thief, another shall punish the organ who violates his duty of punishing the thief. There is no norm $n+2$, securing the efficacy of the norm $n+1$. The coercive norm $n+1$: *If the organ does not punish the thief, another organ shall punish*

---

[8] *General Theory of Law and State*, p. 28.

[9] *Ibid.* p. 29. *Content* should in this particular context be taken to mean *nature* as distinct from specific factual content *i.e.* What a rule actually says.

[10] We shall see later what Kelsen means by this notion of a "norm," and the meaning of his assertion that law is a "normative science." In some circumstances the meaning of "norm" approximates to that of a legal rule; but since the character and the content of the latter notion can easily be confused we should beware of extending the term "norm" beyond the analysis of the prescriptive character of a legal rule.

the law-violating organ, is not guaranteed by a norm of the
$n+2nd$ degree."[11]

The nature of Kelsen's explanation

Kelsen gives to his own theory the title *Pure Theory of Law,* a
name which serves to describe some of the essential characteristics
of his account of law. His object in aiming at "purity" in his legal
analysis is to eliminate alien elements which are not the proper
concern of an account which confines itself strictly to the specifically legal phenomena in the structure of a system of law. He
criticises the way in which contributions to this field of learning
have, during the nineteenth and twentieth centuries, included
ventures into the related but different fields of psychology,
sociology, ethics and political theory. "This adulteration is understandable," says Kelsen, "because the latter disciplines deal with
subject matters that are closely connected with law."[12]

To describe law in terms of what will probably happen, as
Austin does when discussing the part played in a legal system by
sanctions, is to talk in terms of cause and effect, of what goes on in
practice in the actual enforcement of law. This necessarily involves
considerations of sociology, psychology and moral standards—the
elements which Kelsen is at pains to keep separate from his analysis
of the nature of law. In his fundamental thesis that *law is the
primary norm which stipulates the sanction,* Kelsen aims to confine himself solely to an analysis of the prescriptive elements in
law and a legal system. Austin, on the other hand, confuses the
prescriptive character of the legal duty consequent on the sovereign's command, and the descriptive consideration of what will
happen as a matter of practical result. Since such an impurity
exists in his account, his concept of law is faced with this problem
of infinite regression with which it cannot adequately deal.

What does Kelsen mean by his notion of a "norm"? How does
he use it in his account of the prescriptive nature of law? "By
'norm' we mean something ought to be or ought to happen,

---

[11] *Ibid.* p. 29. For Kelsen's general account of the relationship between
validity and efficacy, see *post.* The italics are supplied for easier understanding of the difficult final sentence.

[12] *Pure Theory of Law,* University of California Press, 1967, Chap. 1, p. 1.
For a differing but no less learned approach to discussion of the nature
of law, see Jørgensen's examples drawn from history and sociology in
Law and Society; Akademisk Boghandel, Aarhus, Denmark; 1973.

especially that a human being ought to behave in a specific way. This is the meaning of certain human acts directed towards the behaviour of others."[13] " 'Norm' is the meaning of an act by which a certain behaviour is commanded, permitted or authorised. The norm, as the specific meaning of an act directed towards the behaviour of someone else, is to be carefully differentiated from the act of will whose meaning the norm is: the norm is an ought, but the act of will is an is."[14] Careful consideration of this latter statement will be repaid by a more thorough understanding of the meaning of Kelsen's theory of law. It is central to his analysis that a distinction should be made between what may be called the physical occurrence of a direction or mandate, and its capacity to create a legal effect. The physical consequences of what Kelsen is content to describe as an "act of will" must be considered as something separate from its legal consequences.

Law and fact

The Pure Theory of Law maintains that the nature of law is best explained in terms of a stipulation that, given certain conditions, a sanction *shall be* or *ought to be applied.* Law stipulates that this shall be the case. The stipulations or legal directives represented by the "commands" of the Imperative Theory become reduced in the Pure Theory to conditions which are prerequisite to the order to execute the sanction. Kelsen's theory has usefully been described as consisting in conditional orders to officials to apply sanctions. In other words, given that a certain situation exists which results from a progression of legal acts of various types, a sanction ought, at the end of such a process of development, to be applied; and the sanction is to be applied by an official or organ of the legal system according to which the acts, conditioning the stipulation that a sanction shall be applied, are recognised as being valid legal acts.

This process of the tracing of valid legal connection from the final step of the actual stipulation that an official of the system shall apply a sanction, back to the initial basis for the making of such a stipulation, is called by Kelsen the "theory of concretization." It is his method of describing the progress from the general principle to the particular case. A step-by-step account can be

[13] Kelsen, *Pure Theory of Law,* Chap. 1, p. 4.
[14] *Ibid.* p. 5.

given of the validity of the final order to an official to apply a sanction, in the light of the legal validity of all the conditioning factors which precede the order. The development from the general to the particular—for instance, through a general rule prohibiting theft to a particular case, in which the rule is put into operation by the order to apply a sanction against the thief—is not explicable merely in terms of the physical acts and events which can be observed in practice. It is at this point that Kelsen's theory diverges from most accounts of the nature of law. These acts, he insists, must be considered in the light of the normative relationship which exists between them. The observable events to which we apply the terms legal act or illegal act are natural phenomena but are not as such "objects of legal cognition."[15] By this he means that the attribution of the quality of legality or illegality to physical conduct is not determined by cause and effect, by the laws which govern natural events. The specifically legal significance of an act is represented in the norm which it embodies. The relationship between each norm in the law creating process, between each successive stage in it, is one of imputation and not of causation. The nature of the connections between the various stages in this process of "concretisation" is described by Kelsen in this way: "The norm which confers upon an act the meaning of legality or illegality is itself created by an act which, in turn, receives its legal character from yet another norm."[16]

For example, the order of a court of law to an official to apply a sanction in a particular case will be a valid order if the court was properly constituted in the first place and has adopted the substantive and procedural rules appropriate to the situation upon which the court is adjudicating. In turn, the legal validity of the rules or, as Kelsen calls them, norms which condition the constitution and procedure of the court, may then be tested for their own validity according to the way in which they came into being. If, for instance, reference is made to a legislature having law making supremacy over the courts—such as Parliament in this country—

---

[15] The term "legal cognition" is one which will be encountered again in Chap. 8, in respect of Ross's contention that a satisfactory account of law need not involve an element of specifically legal cognition. The meaning of the term is, simply, the type of perception or understanding on which we base our analysis. "Legal cognition" is thus to be distinguished from "factual cognition" which describes an approach to legal analysis based on the observation of physical acts and events, and their interpretation as such. See, further, Jørgensen, *op. cit.*

[16] *Pure Theory of Law*, p. 4.

then we can consider, the constitution and procedure of that body as the factors conditioning the legal validity of its enactments. Even further back in this step-by-step conditioning process of legal validity, we may come to consider a constitution, written or unwritten, to which all the other norms or conditioning factors down through the legal system are related and to which all are ultimately traceable. At the basis of the whole positive legal system lies the element against which can be tested the legal validity of all the other acts in the prescriptive conditioning process leading to the ultimate valid stipulation to an official to apply a sanction. This final stage in the tracing process is called the "primary" or "basic" norm which stipulates that, if certain conditions of the type just described occur, then a sanction ought to be applied. The notion of the basic norm is thus linked directly with the ultimate stipulation, for it is this fundamental norm which really determines such stipulation, the other stages in the process of development of particular legal stipulation being merely conditions of the basic prescription's being manifested in practice through the putting of the stipulation to a legal official. All the way down the line, the relationship between physical act and legal meaning can be expressed in the form of the statement: "If A is, then B ought to be."

III

The basic norm

The explanation, in terms of a "basic norm," of the coherence and the systematic nature of a legal order connotes the following features. It means, first of all, that a social order is assumed in which the regulations which emanate from the particular system of government or authority which exists are generally effective as methods of social control. On the basis of such an observation an analysis can be formulated which explains the legal system as a particular phenomenon within the general social order; and in this analysis, the idea of a basic or fundamental norm is used to explain the specifically legal meaning of that general efficacy.

An example of the basic stipulation which the fundamental norm of a legal order might be considered to make, is that "the founders of the first Constitution ought to be obeyed."[17] Though

---

[17] Kelsen, *General Theory of Law and State*, pp. 115-116.

different in form, the stipulation of a fundamental norm which refers to a legal order such as our own, which is not founded upon a written Constitution, will not be essentially different.

The fundamental norm, which furnishes the basis for the making of any of the "ought" statements which represent the legal consequences or legal meaning of certain physical acts within the operation of a legal system, is that which gives the legal system its coherence and its systematic form as a particularisation of a prescriptive phenomenon. All the other stages in the process can be tested for their legal validity against this basic norm. Since, however, the basic norm constitutes the final standard of legal validity, its own validity cannot be objectively tested. Its validity, Kelsen tells us, must be presupposed or assumed. When descriptions such as assumption or hypothesis occur in Kelsen's writings, it should be remembered that many of the leading and oft-quoted passages have been translated from the original German. There is nothing in the nature of conjectural assumption about his basic norm, which is *vorausgesetzt* or, literally, presupposed. The idea behind the basic norm could not be more factual. This is that, given a situation in which we can, on the basis of what is going on in the world of legal events around us, talk meaningfully in terms of a "legal system," then, as a matter of logical deduction from our observations, there must have been at some time or times a state of affairs or a combination of various social circumstances which amount to the cause of the present factual situation. Since Kelsen employs the description of a legal system which is "by and large effective," we are enabled in our understanding and application of his theory to start with an appreciation of social phenomena which still give meaning to our use of the description legal system in the context of the physical situation which we observe. In other words the facts and social and physical conditions which have in one way and another, formed the background of the legal system, are connected as a matter of cause and effect with the facts and conditions which now form the present situation which is the context of the continued and continuing system of law.

The very nature of the basic norm is not easy to appreciate, and it may be that difficulties of translation impede adequate interpretation. It has been described as a "mental construct," an idea which the mind of the investigator produces in order to give a satisfactory interpretation of the observable phenomena under

examination. It is suggested that a failure to admit the full consequences of this type of approach to analysis has been the cause of
some apparently sound criticisms of Kelsen's theory which turn
out on further investigation to be misconceived. In particular, critics
have tended to treat the basic norm as if it were something which
exists in a legal system, and this it is not. It represents, rather, the
specifically legal significance of a certain state of affairs which is
attributed to it by the investigator. It is in this sense that we are
to understand such expressions as "the basic norm *of* a legal order."
In his more recent writings, Kelsen has made some slight modifications to the terminology which he uses to describe the basic
norm. He regards it as a "fiction" rather than as an hypothesis; the
former notion is to be distinguished from the latter for the reason
that reality does not correspond to it.[18] Perhaps the term "fiction"
conveys more about the function of Kelsen's method of interpretation than "assumption" or "hypothesis."

Great emphasis is placed by Kelsen on the necessary distinction
between the inherent validity of law and its practical efficacy. His
avoidance of one of the principal inadequacies of Austin's theory
is a consequence of this distinction. In the case of secondary norms
in a legal system—which are all the stages in the validity-
conferring process leading to the stipulation of the sanction other
than the basic norm itself—the question of validity can be
determined according to the stipulations in other norms which are
nearer to the basic norm. When we come to the basic norm,
however, this validity-tracing process has to stop for there is no
prescriptive unit in the legal system under analysis against which
to test validity any further. Since there is no other element in the
nature of law or in the characteristic structure of a legal system
which can be used to demonstrate the validity of the basic norm,
it must be maintained that to assert the existence of the social or
physical conditions forming the background for the basic norm is
necessarily to assert the validity, for the purposes of law, of the
fundamental norm embodied in this factual situation. The basic
norm is, however, of the same character as other (secondary)
norms, inasmuch as it represents what might be thought of as
the legal, normative, or prescriptive significance which is abstracted
from the factual context. It must be taken to be valid if we are to
talk about law at all. "The basic norm is not created in a legal

---

[18] See Friedmann, *Legal Theory*, p. 277.

procedure by a law-creating organ. It is not—as a positive legal norm is—valid because it is created in a certain way by a legal act, but it is valid because it is presupposed to be valid; and it is presupposed to be valid because without this presupposition no human act could be interpreted as a legal, especially as a norm-creating, act."[19]

The notion of "basic norm" thus expresses the legal significance of the factual context of a social order which can accommodate the legal system under examination. It is probably on account of the terminology employed by Kelsen that some of his critics have too hastily concluded that his Pure Theory of Law, based as it is on this "hypothesis" or "presupposition," amounts to no more than a theory of natural law in disguise.

This is simply not so—though a sound understanding of the nature of the idea of Kelsen's fundamental norm is necessary in order to be able to refute such allegations. The basic norm expresses neither pure fact nor pure conjecture; it is, rather, a hybrid of fact and presupposition. The basis of the notion lies within the realms of man-made law, within a positive law environment, and in this it differs fundamentally from the bases of natural law doctrines. In such doctrines the standard of validity by which to test the content and form of positive law lies, as we have seen, outside such an environment. Kelsen admits that the proposition that the basic norm is the ultimate criterion of legal validity in the national legal order does not rule out the possibility of making any assertions about further possible justifications for the law of the system. One might ask, for instance, why the first or basic constitution is to be respected and considered to be legally binding. it might be answered that the founders of the first constitution were empowered by God. One of the essential characteristics of legal positivism is however, that it dispenses with any such religious justification of a national legal order. Invocations of any metaphysical foundations for the legal system would represent an "impurity" in Kelsen's strictly positivistic analysis, however much they might be favoured by extrinsic, non-legal standards. The basic norm is a fiction which is both necessary and sufficient for the positivist's interpretation of law. It is sufficient, since no such external justification is required. It is necessary because the acts of human beings can be interpreted as legal acts only on the con-

---

[19] *General Theory of Law and State*, p. 116: "The Specific Function of the Basic Norm."

dition that the basic norm is presupposed as a valid norm.

Kelsen thus remains firmly within the camp of the positivists. As Raz reminds us: "Kelsen remains faithful to the principle of origin: The identity of a legal system, as well as the membership of a law in a system, is determined solely by the facts of its creation, by its origin. But the source of unity is no longer one legislative body, it is one power-conferring norm. The basic norm replaces the sovereign, otherwise nothing has changed."[20]

Not a theory of natural law

To criticise Kelsen, as some have done, in terms of an alleged reliance on a metaphysical world of conjecture, raised above and divorced from the level of facts, is to exhibit a basic misunderstanding not only of the nature of Kelsen's theory but also of a great amount of legal reasoning as a whole. In this whole matter an analogy might be made between the rules of law and the rules of a game. To say, for instance, that one's opponent's queen in a game of chess is liable to be taken, is not to express something about the physical potentialities of a piece of wood. The rule or combination of rules which leads to the possibility of making a legal statement is not a mere translation of elements in the factual context in which the statement is made; nor are they metaphysical assertions. They are legal conclusions representing the specifically legal meaning of certain combinations of factual circumstances. Kelsen expressly points out that his method of interpreting the factual conditions which are characteristic of a legal system via the notion of "basic norm" does not really involve anything new in the science of law. He is simply making explicit that which is implicit in the assertions of all jurists who consider positive law as a valid system of norms, and not just as a complex set of facts. This remark, moreover, has full application to a positivist account of law which contains an express rejection of conformity with any metaphysical standards of justice or morality. It is in this sense that the notion of the basic norm is a mental construct which "exists in the juristic consciousness"[21] for the juristic interpretation of observable physical phenomena.

In *The Pure Theory of Law* Kelsen answers criticism of his work based on allegations of concealed natural law with an emphatic

[20] Raz, *op. cit.* p. 95.
[21] See *General Theory of Law and State*, p. 116.

denial of the presence of natural law notions in his analysis, for the following reasons. *The Pure Theory of Law* restricts itself to the examination of positive law, and considers it as an "objectively valid normative order." In order to do this, we must adopt the pre-supposition (or the fiction, as he now prefers to call it) of the basic norm (*Grundnorm*) by which we are able to interpret the "subjective meaning" or physical significance, of law creating acts as their "objective meaning"—the specifically legal significance of these acts which we describe as a result of Kelsen's objective interpretation of them. Such an interpretation of physical acts and events is readily distinguishable from a theory of natural law, since the latter seeks the reason for the validity of positive law in another supposed type, or source, of law outside the sphere of positive law. A theory of natural law seeks to base the validity of positive law in a normative order (a system of oughts) to which the contents of a system of positive law may or may not conform.[22] None, however, of the many theories of natural law which have so far been put forward has managed to set out any clear system of principles to serve as a guide or censor for the content of positive law. Still less has any such theory given rise to illumin-ation on the question of the characteristic structure of a system of positive law. For Kelsen, natural law theories amount to theories of justice; and however they are described, he regards them as consisting for the most part of empty formulae. By the methods of natural law doctrine one can, says Kelsen, maintain and even apparently prove opposite postulates. A theory of natural law can be as conservative or as revolutionary as each writer cares to make it; they all consist of assertions which are not proved. Such theories are concerned with political and ideological tasks, not scientific ones, and it is from these external, non-legal standards that Kelsen aims to keep his own analysis free.[23]

Kelsen explains the specific function of the basic norm in terms of the part it plays in an objectively valid legal order. It has been suggested that this fundamental notion is to be understood in this way: if we observe the outward manifestations or workings of a cohesive aggregate of legal rules which are on the whole practically effective, then the basic norm is to be understood as the legal meaning inherent in, or distilled from, the historical fact-situation which has led to what is now seen to be happening.

[22] *Pure Theory of Law*, pp. 217, 218. See *supra*, Chap. 2.
[23] See *General Theory of Law and State*, pp. 9-11.

This description serves as an initial aid to the understanding of the nature of the basic norm. It is also necessary, however, to be able to distinguish the two different senses in which Kelsen uses the word "constitution" in his elucidation of the idea in the basic norm.[24]

The basic norm and the legal system

In Kelsen's terminology, the word "constitution" may be used in a "positive legal sense," or in a "legal-logical" sense; the latter usage is also described at times as the "transcendental-logical" sense, an expression which merely happens to be more indicative of the neo-Kantian philosophical background of Kelsen's method of interpreting legal phenomena. In reply to Stone[25] who, he said, confused the two senses, Kelsen says that he has always maintained a clear distinction between the constitution in the legal-logical sense, which is the basic norm, and the constitution in a positive legal sense, by which he means the type of constitution in a system of positive law to which we should normally apply that term. The difficult usage occurs in the first of these two senses; the idea might, however, be paraphrased in such an expression as "the basis or *foundation* of legal validity in a positive legal system," or the anchor at the end of the chain of legality, as distinct from the basis of the law-creating acts and the institutions within the positive legal system—the constitution in the ordinary sense of the word. The constitution in the positive legal sense is part of the law or norm-creating process within the system of positive law itself, and is elliptically referred to by Kelsen as "a norm of positive law." In contrast, the basic norm which is said to be presupposed in juristic thinking, or the "constitution in a legal-logical sense," is not a part of positive law itself since it is not "posited" or created by the real act of will of a legal organ.

It would be out of place here to consider in detail the misconceptions which have arisen in criticisms of Kelsen's theory. It may be suggested, however, that they are largely attributable to a confusion of the two senses of the word constitution which have just been considered. In particular, the constitution in the

---

[24] For one of the clearest and most detailed of Kelsen's accounts of this distinction see (1965) 2 *Stanford Law Review*, 1128.

[25] See (1963) 26 M.L.R. 34, "Mystery and Mystique in the Basic Norm."

positive legal sense has been taken for the basic norm, which it is not. Even greater feats have been demanded of the basic norm when a political situation is found which does not readily yield a picture of a unified legal system. Kelsen, it is true, refers elliptically at times to the basic norm *of* a national legal order, but this is not something which is yielded by observation. Such an expression refers, rather, to the way in which the notion of the basic norm is applied in an objective legal interpretation of a complex set of physical conditions. A split in governmental allegiance in a country does not, for instance, connote a split in the basic norm,[26] any more than the inapplicability of the basic norm to a disunited political system presents us with a case of juristic schizophrenia!

The use of this important distinction in the description of a particular system of law is this: when the fundamental or basic norm is considered as investing a law-producing agency, the constitution in the legal-logical sense is formed. This agency or organ, sometimes referred to as the "historically first legislator,"[27] may now validly create norms or rules which will regulate the legislating authority, or legislature, itself. The regulating product of the first law-producing agency which refers to the next law-creating organ in the "process of concretisation" of law is the constitution in the positive legal sense.[28] On this basis, the objective validity of the content of the positive legal system is derived from the basic norm; but except for this dependence on the validating or authoritative character of the basic norm, the content of the positive law of the system is completely independent of it. Apart from this single necessary connection, the specific content of the legal order can contain valid laws which may be judged according to non-legal standards as good, bad or indifferent. It is, perhaps, on account of this feature of Kelsen's Pure Theory of Law that some critics have sought to demonstrate its sterility by pointing out that it can serve as an objective analysis of the characteristic nature of any legal system, however immoral or iniquitous its individual positive laws may be. Such criticisms are not only subjective by nature, but themselves depend on

---

[26] For such an allegation, see, for instance, (1967) 30 M.L.R. 156, "Splitting the Grundnorm."

[27] That is, the legislator in the most literal sense, meaning the organ which lays down or sets out the law.

[28] Taken from Allgemeine Staatslehre, Berlin, 1929.

subjective interpretations of fairness and justice;[29] they are concerned with politics and moral ideology, not with law in the strict sense.

Laws and lawyers

We may now refer briefly to the third of the necessary distinctions alluded to at the beginning of this chapter. It is not, of itself, vastly important; but it is a useful and often essential distinction to keep in mind when considering statements made by jurists about the nature of law. The subjects of normative jurisprudence are norms, not actual patterns of physical behaviour. The statements by which jurists describe norms and the way in which they are to be interpreted as elements of a legal system, are not themselves norms. Such statements do not prescribe anything about what is to happen. They are themselves descriptive and not prescriptive, though they refer to something which does prescribe. They descriptively reproduce the "ought" of the norms themselves. In order to appreciate this simple but necessary distinction, we must notice the contrast between law as it comes from the hand of the legislator—the legal norm itself—and the statement which embodies the jurist's description of it. The words of the jurist or the lawyer are norm-descriptive and not norm-expressive.

Validity and efficacy

The basic norm is presupposed to possess an objective validity in relation to the legal order which is founded on it, and the consequent objective validity of all the other norms of the legal order—the secondary norms—is founded on the existence of this primary or basic norm. The general efficacy of a legal order is prerequisite to the attribution to it of a basic norm.

The element of coercion in law does not consist, says Kelsen, in any form of "psychic compulsion," but in the fact that acts of coercion, or sanctions, are provided for by the legal order. Physical coercion is relevant to legal validity only insofar as it forms part of the content of the legal norm. Legal rules are thus rules which provide for sanctions. The quality of legal validity is not affected by the state of mind of any individual who is subject to

---

[29] *Cf.* the attitude of Bentham (p. 39, *supra*) as to valid but unjust laws. See also Chap. 3, *supra*, pp. 59-64.

the operation of the norm. In this context Kelsen refers, for the sake of contrast, to both the questions as to the efficacy of law which were alluded to earlier in this chapter. Whether or not people actually behave in such a way as to avoid the application of the sanction which is stipulated by the legal norm, is a matter which is relevant to the effectiveness of law and legal policy in securing its objects. Whether or not the sanction is actually carried out by the legal officials when the necessary conditions for its application are present, relates to the practical operation and the efficacy of law.

A norm is considered to be valid if, and only if, it belongs to a system of norms and to a system which, moreover, is generally efficacious. These can be regarded as two concurrent conditions which are necessary for the validity of an individual norm of the legal order. On account of the latter condition it can be said that efficacy is a condition of validity; the system of norms has on the whole to be efficacious. But efficacy is a condition of validity, and not the reason for it.[30] The efficacy of law is, according to Kelsen, a matter which is determined by causation, while its validity is explicable in terms, not of causation, but of imputation. A legal order does not lose its validity when a single norm ceases to be effective. Nor does a single legal norm lose its validity if it is only ineffective from time to time. A norm is not, however, considered to be valid when it is never applied; such a norm, having been initially valid on account of its connection with a generally efficacious system of norms, may lose its validity by never being applied in practice. In his *Pure Theory of Law* Kelsen applies the principle of general efficacy to individual legal norms as well as to the basic norm, with the result that widespread inefficacy of an individual legal norm (a secondary norm) may, via "desuetude," produce the same effect as total inefficacy.[31]

On the other hand, just as an individual legal norm which figures in the general picture of legal validity must not be one which is never obeyed or applied, neither can it be of such a

[30] See, generally, *General Theory of Law and State*, pp. 29-42; *Pure Theory of Law*, Chap. 5, pp. 211-214.

[31] This will, presumably, have to happen in accordance with a specific norm of "desuetude" constituting an integral part of the legal order. It would otherwise be difficult to reconcile this problem of the degree of effectiveness of secondary norms with the "purity" of the rest of Kelsen's method of the objective interpretation of legal validity. However, his language in *General Theory of Law and State*, at p. 120, tends to obscure this interpretation. See Raz, *Concept of a Legal System*, p. 60.

nature that it is in all cases bound to be obeyed or applied. The supposed norm would otherwise cease to be a norm at all. In stating a law of nature, for example, no assertion is being made about what shall happen and there is no stipulation or prescription about what is to happen. In Kelsen's words, a norm which prescribes that something ought to be, which we know must happen anyway in accordance with one of the laws of nature, is meaningless.[32] This distinction between human positive law and the laws of nature must be recalled in considering the rejection by Ross[33] of the feature of a specifically "legal cognition" in such an analysis as Kelsen's, together with Ross' method of relating legal validity and factual predictions.

Lastly and very briefly, what is the relationship between fact and what is strictly law? Effectiveness is a fundamental condition for legal validity—this is simple enough to understand—but it is not validity itself. Jurists who carry the original relationship between effectiveness and validity to the length of the identification of the two elements are, according to Kelsen, guilty of distortion in their vain attempt at a simplification of the problem of legal analysis. Furthermore, if the concept of power in the form of overwhelming physical force is used instead of the idea of effectiveness, a similar conclusion is demanded by Kelsen's account; this is, that right cannot exist without might, but is not identical with might.

IV

Kelsen and Olivecrona

Kelsen's analysis of the nature of law is totally dependent on the concept of a norm which is embodied in legal situations and legal acts. The legal system as a whole is the product of certain acts which are all related to a state of affairs which is considered by the jurist to give rise to the notion of the fundamental or basic norm.

For Olivecrona, "law is nothing but a set of social facts."[34]

---

[32] See *The Pure Theory of Law*, p. 213.

[33] See *infra*, Chap. 8, p. 159.

[34] *Law as Fact*, Einar Munksgaard, Copenhagen, 1939; Chap. IV, p. 127. The "second edition" of this book (Stevens, 1971) is an altogether fresh work, though based on the same philosophy. For convenience in the present context, discussion of Olivecrona's propositions in the first edition of his work is retained.

Olivecrona is one of the best known of a group of Scandinavian jurists who deny the necessity of adopting the type of normative approach to legal analysis which underlies the whole of Kelsen's juristic method. His disagreement on some fundamental issues with Kelsen's legal analysis may appear surprising when viewed in the light of one of his principal contentions. "Law," says Olivecrona, "consists chiefly of rules about force."[35] The essential element of regulated force is thus present in the analysis of each jurist. It is, however, in the method by which this regulated force is interpreted by Kelsen and Olivecrona respectively that a notable difference of opinion between them is to be found.

Olivecrona maintains that the prescriptive character of law can be represented in exactly the same way as any other social phenomenon, in terms of facts and by means of a description of the causal relationship between one fact or set of facts and another.

Questions as to the validity of law arise from the problem of what is often called the "binding force" of law. The relationship between law and fact was examined in the two preceding sections and it was seen that, according to some views of the nature of law, a separation is to be made between law and fact and between the validity of law and its practical effectiveness. Kelsen's analysis of law rests on a separation between those different features which are related to each other in complex ways but which are not to be identified with each other.

Olivecrona expresses a view similar to that of Kelsen, by saying that the binding force of law must be something different from the fact that we expose ourselves to the risk of sanctions when we overstep certain limits drawn up by the law. He also states that "the rules of law have a firm grip over us. But this is not what is meant by their binding force. The binding force is definitely not the same thing as the fact that unpleasant consequences are likely to occur in case of unlawful behaviour. If this were what we mean by the binding force, we might as well say that there is a binding rule forbidding people to put their hands into the fire."[36]

The proposition that the binding force of law—an idea which is closely allied to the notion of legal validity—does not exist as a fact is given a new twist by Olivecrona. He asserts that it exists "in the imagination only"[37] and at times goes even further, to

---

[35] *Ibid.* Chap. IV, p. 134.
[36] *Law as Fact,* p. 12.
[37] *Ibid.* p. 15.

condemn the idea of the binding force of law as nonsense. He insists on the interpretation of facts as facts and as nothing more. It is in the light of this feature of his account that his comment on the Pure Theory of Law should be interpreted: "It is impossible to explain rationally how facts in the actual world can produce effects in the wholly different 'world of the Ought.' At one time Kelsen bluntly declared that this was in fact 'the Great Mystery.' That is to state the matter plainly. A mystery it is, and a mystery it will remain for ever."[38]

In order to be able to attach any meaning to Kelsen's explanation, it is essential to distinguish between prescriptive and descriptive elements in law. The legal or prescriptive significance of physical acts and events connected with a legal system is not identical with those acts and events; but it would be somewhat distorted to assert that all talk of their legal significance is imaginary or even nonsensical merely because that significance is not identical or synonymous with the acts or events themselves. Words have to be examined in the context in which they are or have been used, if we are to appreciate their meaning. This consideration applies to the analysis of the meaning of legal concepts; and it can usefully be applied to the meaning which Olivecrona can be deduced to attach to his own notion of fact. In relation to Kelsen's theory of law, the meaning, for Olivecrona's assessment, could either be made wide enough to cover also the legal significance of a norm-creating act as something separable from it; or such a meaning could be excluded because of the absence of identification with the fact or physical act itself. Olivecrona comes down squarely in favour of the latter alternative.

This is, however, to exclude a very great deal from the category of meaningful statements. The argument has been advanced that Olivecrona, together with other Scandinavian "realists" who adopt an approach similar to his, are offering a peculiar and unnecessary alternative in the analysis of legal concepts, including primarily the concept of law itself.[39] Is it necessary, runs the argument, to treat all statements which are not simply descriptive of events, as being descriptive of imaginary events, or psychologically induced fictions? The example is taken of a goal in a game of football. A piece of inflated leather flying under or over a set of wooden posts is not a goal; neither is the converse proposition

[38] *Ibid.* p. 21.
[39] See *e.g.* Marshall, "Law in a Cold Climate," 1956 *Juridical Review.*

true. A goal is a meaningful concept describable as the rule-based significance or meaning of such a physical or factual event. A goal is not something in the world of the supernatural, it is not metaphysical, it is not imaginary and it is not a nonsense.

Olivecrona continues, "The sole basis for the nebulous words about the supernatural relation of the 'ought' is a verbal expression in conjunction with certain emotions. The word ought and the like are imperative expressions which we use in order to impress a certain behaviour on people. It is sheer nonsense to say that they signify a reality. Their sole function is to work on the minds of people, directing them to do this or that or refrain from something else...."[40] By means of such expressions, we are told, the lawgivers are able to influence the conduct of state officials and of the public in general. "The laws are therefore links in the chain of cause and effect."

The legal imperative

In this account of law, which appears to be so very different from that of Kelsen, two elements are included which are similar to ones used in that theory. These are the idea of the imperative element in law and the particular concern with state officials. In his description of the nature of legal norms, Kelsen uses the expression "depsychologised commands." Olivecrona is one of the leading critics of the Imperative Theory of law, and he must find some means of expressing his own views in which he does not have to resort to the direct and personalised notion of a sovereign. His method of explanation of what he admits to be the imperative element in law is therefore described by the notion of "independent imperatives." This is the term which Olivecrona uses to describe the character of rules of law. A command in the true sense implies a personal relationship, but the words which are characteristic of commands can also be used in situations which do not involve any such relationship, and can have an effect which is similar to, if not identical with, their effect in that type of relationship. Such imperatives are said by Olivecrona to function in a way which is independent of any particular person issuing the commands.

It might seem that Olivecrona's "independent imperatives" serve only to express the same sort of idea which Kelsen referred

[40] *Law as Fact*, Introduction, p. 21.

to as "depsychologized commands" representing the meaning of physical acts for the purpose of the legal system. The explanation which is attached by Olivecrona to the use of this term demonstrates, however, that his notion is restricted to the description of a physical state of affairs. In our minds, he says, the imperative expression is connected with the idea of an action, and it is on account of this purely psychological effect of the imperative form of the law that we feel ourselves to be under a legal obligation, that we feel bound. It is merely this which amounts, for Olivecrona, to the binding force of law.

It is suggested that this initial account of the real nature of the reason for which law is regarded as binding contains the seeds of a confusion between two related but essentially separable questions. One question relates to the nature of law itself and the other to the reasons for which people obey law or feel, in a subjective way, under a legal obligation. An effect on people's minds may, in fact, be produced by all sorts of combinations of physical circumstances and mental processes. With regard to mental attitudes to law, such an account can only lead to the widest subjectivity. In the light of an analysis of law such as that put forward by Kelsen, Olivecrona's picture, and especially his interpretation of facts, seems somewhat oversimplified. It is capable of leading to a confusion of the validity and the efficacy of law, and also between reasons for appreciating legal obligation and motives for obeying law.

At the end of the chapter of *Law as Fact* throughout which Olivecrona levels explicit or implicit criticism at Kelsen's theory of law, is this passage: "In reality, the law of a country consists of an immense mass of ideas concerning human behaviour, accumulated during centuries through the contribution of innumerable collaborators. These ideas have been expressed in the imperative form by their originators, especially through formal legislation, and are being preserved in the same form in books of law. The ideas are again and again revived in human minds, accompanied by the imperative expression: This line of conduct shall be taken, or something else to the same effect."[41] For Olivecrona, a fact is something which possesses objective reality—the quality which he expressly denies to Kelsen's notion of the "ought." His explanation therefore combines two aspects of the same feature, namely, the factual description of the evolution of legal ideas and the descriptive

[41] *Law as Fact*, p. 48.

consideration of the effects which these have when they are again and again revived in human minds. It may, however, be suggested that such a descriptive consideration is neither necessary nor sufficient to account for the essential and distinguishing characteristics of the concept of law. The combined effect, on the other hand, of the separation and interrelation, in Kelsen's theory of law, of descriptive and prescriptive elements in an explanation of law, of the essential character of law and its actual content, and of the validity and efficacy of law, is to arrive at an interrelation of factual and conceptual expressions which is both sufficient to afford an answer to the question: What is law?—and necessary, if the legal meaning and significance of the Physical aspects of legal rules and legal institutions is to be brought out.

CHAPTER 7

LAW, FORCE AND AUTHORITY

Introductory

THIS chapter deals with three principal relationships. Section I discusses connections between law and force—that is, physical force and physical power. Section II deals with the notion of power considered from a different angle—with the element of authority in law. Section III contains a brief review of some notable interpretations of the nature of International Law, and, as in the first two sections, the account consists of an outline only. Much more could be said on each of these matters, but attention will centre on some principal points of comparison. The last section of this chapter takes a look at some opinions about the way in which the character of law is to be described in its relation to factual situations and physical events. At the beginning of Chapter 8 it will be seen how one view of this relationship can influence the manner of accounting for the place and function of legal institutions, especially the courts, within a system of law. The three relationships dealt with in this chapter may be given the titles: Law and Force, Law and Authority, and Law and Reality. These headings recall three differing approaches to legal analysis which have so far been encountered, and further attention will now be given to characteristic points of some leading accounts of law.

I

Law and force

The very expression "binding force of law" indicates that the obligatory character of valid laws and of the legal system in which they figure may well have something to do with force—physical force. It is also fairly clear that law cannot be characterised in terms of force alone without the addition of some element by which to confer legality on its exercise. The meaning of the added condition "binding" must be considered. This notion has implications of regularity, legality, authority and consequent legal obligation, and a brief résumé of the conditions which were attached to physical force in the theories so far studied may be useful.

The "binding" or obligatory character of the law of nature lies essentially in the moral worthiness of such a source of human regulation to be obeyed by man.[1] In the development of natural law doctrine it is possible to detect an interplay between the fateful forces of nature in numerous guises and the moral superiority of the higher law which contains, *ex hypothesi*, the ultimate standards of righteousness. The power and authority of natural principles is usually endowed, however, with a moral quality which is understandably attributed to the natural order, which governs everything. A fatalist philosophy need not come to conclusions founded on ethical characteristics, but if man is in the hands of fate and at the beck and call of nature it is comforting to presuppose a morality and a justice behind all nature.

The position of human positive laws is different in that men have the faculties of freewill and reason and have a choice as to what laws they will make for themselves and for their fellow men. They all have a choice whether or not to obey those laws. The exercise of this choice may be conditioned by a number of factors. First, laws may fail to achieve any substantial degree of efficacy if they do not comply with certain minimum moral standards accepted by those whom it is sought to regulate. Secondly, law as a whole may suffer from a similar incapacity if there is not the physical might to enforce it. As to the first point, it was argued in Chapter 2 that the character of positive law lends itself to satisfactory analysis without the assumption that the Is of positive human law necessarily involves an Ought of some standard of morality. The second question, it will be noticed, concerns law as a whole rather than individual laws. To regard force as a necessary element in human regulation is simply to represent what goes on in the operation of a typical modern state, however democratic or otherwise it may be. The law-enforcing authorities have at their disposal the mechanisms by which to put into operation part of the physical power of the state; the ultimate exercise of such force consists in death or the deprivation of personal liberty, though there are many other sides to its use besides these extreme ones. On a view which regards the fulfilment of certain moral standards as being necessary for regula-

---

[1] It has sometimes even been based on the scientific necessity that such "laws" will be obeyed.

tions to attain the status of legal validity, even a single regulation might be condemned as immoral and might therefore be regarded as non-legal, despite the general righteousness of the system of order. If, however, the regulations of the system were seen to be generally enforced, the relative absence of enforcement of a particular legal provision, the fact that it was not often enforced by the officials of the legal system, would not necessarily attract the same compelling reasons for exclusion from the category of "law." A law may be regarded as a valid law before it is ever put into operation by the decision or the action of a law official. If, however, the particular law was deliberately and consistently ignored even when occasions arose on which it could suitably be applied, a different construction would be required. The view that no regulation becomes law until it is the subject of a judicial pronouncement would not accord with this construction, though the justification of that view would be limited to the discussion of laws in the form of particular legal provisions, as distinct from an explanation of the character of law in which the very position of the courts themselves and the reasons for the legitimacy of their action may also be considered.[2]

Similar considerations may in certain instances apply to morals and to force, as they each figure in an analysis of the nature of law. A common feature may be seen in the generality of moral worthiness and the generality of official enforcement, which analyses based respectively on morality and force would require. On the other hand, the place of morality in a characterisation of law differs from that of force, since it can involve the attribution of a subjective standard of assessment at every stage in the legal process. Accounts of the nature of law which are based on value-judgments contend that morals condition and govern legality. Legality, on the other hand, can itself be found by empirical observation of modern legal systems to condition the exercise of physical force. Regulation of physical force is necessary if legal order is to be distinguished from anarchy. The respective elements of morality and force as they figure in a characterisation of the nature of law are generally to be regarded as making the same type of contribution only on the assumption that iniquity is to be regarded as synonymous with anarchy. Moreover the incidence of force and the incidence of morality in a legal system differ according to whether the concept of law or an individual law is being considered. Both elements can be related to the character of law, though for different reasons. A moral judgment may, how-

[2] See Chap. 8, pp. 171-173, *infra*.

ever, be passed on the claim to legality of a particular regulation, while the exercise of force cannot realistically be considered in direct connection with each individual positive regulation within a generally enforced system of laws unless one of the excesses of Austin's formulation is to be reiterated.

A division between laws and morals was made by Bentham, but it was left to his successor Austin, in his version of the Imperative Theory of law, to elaborate on the place of force in the operation of laws. It might be thought remarkable that the theory which traditionally goes by this name is generally associated with the work of Austin, although it was Bentham's account which really stood or fell by the notion of the sovereign order or command, without going into great detail about the force which may be expected to result from a breach of the duty created by that order. In distinguishing his own account from that of Bentham by expressly refusing to consider rewards as sanctions, Austin gave a new and rather different form to a theory originated by Bentham. It was on account of Austin's use of the notion of force, expressed in terms of sanctions resulting from breach of legal duty, that Kelsen was able to point to one of the theory's major inadequacies. For Kelsen, laws are laws if they are part of a process which involves the stipulation of physical force under certain conditions. Law is the primary norm which stipulates that the regular use of physical force shall ultimately, on the basis of certain conditions traceable through the valid stages of a legal system, be applied. On this view, given that a generally effective system of ordered enforcement exists, law is essentially sanction-stipulating as distinct from sanction-applying. Whether or not it is in fact sanction-applying does not depend upon its validity as law but upon its practical effectiveness as a form of coercive regulation.

For Olivecrona the binding force of law is something which exists only in the imagination. It is not for him a "reality." Law consists of rules about force, and legal phenomena are to be examined in terms of empirically verifiable propositions which are directly about what goes on in fact. In the back of the minds of all the populace lies an awareness of the central and organised physical force which is the monopoly of the state. Olivecrona does not even admit that law may be upheld by force or guaranteed by force. Such a formulation of the nature of a legal order would involve a dualism which he is not prepared to accept. In his view law is regulated force; the binding force of law is represented as consisting essentially in the physical force itself, with attention to its specifically binding quality limited to the impression created by the ideas which are again and again revived in people's minds on the basis of the physical power at the disposal of state organs.

Olivecrona, like Kelsen, clearly directs his analysis towards the character of law as a whole phenomenon, as distinct from the more atomic explanations of Bentham and Austin. The similarity of expressions chosen by each of these jurists to represent the prescriptive character of positive law in such a way as to avoid the overdirect and personalised notion of "command" was noted in Chapter 6. Another feature common to their accounts is a concern with the monopolisation of force within the state machinery.

Kelsen notes the paradoxical characteristic of law, that force is used in order to prevent the employment of force in society. This apparent antinomy leads to the doctrine of anarchism, which holds that force should be precluded from playing a part even in the stipulation of the legal sanction. The antinomy is, however, only apparent, since the law which makes for peace consists of organised force.[3] The law attaches certain conditions to the authoritative employment of force, and the authoritative use of force is made the monopoly of official state organs. So far this account seems indistinguishable from that given by Olivecrona.[4] The Swedish jurist remarks that actual violence is in practice kept very much in the background in the operation of the state legal system. This factor represents a real advantage to the smooth operation of the state legal machinery but it has also, he says, served to give the impression that physical force or violence is alien to law or that it is of only secondary importance. The essential conditions for the effectiveness of the state force in the accomplishment of its necessary role in the preservation of order are that it should be organised and that it may, owing largely to its organised character, be of overwhelming strength in comparison with any possible opposition. Force must be the monopoly of the state organisation, and the use of force by this organisation must be harnessed by means of rules.[5]

Thus, in the treatment which they each give to the place of force in an account of the nature of law Kelsen and Olivecrona put

[3] *General Theory of Law and State*, p. 21.

[4] See *Law as Fact*, Chap. IV, generally.

[5] *Law as Fact*, p. 172. It is arguable, however, that when Olivecrona comes to examine the nature of the vital element in this explanation—that of a rule—he really gives an account, not of the nature of legal rules, but of the reasons or motives for which people obey them.

forward some similar propositions. It is in their respective attitudes to the way in which conclusions as to the use of force are best to be represented that fundamental differences of opinion arise. In particular the role of force in Kelsen's account is integrally connected with the postulation of a basic norm of a legal system, against which the legal validity of all the intermediate stages or secondary norms leading up to the stipulation of a sanction in any particular case may be tested. Force is central to Kelsen's analysis, but it is interpreted as part of the content of the sanction-stipulating norm. The legal norm, whether it be the primary norm or one of the secondary norms, is in turn characterised by Kelsen as something necessarily distinguishable from plain facts such as the actual exercise of physical force. Though law relates to the force within a system, law and force do not attract the same kind of analysis. Kelsen insists on the distinction between the efficacy or effectiveness of legal norms, which will vary in accordance with the extent to which they are finally enforced, and the validity of law which is related to efficacy but which is not identical with it. The validity of a legal rule is all that is necessary for its existence as such, provided of course that the provisions of the legal order as a whole are generally enforced by the official sanction-applying organs of the state. Validity and efficacy may coincide in particular cases of the application of valid rules or norms, but at the level of secondary norms they need not necessarily do so.

II

Law and authority

The account given by the eminent sociologist Weber is naturally framed in sociological terms and considers a legal order as a type of social phenomenon. He deals with the way in which authority establishes itself in society. Legitimate domination, he says, begins in a "charismatic" form, whereby a kind of personal ascendancy is attributed to a particular individual. Even at the end of a régime, the person enjoying this charismatic aura of authority may still be able to exercise personal power to an otherwise inexplicable extent.[6] The next typical stage in the development of authority consists in the passing on of the personal power by those endowed with a

[6] See Lloyd, *The idea of Law*, Pelican 1964, p. 30, commenting on the last days of Adolf Hitler in a Berlin bunker.

charismatic aura to their successors in title. In this stage of social development a significant step can be detected from government by men to government by law. We now begin to speak of rules of succession, and an element of continuity has been introduced. The third and final stage which typifies this development is that at which the personal ascendancy and also its attenuated form as a title to succeed can fade into the background, leaving only the essential belief in the legitimacy of the governmental authority. The name which Webber gives to his final development of authority is "legal domination," but it should be remembered that all three forms which he outlines are forms of legitimate domination. Where the attitude of a legal analyst such as Hart differs from that of Weber is in the treatment which is made of the available material. While Weber asks how legitimate domination can be described as arising in a social order, Hart is concerned with what that legitimate domination is and with the way in which it can best be represented as a characteristic element in the structure of law. It must be noted that Weber's so-called "ideal types" of authority are intended only as models for the stages of development which authority can be expected to undergo in society. All three represent a potentially legal authority, even though that term is reserved by Weber for use in a stricter sense to signify the final stage of de-personalisation of governmental authority. All three stages may be analysed by such a method as that adopted by Hart, in terms of the attitude of people within the legal system, in which one such type of authority prevails, to the rules and standards of legal validity which depend on that authority. From this point of view each stage may be seen as a legal situation distinguishable from that which Hart calls a "pre-legal" world. Whether the particular manifestations of legal authority are to be described as personal (charismatic) or impersonal (legal) is of no account in a positivist analysis of the nature of law. However, with his account framed in terms of sociological facts, Weber is able to avoid the over-ambitious attempt of an analysis such as that of Austin to account for both the physical signs of legal authority and the legal significance which is to be interpreted from the acts and events themselves. Such a demarcation in legal theory has good reason behind it, for it can assist in avoiding circularity of description and muddled thinking. The separation of different questions within the field of varied aspects of law becomes most distinct in Kelsen's Pure Theory of Law, and its effect will now be considered in relation to the account given by Gray of legal authority in society.

The American writer Gray took a view of the nature of law which appears to English eyes as lying midway between that of Austin and the accounts of more modern legal writers. He is, however, closer in the view he takes to Austin's notion of law as the *fiat* of the sovereign; in a sense Gray replaces this with an emphasis on law as the *fiat* of the judges. In both approaches the principal assertions tend to concern individual positive laws rather than the general characteristics of law as a whole. The following chapter is devoted to a discussion of approaches to legal study which have centred on the position and function of the courts in the legal system, and that aspect of Gray's work will be included. The matter to be discussed here is the way in which he deals with the notion of authority in a legal order, and to do this a search must be made behind the courts and judges for the elements of the system which ultimately influence the law-making powers of the judges themselves. Gray calls these influences the "real rulers of society" or the "ruling spirits of the community." A defect of Austin's description of the sovereign's powers lay in his failure to give an adequate account of the *reasons* for which the orders of the sovereign are to be regarded as authoritative. He was, in a way, putting the cart before the horse, for without law there would be no sovereign and no inheritance. Gray was clearly aware of this inadequacy, and he compensated with his description of forces or powers lying behind the organs which are parallel, in his account, to the law-creating organs in Austin's theory.

One of the central propositions in his book *The Nature and Sources of the Law* is this: "The true view, as I submit, is that the Law is what the judges declare: that statutes, precedents, the opinions of learned experts, customs and morality are the sources of the Law; that back of everything lie the opinions of the ruling spirits of the community, who have the power to close any of these sources; but that so long as they do not interfere, the judges, in establishing Law, have recourse to these sources."[7] These "ruling spirits" therefore represent the anchor for the chain of legal acts, especially for those of the courts, who would otherwise have a

---

[7] *The Nature and Sources of the Law*, 2nd ed., pp. 283-284. Under "morality" Gray includes principles of fairness and general equity. It is, incidentally, remarkable that this vital passage occurs almost *en passant* in a chapter on Custom, and also that the "ruling spirits of the community," though of fundamental importance in Gray's account, do not figure in his index.

free hand in lawmaking. Whoever or whatever these ruling forces are, it is they that possess the ultimate power to regulate the particular legal order with which they are concerned. At some points in Gray's account they are apparently highly personalised, but at others they evaporate into spirits. The problem of description is set by Gray himself. "To determine who are the real rulers of a political society is well-nigh an impossible task—for Jurisprudence a well-nigh insoluble problem"; and very soon afterwards he says that the "real rulers of a political society are undiscoverable."[8] This idea is central to Gray's account of the nature of the law, and yet it is described as being remarkably elusive. For Kelsen, however, the idea fails to constitute a juristic problem. The attitudes of Gray and Kelsen may be compared in order to discover the reason for this difference of opinion.

Who or what are these "real rulers?" How do they function? As to the first question, a possible solution to this problem of the power behind the law might be found in the participation in government of the general electoral body, which Austin at one point included in his notion of sovereignty. This is not, however, what Gray means. For him the notion of sovereignty is superfluous. To divide the members of a state into rulers and ruled and to call the former sovereign and the latter subjects gives us no help in understanding the nature of law. Nor, he says, are the real rulers synonymous with the state itself; in fact they create and uphold the state. They are endowed with the power to create the rules of succession themselves. All we have up to now is a vague impression of what the "real rulers" are not. Gray goes on, however, to refer to the "real rulers" of society as a "personified abstraction," and it is in this description that we may find a key to the understanding of Gray's idea which can serve to indicate both the merit of the idea itself and the weakness resulting from the way it is expressed.

An abstraction is, in the light of the account which was given of Kelsen's analysis of law, a convenient and indicative term by which to describe the notion of the basic norm, the notion described by Kelsen himself as being of fictional or hypothetical quality. This feature constitutes the merit and realism of Gray's notion, but its personalisation represents a weakness. Gray was still, rather like Austin, trying to delineate a specific body or entity from which legal power and authority is derived. It is as

[8] *Op. cit.* pp. 76, 77.

though he could not envisage the existence of such authority without at the same time thinking in terms of its practical exercise in specific cases. According to Gray law is derived from sources. When the courts make pronouncements on the basis of those sources, then and only then is actual law created. Behind the courts lies the power of the ruling spirits of the community, which represents the ultimate influence on the authoritative character of judicial decisions. Even here, however, Gray goes in search of a source of this authority on the same plane as the rest of the legal order. In his "personalised abstraction" we can see an indication of a move towards the type of analysis employed by Kelsen and Hart, together with an unwillingness to make the final break between the social facts and the legal interpretation which may be to be placed on them.

The might of the real rulers creates and upholds the State and thus exercises a binding effect in influencing the coherence of society and its laws. Since the real rulers are said to determine whether a rule laid down by the courts can constitute valid law within the limits which they set on the courts' choice from sources of law, they might also be thought of as lying behind the binding force of law. The real rulers of society are the highest authoritative influence on the validity of that society's body of laws. Legal validity cannot, on some views which have been considered in previous chapters, be derived immediately from facts, and therefore something lying behind the laws, or at least some notion which is distinguishable from their specific identity, appears to be necessary for a satisfactory account of the nature of law. Gray certainly makes a step in this direction, but Kelsen rejects the way in which he makes it. For Gray the problem of discovering the real rulers of the community, the influences which ultimately dictate the lawmaking powers of the courts, is insoluble. For Kelsen it is unnecessary. In Kelsen's analysis the State is the valid constitution. At the fundamental level at which the elements which give coherence to the legal order of a society are to be examined efficacy is presupposed, by means of the notion of the "basic norm," to constitute the validating influences within that order. The "real rulers" are therefore to be regarded as the organs by whose acts norms are created which are generally efficacious in the form of a general order. At this basic level of sociological and political fact the notion of "ruling spirits of the community" may be regarded as one of the unspoken characteristics of the general efficacy which constitutes only the background for Kelsen's initial hypothesis of validity.

III

International law

While natural law doctrines prevailed, the problem of the character or foundation of internal law hardly arose. The doctrines of Grotius in the seventeenth century could ultimately be traced back to Aristotle's conception of the way in which law and man's reason are intimately connected. The highest law, constituting the authority behind all forms of law, including the law governing mankind, was the law of nature, and this law applied both within states and between states. It was usual to conceive of municipal law and international law[9] as being of the same nature, since theory made no particular demand to consider each separately.

A break with the approach of Grotius was made by Hobbes, who, while admitting certain principles as "natural," indicated that the instrumentality of positive law was to be regarded as predominant as a source of legislation within a state. The true separation from natural law tradition came, however, with Hume and Bentham, and the critical approach of these two great philosophers formed the basis of Austin's theories of law and sovereignty and of his consequent attitude to the nature of international law. The combination of indivisibility and illimitability as necessary characteristics of Austin's sovereign led to his exclusion of what is now known as public international law from the ambit of the term law when properly used. It is apparent, even in the modern form which international law assumes—with the United Nations Organisation, the International Court of Justice and a whole mass of treaties and treaty organisations—that the use of physical coercion and enforced sanctions cannot be described as coincidental in municipal, or national law, and international law. The two situations do not possess the same characteristics in this respect. This is not to say that international law cannot be analysed in terms similar to those which legal theorists may apply in the sphere of municipal law. However,

---

[9] At that time the law which governed the relations between states was not as yet known as "international law"; the term was, incidentally, first coined by Bentham.

these two spheres of regulation should not simply be assumed to possess the same characteristics merely on account of their common name "law." Throughout the relatively short history of international law more assumptions seem to have been made in the examination of the character of international law than in any other part of legal theory. Assumptions may result in a number of differing conclusions. To insist, for instance, on the Austinian idea of law as a sovereign command backed up by the threat of a sanction, is to exclude international relations from the meaning of law, for this is a necessary result of the initial definition. On the other hand, the assumption by Kelsen of a basic norm of international law which is related to that of a national legal order may not appear to be wholly justified. In Kelsen's view, however, the fundamental assumption required for the interpretation of a social order as a legal order is itself of a fictional nature, and the problem of distinguishing international law from municipal law— or, at least, of refusing to see a necessary relation between the nature of one and the nature of the other—becomes more difficult to solve than the version of the problem involving Austin's theory.

It might at first seem remarkable that Austin and Kelsen put forward opposing views of the character of international law, for, although Kelsen appreciated and avoided Austin's error of identifying the breach of a legal rule with the probability that a sanction would be applied, both he and Austin place great emphasis on the element of physical constraint or coercion in law. Since the feature of organised sanctions is found in both accounts, they might both be expected to maintain that international law lacks one of the essential characteristics of law. The difference between their approaches lies, however, not in the presence or absence of the element of force in a theory of law, but in the way in which it is treated by the particular method of interpretation adopted by each of these writers.

Enough has been said already to dispel the misconception, manifested by some critics of Kelsen, that the basic norm of a national legal order is itself a part of that order or the basis of the physical acts upon which the order operates in practice. It is a method of interpreting facts, and the expression "basic norm *of* a national legal order" may be understood as the basic norm *as applied* to a national legal order. It is a fiction, not in the sense of a mere invention of fact, but in the sense of a mental assumption necessarily adopted in the interpretation of legal phenomena. The notion of a norm represents the expression of legal meaning.

The coercive acts to which the basic norm of international law relates are found by Kelsen in armed reprisals and war, the difference between the two being one of degree only. The meaning of law is not to be found in facts alone: an assumption must be made, in Kelsen's view, in relation to those facts. It is on account of this method of interpretation of fact that Kelsen is able to apply his analysis both to municipal, or national law, and to international law. It might, however, be asked whether in so doing Kelsen makes an assumption—this time of a rather more mundane variety—as to the facts which form the basis for statements about international law. Traditional theory, he says,[10] sees in national law and international law two different, mutually independent norm systems. This construction of the situation is referred to as "dualistic," or, more accurately, "pluralistic," as an indication of the several different systems of law. Such a view of the world legal situation is, however, untenable if both the norms of international law and those of the national legal orders are to be considered as simultaneously valid legal norms. The unity of the supposedly separate orders—national and international—is asserted by Kelsen on the ground of a lack of contradiction between them. No one can serve two masters, and it is impossible for consistent legal theory to regard both international and national law as simultaneously valid legal orders. What is traditionally regarded as a conflict of norms—the contradiction, for instance, of an international treaty by a specific provision of municipal law—is not really a conflict of norms at all: it is merely a factual conflict and as such is analogous to the conflict within municipal law of norm and delict. The delict or "wrong" is not a negation of law but rather a condition for the legal stipulation. There is no "logical contradiction" between a norm of international law and a norm of national law, even if the latter is, by the standards of international law, delictual.

International law arose out of traditional natural law doctrine, and much of that doctrine was concerned with the relation of law to moral and ethical standards. Some recent formulations have sought to establish the basis of international law as morality itself, but expressions of such a view may assume at least two different forms: first, it is sometimes asserted that international law possesses the characteristic of morality in its very nature; secondly,

[10] *Pure Theory of Law*, Chap. VII generally.

the related but different view may be taken that obedience to international law represents a moral obligation. It might be maintained that international law is founded on moral obligation and that the rules of international law are to be regarded as moral rules. A separation must, however, be made between the nature of law itself and the reasons for which legal rules ought to be obeyed. Even the early positivist approach of Bentham was consistent with the central maxim: Obey punctually, censure freely. Apart from those which specify a minimum moral content for any of the particular rules which are constructed on this basis, the views which concern themselves with a moral obligation in international law contribute nothing to an account of its nature. Such views amount merely to exhortations that something be accepted as a matter of moral obligation, without first saying what that something is. Both censure and approval require a subject-matter to which to relate.

Other theories have been content to describe the acceptance by States of the rules of international law without necessarily indulging in overtones of morality. The voluntary "reception" of the international rules by the national legal order presupposes what is generally called a "dualistic" view, which simply means that the two forms of regulation are thought of as initially separate.[11] By the notion of acceptance a dualistic account is able to treat national sovereignty as consistent with the existence of supranational rules of international law, for the two orders are thought of as being neither coincident nor incompatible, but complementary. This account, however, cannot by itself furnish an analysis of the character of international law, for the particular rules of a supranational type which are voluntarily received into municipal law will probably vary from state to state.

Writers who attempt to extend the usage of "law," in the sense in which that term is used to refer to municipal law, to international rules and relations, usually offer one of two alternatives to the Austinian exclusion of these rules from the category of "laws properly so called." One such alternative is to expand the notion of sanctions to cover war and international reprisals, but such measures have been described as "the very symbols of inter-

---

[11] It need hardly be pointed out that the rules known as "Private International Law," otherwise referred to as the "Conflict of Laws," are themselves included in the particular provisions of a positive legal order.

national anarchy"[12], and it is hard to disagree with such a view when it is remembered that war and reprisals are employed as self-help by the States which are themselves the subjects of international law. The other alternative is not to expand the notion of sanction but to extend the sphere of reference of the word "law" itself. Two things may be said about this attitude: first, an analysis which describes its object in such a way as to include something which has not yet been proved to lie within that object may appear naïve; and secondly, there is the positively detrimental effect on the analysis of the nature of municipal law, for the description settled on may be so wide as to be meaningless.

The conclusion that there are obstacles in the way of all these differing approaches to the nature of international law may lead to two attitudes which may themselves be coincident with or contrary to each other. One view is that the question, whether international law is "really law," represents a mere verbal dispute, and that it has only survived as a live issue because a relatively trivial question as to the meaning of words has been mistaken for a real issue of substantive analysis.[13] The other may be described as a kind of "openmindedness" towards the question. The former view is adopted by Williams[14] and the latter by Hart.[15] In this case the respective attitudes are contrary to each other, for Hart does not share Williams' view that the nature of international law involves a merely verbal dispute.[16]

Hart's approach to legal analysis consists of an elucidation of the concept of law, as distinct from a "definition" of the sort encountered in Austin's explanation. Once we free ourselves, says Hart, from the assumption that international law must contain a basic rule, the question to be faced is one of fact. Kelsen interprets the facts as the foundation for the basic norm of international law, but the justification of this particular form of "assumption" may be questioned. Hart, on the other hand, chooses to interpret the facts as constituting not a system but *a set* of rules. There is as yet no basic rule providing general criteria of validity for the rules of international law. In this way a view of international law can be taken which demands or assumes neither more nor less than what is offered by the facts and which demonstrates

[12] Friedmann, *Legal Theory*, p. 577.
[13] See *supra*, Chap. 1, *supra*.
[14] See (1945) 22 B.Y.B.I.L. 146.
[15] See *The Concept of Law*, p. 4, and Chap. 9 generally.
[16] See Chap. 1, *supra*.

the similarity of international to municipal rules and yet stops short of treating all of them as part and parcel of the same thing.

IV

Law and reality

Enough has already been said about the various possible usages of the word "law" to enable a distinction to be made between prescriptive and descriptive elements in law and legal analysis and to indicate the separation of normative and casual relations, with their corresponding methods of interpretation.[17] Some particular reasons for making these distinctions have been considered in previous chapters. It is improbable that everyone will have agreed with the various justifications for some of the approaches which have been examined, but the possibility of argument based on normative concepts as distinct from observations of fact cannot be denied, whatever may be thought of its application to any particular case. Ross, whose views, for the purposes of the present discussion, are very similar to those of Olivecrona, has denied that legal analysis requires a "normative cognition"[18] in order to represent the essential character of law. For Olivecrona law is nothing but a set of social facts. Law in his view consists chiefly of rules about force, but even the notion of a rule is explained in purely causal terms, the "independent imperatives" of law being described in terms of the effect of certain methods of law-making, coupled with the organised monopoly of power possessed by the State, on the minds of people subject to the system. The similar method adopted by Ross will be discussed in the following Chapter, for the facts upon which he concentrates differ somewhat from those at the basis of Olivecrona's account.

The subject-matter of the present section is related in many ways to both the discussion of law and force and to the section about legal authority. It concerns, however, certain methods of interpretation and analysis rather than any particular subject-matter to be investigated. With regard to force, Austin saw how regulation of physical coercion was necessary in order to produce legality. "It has often been affirmed," he said, "that 'right is might' or that 'might is right'. But this paradoxical proposition

---

[17] See Chap. 2, esp. sections I and IV, *supra*.
[18] See p. 159, *infra*.

(a great favourite with shallow scoffers and buffoons) is either a
flat truism affectedly and darkly expressed, or is thoroughly false
and absurd."[19] He was fully aware that something has to condition force in order to produce the legality of actions, but in the
account which he gives of elements in positive laws he still represents law and sanctions in the language of probability. Kelsen's
completion of the separation between law and fact in this respect
represents an account which both asserts the normative character
of human positive law and goes on to infer the necessary consequences from the initial proposition. "If the validity, that is,
the specific existence of the law, is considered to be part of natural
reality, one is unable to grasp the specific meaning in which the
law addresses itself to reality and thereby juxtaposes itself to
reality."[20] Although, in other words, law is obviously related to
fact and conditioned by it, it is not to be explained purely in
terms of fact.

The title of one of Olivecrona's best-known works is *Law as
Fact*, and his treatment of law lives up to this title. Although Ross
speaks in terms of "legal norms," he nevertheless claims that the
method of interpreting this subject-matter can be non-normative;
the two propositions are not, to him, inconsistent, and he thereby
adopts a methodology similar to that of Olivecrona. Ross does
not, however, go so far as to condemn a normative approach to
the subject matter of legal analysis as nonsense. But even though
he uses the word "norm" his view of the nature of law, and consequently of the interpretation to be adopted in its analysis, is
empirical.

By contrast, another Scandinavian jurist, Castberg, insists on
the normative character of law, and his views should not be confused with those of other "realist" jurists of Scandinavia. For him
a normative proposition does not express a straightforward connection of fact, and a remarkable resemblance to Kelsen's analysis
is shown when Castberg says: "A positive legal order constitutes
a system of norms. Its authority is based on a postulate of the
validity of this system of norms. But the postulate of validity is
established also in view of the social fact that the system is on
the whole accepted by public opinion and maintained by organised
force."[21] He points out that "realist" explanations of law which

---

[19] *Province of Jurisprudence Determined*, Lecture VI, p. 285.
[20] *Pure Theory of Law*, p. 213.
[21] *Problems of Legal Philosophy*, p. 27.

rely on the non-normative or even anti-normative approach tend to interpret law partly as the expression of a complex of sociological probabilities, and partly as fact about the psychological condition of people subject to law. But in so doing, says Castberg, such theories tend to obliterate precisely what is characteristic of human positive law and to obscure the real meaning of statements about "valid law" which rely on a presupposition of legal validity, if a set of facts is to produce law. A normative statement cannot, unlike a statement of fact, be true or false, but it can be correct or incorrect. In this, Castberg expresses a point of view which is the same as that of Kelsen; but, for him, Kelsen's analysis appears incomplete. Legal reality, Castberg says, is too complicated for Kelsen's view to be sufficient in itself to solve the problem of legal validity. He asks what conclusion is to be drawn if the courts override the law which has been created in accordance with the rules of the constitution. Are not the decisions of the courts, he asks, just as much legal reality as the pronouncements of the legislator?[22] It is true, of course, that we might just as easily take our point of departure, as Castberg calls it, in the decisions of the courts and then go on to formulate the fundamental norm of legal logic in accordance with these. It is hard to see, however, that such a view demonstrates that Kelsen's analysis is incomplete in the way claimed. The very decisions of the courts derive their legality from a fundamental norm, and it does not appear to matter whether such legality of action is derived immediately or only indirectly from the basic norm. The concept of the basic norm will simply have to be redirected at an amended set of social facts. These are features of what Castberg calls "reality," which themselves form the factual basis for a juristic assertion in terms of the fundamental postulate of valid legal acts within the system.

Kelsen's idea of the fundamental norm has been criticised by Hart, who regards the postulate of validity to be interpreted into the basis of the generally effective order as being a "needless reduplication."[23] If a constitution, he argues, is a "living reality," then this is tantamount to saying that the constitution is accepted as such and that it exists. For the purposes of Hart's own account it would indeed be superfluous to add that the basis of the actual order ought to be accepted; it is accepted, and that is enough. It

[22] *Op. cit.* p. 45.
[23] *The Concept of Law*, p. 246, n. 3.

will have been noticed, however, that the nature of Hart's theory is different from that of Kelsen; for although Hart indicates that concepts based on the existence of a legal system enable different types of statement to be made from those which relate simply to facts and to causal relations, he nevertheless manages without the strict logical separation of Is and Ought employed by Kelsen, and he analyses legal rules in terms of the "internal aspect" of attitudes to legal authority and the criteria of legal validity, instead of using as a starting point the logical character of the normative legal Ought. The fact of acceptance of a legal order, and therefore of its existence, is taken by Kelsen as the basis for making normative propositions. In his account, inquiries into the factual background relating to the basic norm do not extend beyond the established fact of the existence of this order, and the logical presupposition has to be made of a conditioning influence inherent in these basic facts by which the consequent acts of the legal order may be interpreted as *legal* acts. In one sense Kelsen is making explicit that which is implicit in Hart's account. It may, at worst, be a truism to point out the reasons for what is taken for granted, but is hardly mystifying. Against this view may be set Hart's general attitude to rules, for in the use of his notion of the acceptance of rules he is both indicating the legal consequences of sociological fact and also avoiding questions as to the specific source of rules or norms. It seems that this latter problem can only be solved in terms of a presupposition or hypothesis if infinite sociological *regressus* is to be avoided.

CHAPTER 8

PREDICTIONS AND THE CENTRAL POSITION OF THE COURTS

I

Introductory

IN the previous chapters the interplay of two different approaches to legal analysis has been observed, sometimes called the "normative" and the "non-normative." The former treats law as something of a rather different nature from a complex series of physical and social facts. The latter describes the nature of law and the character of a legal system simply in the manner of a natural science of causes and effects.

In natural law doctrine, including Blackstone's version of it, a confusion was apparent between the prescriptive and descriptive meanings of the word "law." Even the corrections offered by Bentham and Austin still placed too much emphasis on factual probabilities in the operation of law. Hart's account of law as a system of rules represents a substantial advance on earlier legal theory in its shift of attention to the analysis of rules and of the reasons for legal obligation. Kelsen goes even further, to a sharp division between fact and law and between the relations of causation and imputation. In this change of view lies an increasing emphasis on the normative character of positive law.

Naturally enough, the foundation even of a normative approach to legal analysis, as distinct from a purely causal approach, is ultimately to be traced to factual situations and events. It is, however, in the method of interpreting these facts and the specifically legal relationships which they embody that the separation of normative from non-normative analysis is to be found.

Some tendencies are apparent to revert to an empirical analysis which not only diverts attention away from the type of separation insisted on by Kelsen, but expressly rejects it as "imagination" or "nonsense." Such is the opinion of the Swedish jurist Olivecrona, a Scandinavian realist. His views involve the rejection of anything of a metaphysical or conjectural nature, indeed of anything inconsistent with a view of law as the complex interaction of a set of social facts. He expressly rejects the type of tenet of legal analysis which Kelsen went so far as to describe as the unspoken hypothesis which is really used by every jurist in his description of law and legal relations.[1] Admittedly, this assertion by Kelsen might be regarded by sceptics as a claim that he can see other jurists doing something of which only he is aware, and of which they are not. Not unnaturally, a common reaction is to say that it is really Kelsen who is romancing.

In many textbooks the term "realist" is applied to two groups of legal writers, the Scandinavian realists and the American realists. Of the two, it is the Scandinavians who adopt a more philosophically-based scepticism, involving in many instances the rejection of earlier approaches to legal analysis as being based on metaphysics or as amounting to imagination or nonsense. It would, however, be a most unrealistic treatment of all Scandinavian jurists to force them into one general category. The views of Castberg, considered briefly in the previous chapter, are very much at loggerheads with most modern legal thought in Scandinavia. Even among those who share the "anti-metaphysical" approach, as they like to call it, there are great differences of opinion. Ross, for instance, admits to the influence of Kelsen's teaching on his own views, even though he goes on to reject a normative analysis framed in terms of "ought propositions."[2]

Apart from sharing a common appellation, the Scandinavian and American realists have little else in common save that both movements have exhibited dissatisfaction with earlier products of positivism. The American realist movement in jurisprudence does not share the philosophical background of modern Scandinavian legal studies. The amalgam of some notable characteristics of the United States legal and constitutional system has provided a uniting force behind modern American legal study which is of even greater local significance than the philosophical background of the Scandinavians. These characteristics include, principally, the powers of the Supreme Court under the Fourteenth Amendment to the Constitution, the variation in state laws, and

---

[1] See *supra*, Chap. 6, p. 124, as to Kelsen's description of the necessary role of his construct, the basic norm, in an adequate analysis of the relationship between fact and law.

[2] It should be noticed that though Ross himself uses the term "norm" in his own analysis, his rejection of a normative approach or of "normative cognition" is to be understood in the sense of that notion indicated in the text.

the nature of the federal system and its consequences in the administration of law.[3]

Few, if any, of the modern American legal realists are really as concerned as the Scandinavians with questions as to the *nature* of law, though many of them touch on this problem in the course of studies which have more to do with the practical administration of the judicial process. While all legal analysis must, of course, make some provision in its formulation for the application and administration of the law, most of the American realist approaches concern themselves with this question alone. They concentrate on the meaning of law to the people subject to it, its significance to the ordinary man seeking legal advice, on the inability of rules alone to yield a prediction of the outcome of litigation, on the facts which have in the first place to be found in order that the judicial decision and the legal rules will have something on which to operate.

Despite the obvious differences in both origin and object which exist between the Scandinavian realists and the American realists, and despite the fact that the American movement constitutes far less a school of thought than the Scandinavian, some similarities in approach can usefully be indicated. Both movements are radical and iconoclastic in their purpose, and this attitude is reflected primarily in their respective attitudes to legal rules. Scandinavians treat the notion of a valid rule as something which exists in the imagination only; the American realists emphasise the impracticability of describing the judicial process, or of predicting its outcome, solely in terms of legal rules. Thus the Scandinavians concern themselves primarily with the character of legal rules, while the Americans examine the content of law and the interaction of rules, policies and principles within a legal system. A common tendency is to minimise the normative character of law and to investigate legal problems by means of the methodology of the physical or empirical sciences. It is remarkable, however, as Lloyd points out,[4] that, "although the Scandinavians are the most extreme of empiricists, it is the Americans who primarily stress the need for factual studies in working out proper solutions for legal problems, and the Scandinavians who appear to rely mainly on argument of an *a priori* kind to justify particular legal solutions or developments." Yet another common feature is a concern with

---

[3] For a fuller account, see *infra*, pp. 175-176.
[4] *Introduction to Jurisprudence*, 3rd ed., p. 514.

psychology and behaviouristic studies, though different conclusions are drawn from such observations. Finally, not without connection with the last feature, is the attention paid by many
Americans and some Scandinavians to the prediction of future
judicial action—though, again, the differing backgrounds to each
movement are reflected in the varying attitudes to this aspect of
a legal system.

II

Courts and predictions

Having indicated some of the characteristics of Scandinavian
realism and American realism, with their similarities and differences, attention may now be directed away from generalisations
about forms of modern realism and towards an important feature
which is shared by many of the realist accounts, but which is not
exclusive to them. This is the concentration on the position and
functions of the courts in a legal system and the ways in which
these have been described by various legal writers, and on the
aspect of prediction of judicial action which is a feature common
to some, but not all of, these accounts.

The views of Ross, though very similar to those of Olivecrona
and other Scandinavian jurists, are considered in the present
chapter on account of their notable resemblance to some modern
American attitudes to law and predictions of legal action. As for
the Americans themselves, attention both to the position and
functions of the courts of law, and to the predictability of future
judicial action, is shared by most modern legal writers such as
Frank and Llewellyn and is originally to be found in the writings
of the father of the American realist movement, Oliver Wendell
Holmes.

Consideration will also be given to Gray's account of law which
is to be found in his book *The Nature and Sources of the Law*.
Although Gray was not really in the tradition of the realists as a
whole, the emphasis placed by him on the judicial function played
a substantial part in the development of legal thought in America.
Gray's analysis represents the transitional process from the old
analytical positivism to the new-style methods of legal investigation
which have been concerned, at least in part, to avoid the sterility
of some of the earlier forms which positivism assumed.

III

Ross and valid law

An exposition of Ross' views will indicate not merely an attitude shared by many other Scandinavian writers but also his indebtedness to Kelsen, which he acknowledges. Beyond the realism which Ross claims for his approach, special emphasis must be laid on his description of the position of the courts in a legal system.

There are two principal aspects of the way in which Ross highlights the position of the courts. The first, reminiscent of some modern American attitudes, is his emphasis on the prediction of future judicial action. For Ross, this element of prediction is entailed as a consequence of his characterisation of the notion "valid law." The other aspect, which is clearly reminiscent of Kelsen's views, lies in his conception of legal norms as directives primarily to the courts and only secondarily to the people who are generally subject to a system of law.

Even greater than Kelsen's influence on Ross was that of Axel Hägerström, whose method is apparent throughout Ross' work. The standpoint taken by Ross can be appreciated in outline from the following statement in the preface to his book *On Law and Justice*: "I reject the idea that legal cognition constitutes a specific normative cognition, expressed in ought-propositions, and interpret legal thinking formally in terms of the same logic as that on which other empirical sciences are based (is-propositions)."[5] Ross maintains that Kelsen's principal aim in the presentation of his Pure Theory of Law was to free the study of law from all traces of sociology, or "considerations referring to the actual course of events." So expressed, the aims of Kelsen would appear to the newcomer as singularly unconnected with reality. In Kelsen's analysis, however, "law" assumes a very special meaning which can only be understood in its particular context.

For present purposes the most important part of Ross' book is his examination of the concept "valid law." Many propositions about law employ this term, but their meaning cannot be fully

[5] Ross, *On Law and Justice*, Stevens and Sons Ltd., 1958, preface, p. x. Ross modifies his views somewhat in his more recent work *Directives and Norms*. A norm is to be defined as a directive which corresponds in a particular way to certain social facts, but it is to be defined neither merely as a linguistic phenomenon (the meaning content which is a directive), nor merely as a social fact; *op cit.*, Chap. 4.

elucidated without an understanding of that notion itself. Ross maintains that much of the apparent disagreement between legal writers can be traced to the fact that their works are based tacitly on different assumptions as to the meaning of this concept. This problem, he says, is peculiar to the study of law and without parallel in the natural sciences. Nevertheless, he proposes to employ an examination, based on is-propositions, of the type involved in the methods of observation and verification of the empirical sciences. His methodology is based on a reinterpretation of validity in terms of social facts.[6]

In his preliminary analysis of the concept of valid law Ross uses the analogy of a game of chess. In employing such a set of rules to serve as a model for the concept of law—a set of legal rules—he gives us a foretaste of his own interpretation of the concept of valid law. "The norms of chess are the abstract idea content (of a directive nature) which makes it possible, as a scheme of interpretation, to understand the phenomena of chess (the actions of the moves and the experienced patterns of action as a coherent whole of meaning and motivation, a game of chess; and, along with other factors, within certain limits to predict the course of the game."[7]

He labels as directives the primary rules of chess, and under the term primary rules he includes those which govern the arrangement of the pieces, the moves, the permitted methods of taking, and excludes from the term such things as the gambits of chess. He notes, in particular, the way in which such directives are *felt* by each player to be binding. In his view a rule of chess is valid if, within a certain framework, this rule is effectively adhered to, and because the players feel themselves to be socially bound by the directives contained in the rule. Two elements thus combine to produce the validity of a rule: first, the effectiveness which is stated in the conclusion from external observation, and second, the way in which the rule is felt to be binding by the people who make use of it as such.

A parallel examination of chess and law leads Ross to the following conclusion as to the validity of law: " . . . 'valid law' means the abstract set of normative ideas which serve as a scheme of interpretation for the phenomena of law in action, which again means that these norms are effectively followed because they are experienced and felt to be socially binding."[8] In a footnote to this pro-

[6] *Cf.* Olivecrona, *Law as Fact*, Chap. IV, p. 127.
[7] *On Law and Justice*, Chap. 1, p. 16.
[8] *Ibid.* p. 18.

position he adds the words: "By the judge and other legal authorities applying the law."

Like other positivist jurists before him, Ross sets out to answer the question how the rules or norms of law are to be distinguished from other types of rules or norms. It is important to notice that he confines his description of law to an individual *national system of norms*. He expressly states that he does not attempt a definition of law, which, he says, has never been realised. He gives as the reason for earlier misguided attempts to define law in order to distinguish it from other kinds of social norms, the failure to consider a national system of legal norms as an individual whole. The distinctions which Ross proceeds to indicate are accordingly to be gathered from his treatment of the distinguishing characteristics of an individual national law system.

He initially divides the norms of law into "norms of conduct" and "norms of competence or procedure." The former include those norms which prescribe a course of action, for example, the rule that the acceptor of a negotiable instrument shall undertake to pay it according to the tenor of its acceptance. The second group includes those which create a competence, or a power or authority. These are directives to the effect that the norms which come into existence in conformity with a declared mode of procedure shall be regarded as norms of conduct. A similar distinction is to be found in Hart's separation of duty-imposing and power-conferring rules, and Ross' description of his "norms of competence" is reminiscent of Hart's references to the "criteria of legal validity." For Ross, a norm of competence amounts to an indirectly expressed norm of conduct. He gives as an example the norms of a Constitution which regulate the way in which new legislation is to come into being; they prescribe behaviour through the norms of conduct which are produced by legislation. In a way which is typical of his method of legal analysis, norms of competence are said to be "reductible" to norms of conduct.[9]

Since norms of conduct are characterised as directives, the question naturally arises: To whom are they directed? Herein lies the particular significance of the position of the courts in the legal system. Ross says: "If it must be assumed of any statutory provision that it does not contain a directive to the courts it can be regarded only as a moral-ideological pronouncement without legal relevance. Conversely, if it is established that a provision does

---

[9] See Raz, quoted at p. 98, *supra*.

contain a directive to the courts, then there is no need to give the private individual any further instruction as to his conduct."[10] Indeed, the norm directed to the individual is of such a secondary nature that it is referred to as a "derived and figurative norm." The judgment of the court, thus affected and influenced by such directives, forms the basis for executive action which will potentially constitute the exercise of physical force. The ultimate right to the exercise of this physical force is the monopoly of the public authorities of the State. In a summarising passage which is reminiscent of Olivecrona's account, Ross says: "A national law system is an integrated body of rules, determining the conditions under which physical force shall be exercised against a person."[11]

Having thus described the distinguishing characteristics of a national legal system, Ross proceeds to discuss the meaning which he attributes to expressions about the concept of validity with reference to that system. He adopts an initial hypothesis which is somewhat reminiscent of Kelsen's basic presupposition but which differs from it especially in the consequences which it entails. The hypothesis is that a system of norms is valid if it is able to serve as a scheme of interpretation of a corresponding set of social actions. One of the principal consequences of the understanding produced by such an interpretation is the ability to predict certain future action. Since the legal norm is, according to Ross, a directive primarily to the courts, such future action will be that of the courts. The ability to understand the national legal system as a "coherent and meaningful whole" is based on the fact that its norms are effectively complied with, and this compliance is, in turn, engendered by a feeling that the rules are socially binding. These propositions are combined in the following statement: "A national law system, considered as a valid system of norms, can accordingly be defined as norms which actually are operative in the mind of the judge, *because* they are felt by him to be socially binding and therefore obeyed."[12] The corollary, therefore, is that the effectiveness which conditions the validity of the norms is to be sought in the judicial application of law as distinct from the attitudes to the national legal system of the mass of private individuals. The decisiveness of

[10] *Ibid.* pp. 32-33. See Hart, *The Concept of Law*, p. 114, where he says it is conceivable that the subjects of a legal system might merely "follow like sheep."

[11] *Ibid.* p. 34. The terminology, though not the substance, of this passage is reminiscent of Kelsen; see esp. pp. 118-120, *supra.*

[12] *Ibid.* p. 35, italics supplied.

judicial pronouncements is, in his opinion, so great that it does not make any difference whether people obey or disobey a legal rule. "This indifference results in the apparent paradox that the more effectively a rule is compiled with in extrajudicial life, the more difficult it is to ascertain whether the rule possesses validity, because the courts have that much less opportunity to manifest their reaction."[13]

For Ross, law consists of a system of norms which are directives primarily to courts or judges. He emphasises, however, that a purely behaviouristic interpretation of the judges' actions achieves nothing in the analysis of law.[14] In his view, the internal aspect of law is to be represented as a feeling of being bound or, in his own words, by the expression of "a certain ideology which animates the judge and motivates his actions." As with Hart, the external aspect of law is described as the outwardly observable and regular compliance with a pattern of action; but the internal aspect is represented as the experience of this pattern of action (by the judges, by the courts) as being a socially binding norm.

Hart agrees[15] that the distinction between such regularities and certain "emotional experiences," can be drawn. It is not, however, coincident with his distinction between "internal" and "external" elements which characterise the difference between regularities and regulations; nor are the consequences of the use of the distinction the same. In particular, the type of separation upon which Hart insists is one which is used to divide "two radically different types of statement for which an opportunity is afforded whenever a social group conducts its affairs by rules."[15]

Predictions and legal validity

Let us now look further into the element of prediction in Ross' account, as it is connected with judicial decisions. His concentration on the position of the courts is a feature which his theory shares with the views of some modern American legal writers, many of whom also concern themselves with the prediction of judicial be-

[13] *Ibid.* p. 36.

[14] With this attitude may be compared some American views, which favour both predictions and behaviouristic studies; see section IV of this chapter.

[15] In his review, "Scandinavian Realism" of Ross. *On Law and Justice*; (1959) C.L.J. 233. In *The Concept of Law* Hart specifically denies that internal attitudes are feelings; see *supra*, Chap. 5, p. 108.

haviour. Most of these American writers are concerned with a different type of investigation from that of Ross, but inasmuch as they appear to be dealing with ideas on the nature of law, they share with Ross the weakness in their "predictive" analysis of legal validity.[16]

Legal norms assist in predicting the course of the practical administration of law. Ross appears to be forced to this proposition by his refusal to consider law itself as a system of *ought-propositions*. A retrospective review of the specific content of existing law reveals something which cannot be altered merely by the way in which it is described; it has certain characteristics, and it has a certain content. When, however, a forward-looking point of view is adopted, the position is different. As long as an adequate explanation has been given, the notion of law will continue to possess certain characteristics; the same applies to the term "national legal system." But a different kind of statement is clearly involved if it is said that the specific content of positive law *probably will be* such and such—in other words, if a prediction is made about it.[17]

With regard to the validity of law and its efficacy, the necessary distinction insisted on here between identity and mere coincidence may be further brought out with reference to Ross' section on the "Verification of Propositions Concerning Norms of Conduct," in which he says that "a rule can be valid law to a greater or lesser degree varying with the degree of probability with which it can be predicted that the rule will be applied."[18] The practical application of a legal rule may certainly be related to a statement about validity in relation to it, but it is not the reason for which is made that statement. Such a reason must be found in the valid authorisation behind the application of the rule. The statement that a rule is valid, and the statement that it is always or usually applied, may indicate a coincidence of validity and efficacy, but they will neither describe nor offer any evidence for the identification of the two.

Further, what is the justification of a strict insistence on an examination of law which, using the empirical methods of physical science, arrives in this way at a notion of "relative validity"? The

---

[16] The basis for Ross' statements about such predictions is more complex than that found in the American views which are considered in section IV of this chapter.

[17] The fault in such terminology was noted above in connection with Austin's use of the notion of sanction; see, Chap. 6, pp. 114-117, *et seq.*, *supra*.

[18] *Op. cit.*, p. 45.

practical application of a legal rule, upon which observations can be based as to the relative efficacy of the stipulation contained in it, is by nature variable. The only prediction that can really be made is that, so long as the legal system remains generally efficacious, any particular judge will probably apply the relevant valid legal rule which receives its validity from the determining criteria of the system. Moreover, if a rule could be valid law to a greater or lesser degree, depending on the predictability of its application, then the highest conceivable degree of validity would be possessed by a rule which could, given the correct background information, be predicted with certainty. Ross himself says that the degree of probability "depends on the material of experience on which the prediction is built." Certainty in prediction would, on this basis, indicate that the background information or "material of experience" tells us that the rule is always followed. With this approach may be contrasted that of Kelsen. In his discussion of the distinction between validity and efficacy[19], Kelsen states that a rule whose operation is certain is part of the law of *nature*. Analysis of it in terms of prescription would be quite meaningless.

This predictive aspect of Ross' account has also attracted criticism from Hart[20]—of a kind which is equally applicable to some American views which are shortly to be considered. Even if the expression "This is a valid rule of law" means in the mouth of an ordinary person, a prediction of what a judge will do and say, on the basis of his special motivating feeling, this cannot be what it means to the judge himself. He is not engaged in predicting his own feelings or behaviour, nor those of other people. In the terminology of Hart's own approach to the concept of law, the judge's admission of such and such a rule as a valid rule of law represents an "act of recognition." Moreover, even if expressions about valid legal rules made by people other than the judges were to be represented as predictions of judicial behaviour, the basis for such expressions would be the knowledge that judges themselves employ the idea of valid rules in the non-predictive sense indicated above. In other words if it

---

[19] See *supra*, Chap. 6, p. 128.

[20] "Scandinavian Realism" (1959) C.L.J. 233. Ross replies to this criticism in his review of Hart's *Concept of Law* in (1961) Yale L.J. 1962. He indicates the unfortunate translation of the Danish *gældende ret* as *valid law*, whereas its meaning is really *existing law* or *the law in force*. However, analysis of these notions in terms of predictability would appear to produce no more than a truism, unless, with some American jurists shortly to be mentioned, a behaviouristic investigation is added to the initial analysis.

were said that the instruction to the private individual manifests itself through his knowledge of the reactions which he could, under certain conditions, expect from the judge, it would be a strange state of affairs if recourse became necessary to yet another set of predictions in the inquiry into the position and authority of the judicial organs within the system of law in question. Since it is unlikely that Ross intended to formulate the authority of the judges in a way which would have them according validity to a legal rule on the basis of predictions as to their own future action, the characterisation of valid law as predictions may be confined to statements *about* law made by legal theory, as distinct from statements *of* law made by the judges.[21] There still remains, however, the second of the two objections.

Ross' primary and prominent emphasis on the position of the courts in a legal system itself affords a ground of criticism. The norm directed to ordinary citizens is, according to him, only derived; the real legal norm is the directive to the courts. Kelsen said that one type of valid legal norm is, as it were, "directed" to the courts or judges; but for him this was only one of the steps in the "gradual concretization" of law, which served both to indicate the constitutive character of the judicial decision and, at the same time, to represent the particular place which the judicial organs occupied in the system as a whole. For Ross, the legal norm is to be explained in terms of predictions and feelings of being bound, with the help of the methods of an empirical science, and it may perhaps seem strange that, on the basis of such an approach, the regulation of ordinary people's behaviour should become the subject of a merely "figurative" norm. Arnholm[22] asks whether, if a legal rule in fact influences the activities of both courts and citizens, if it in fact aims to influence the conduct of both (so far as it has any purpose at all), there can be any sense in discussing which is the real, and which the derived, norm. According to this critic, inasmuch as a legal rule is the result of an intention behind the acts of the legislature, this intention is aimed primarily at the activities of the citizens. With Kelsen, on the other hand, a thoroughgoing normative approach to the analysis of law facilitates an adequate account of the relative positions in the system of both the legislature and the courts in such a way that neither is given undue prominence and yet which, by virtue of the special nature of the inquiry, is able to avoid the

[21] *Cf.* Kelsen's distinction; *supra,* p. 128.
[22] Vol I, *Scandinavian Studies in Law,* pp. 43-45.

type of criticism levelled by Arnholm at Ross.

An analysis which concentrates on the position of the courts in a legal system is inherently neither more or less realistic than any other. A lack of realism may, however, be found in the combination of this concern with the attention given by Ross to the element of prediction in his scheme of legal analysis, particularly in the way in which this combination produces the idea of "relative validity" as a consequence of relative predictability, and also in the way in which it reduces the relationship between legislature and ordinary citizens to a distinctly secondary element in legal regulation.

Ross' identification of effectiveness and validity via the device of prediction runs counter to a distinction which is of vital significance in Kelsen's *Pure Theory of Law*. For Ross, "a doctrinal study of law which ignores the social function of the law must appear unsatisfactory when judged by the criterion of the interest that lies in the predictability of legal decisions."[23] It is suggested, however, that there is room for doubt whether the particular method chosen by Ross for his investigation of legal phenomena can satisfactorily bridge the gap between "doctrinal" and "sociological" approaches to law in a realistic way and without distortion on either side.

IV

Some American approaches

The attitudes to law and legal study which are to be dealt with in this section involve juristic concentration on the prediction of judicial action. Like Ross, the writers who adopt such an approach maintain the importance of looking at what the courts do in fact, though their reasons for doing so are rather different.

A great deal of work which has been done during the present century in the United States of America in the furtherance of legal knowledge has concerned the forecasting of judicial treatment of legal rules and principles. The movement which has made the task of prediction one of its chief objects of attention is generally known as realism.

The common name "realism" must not be allowed to give the impression that American realists offer their own version of a basic theme which they share with their Scandinavian counterparts. The present chapter is concerned, not with realism as such, but with

[23] *On Law and Justice*, p. 20.

approaches to law which focus attention on the place of the courts in a legal system. It is this shared emphasis, rather than the mere label which is commonly attached to them, which merits the treatment of Ross' theories and of the views of some leading American writers in the same section of this book.

John Chipman Gray

The view of law propounded by Gray at the beginning of this century does not usually lead to his being classified as a realist. His notion of the "real rulers of society" was considered in the previous chapter; despite, however, the innovation in legal theory which his idea may have afforded, the remainder of his account of law in terms of the actions and determinations of the courts has stronger affinities with the Austinian definition based on the actions and pronouncements of a sovereign.

The father-figure in the American realist movement was the great judge and jurist Oliver Wendell Holmes, whose early writings in fact preceded Gray's juristic work. Holmes' view of law contains an emphasis on the prediction of judicial action which is not to be found in Gray, but which has since been turned into the chief concern of modern American legal writers. Holmes himself, however, did not acknowledge any greater affinity to the realists than to any other school in jurisprudence.

So great, however, was the emphasis given by Gray to the central importance of courts and judges in a legal system, and so useful is a general view of his ideas on the nature of law for a comparative study of legal theory such as the present, that any adequate treatment of American legal thought during this century must take some account of his views.

The nature and sources of the law

Such was the emphasis placed by Gray on the creative nature of the judicial decision that he even insisted on reducing legislative enactments to mere *sources* of law.

Gray gave the following definition of the law: "The Law of the State or of any organised body of men is composed of the rules which the courts, that is, the judicial organs of that body, lay down for the determination of legal rights and duties."[24] In his opinion,

[24] *The Nature and Sources of the Law*, 2nd ed., p. 84.

the reason for a difference in the formulations of law given by others is attributable to a failure to distinguish between the law and the sources of the law. It should be noticed immediately, of course, that his concern is with "the Law."[25] Some doubt must therefore arise as to the justification of his startlingly brief assertion about the reason for differences in accounts of the nature of law. Gray seems, from this introductory proposition, to be concerned with the law as the aggregate of individual positive legal rules. Elsewhere, however, he expresses himself in terms which give a less atomic account of law, and inconsistencies consequently arise within his ideas.

It has, according to Gray, been called an absurdity to say that "the Law of a great nation means the opinions of half-a-dozen old gentlemen, some of them, conceivably, of very limited intelligence." Yet "no rule or principle which they refuse to follow is Law in that country."[26] On the other hand, the courts do not enjoy unlimited freedom in arriving at their decisions, for they are directed to certain recognised sources. In this rather vague way, and with the assistance of his somewhat amorphous notion of the "real rulers" of society which lie behind these sources, Gray goes some way towards anticipating the criticisms by Kelsen and Hart of explanations of law which concentrate exclusively on the position and function of the courts in a way which disconnects them from their regulated background.

At two other points in a chapter entitled "The Law" Gray shows some awareness of faults in previous approaches to legal analysis which have subsequently received even more criticism. In a cryptic sidenote he makes a distinction between "a Law" and "the Law," and begins the accompanying text by saying that the two usages must be distinguished. Austin, he continues, defines the law as being the aggregate of the rules established by political superiors. He also quotes Bentham, who said that "*Law*, or *the Law*, taken indefinitely, is an abstract, and collective term; which, when it means anything can mean neither more nor less than the sum total of a number of individual laws taken together." This is not, says Gray, the ordinary meaning of the term "the Law." The conclusion he reaches is not, however, particularly illuminating. A law, he says, ordinarily means a statute passed by the legislature of a state; the law repre-

---

[25] Gray uses the capital letter throughout the work under discussion.
[26] *Ibid.* Note Gray's account of the position of "principle" in the explanation of the nature of the judicial decision; *cf.* Dworkin's criticism of Hart, *supra*, Chap. 5, p. 105.

sents the whole system of rules applied by the courts, and not the aggregate of a superior's commands.

Law and sources of the law

Gray ascribes two principal functions to his "real rulers of society," alternatively called the "ruling spirits of the community" or the "rulers of the State." First, they are responsible for creating the judicial organs of the community; second, they lay down limits for the action of these organs by indicating and controlling the sources from which the courts or judicial organs choose in creating "the Law."

The sources of the law comprise statutes, judicial precedents, opinions of experts, customs and "principles of morality" under which term Gray includes considerations of public policy. The contents of this list anticipate the attention paid by some modern American writers to the part played by social factors in the contents of the judicial decision. It is worthy of note, however, that even statutes are listed merely as *sources* of law. Any division of law into legislative law and judge-made law is rejected by Gray; all the law, he says, is judge-made law.

The principal reason for this humble position in Gray's account of statutory law is expressed in his assertion that "the courts put life into the dead words of the statute."[27] This is indeed true in a great many of the cases in which attention is justifiably focussed on the creative or constitutive character of the judicial decision. Books and articles abound with references to "statutory interpretation" which frequently connotes considerably more than that expression might indicate. Two reasons exist, however, for restricting this attention. First, the law which regulates the behaviour of the proverbial man in the street includes the text of statutes just as much as the law reports; in an era of the proliferation of administrative statutes containing penalty clauses, probably more so. Perhaps this consideration was present to Holmes' mind when he said[28] that, in our concentration on the actions of the courts, we may focus our attention on the "bad man." Second, and more important, even within the area of judicial activity for which a place must be found in any adequate analysis of the nature and structure of a legal system, the scope for genuine creativity is severely limited. It is only

[27] Gray, *op. cit.*, Chap. V, p. 125.
[28] Holmes, *The Path of the Law*, pp. 171, 173; *infra* p. 174.

infrequently that the courts hand down such significant decisions as *Donoghue v. Stevenson* or *Rylands v. Fletcher*. Furthermore, a feature even of the most creative of judicial decisions which a lawyer is accustomed to meeting in the system of precedent in this country is the unwillingness of the courts to arrive at a decision about some novel situation without at least some reference to authorities which might be found, despite the tenuous connection which sometimes exists.

Authoritative decisions

In addition to these practical considerations restricting the genuinely creative character of judicial decisions, another very important criticism of the type of approach taken by Gray is its relative failure to take into account the authoritative nature of the judicial decision. Benjamin Hoadly, Bishop of Bangor, achieved unsolicited celebrity in the law books by making the following statement: "Nay, whoever hath an absolute authority to interpret any written or spoken laws, it is he who is truly the Law-giver to all intents and purposes, and not the person who first wrote or spoke them."[29] This passage is quoted by Gray in his chapter on the courts, but the matter is left at that, without any indication of the character of what is, for legal theory, the central notion in the passages. That is the notion of authority.

In a later chapter entitled "Statutes"[30] which deals specifically with the judicial interpretation of statutes, Gray is particularly concerned with the judicial function of reading into a statute the probable intention of the legislature, especially in cases in which the point in issue could not have been present to the legislator's mind owing to the occurrence of novel circumstances. Such an account is of course more "realistic" by far than Blackstone's notion of the courts' mere discovery of already-existing rules. But Gray's method of relating the function of the courts to the legislature is still not a satisfactory explanation for the purposes of legal analysis. In particular, it cannot furnish a description of the nature of the position of the judicial organs of a legal system within the authority-based relations upon which the system operates. Gray's account is therefore to be distinguished in this respect from that of Kelsen and that of Hart. Even his use of the notion of the "real rulers of society" cannot

[29] Sermon preached before the King, 1717, p. 12.
[30] *Op. cit.* p. 152 *et seq.*

save his theory from this criticism. In particular, no provision is made for notions of a specifically legal significance, such as the basic norm in Kelsen's theory or the rule of recognition in that of Hart. These notions lie behind the positive legal institutions of the legal system, including principally the legislature and the courts. This element of the authoritative basis and coherence of a legal system is frequently hinted at by Gray, but inadequately pursued. For him, it is the "real rulers of society" or, in this instance, the "rulers of the State" who are responsible for creating the courts and for exercising power over the sources of law from which those courts choose. In contrast to Hart's explanation of the nature of law, Gray's treatment of these matters provides no common basis upon which to relate both the authority of the courts to reach valid decisions and also the "criteria of validity" which explain the reason for which certain sources of law are recognised as providing the material for a valid and authoritative choice. In contrast to Kelsen, Gray's account involves the omission of one of the integral stages from the gradual process of "concretization" of law. Kelsen's criticism of the notion of the "real rulers of society" in Gray's account has been considered. Let us now look at Kelsen's opinion of an account which concentrates on the position of the courts in a legal system at the expense of a failure to indicate their relationship with other legal, norm-creating organs.

For Kelsen, the judicial act is but one stage of the law-creating process which is regarded as complete only on the stipulation that a sanction shall be applied. Its two principal functions are the determination whether the conditions specified by the general, abstract norm are present in the particular case, and, if these are present, the stipulation that the sanction shall be applied. In each case, the judicial decision has a constitutive character. Kelsen also accommodates cases in which there is no general norm providing for a certain situation, by saying that other norms of the legal order may authorise the stipulation of a sanction in one direction or another, provided that the court finds the lack of a general norm suitable for the particular case to be unsatisfactory, unjust or inequitable. There is, however, only a difference in degree between this case and one in which the court applies pre-existing law; for in one sense, in ordering the sanction, the court is always in the position of legislator because of the constitutive character of any judicial decision. On the other hand, paradoxically, it could be said that a court always applies pre-existing law, whether such law is "substantive" or merely "adjective"; this is so, in other words, even if the court is only administering the general norms which regulate its own existence and procedure. In this way a creative function is imputed to the courts, while at the same time the regulation of the courts themselves is accommodated in Kelsen's theory.[31]

A similar treatment of the creative but regulated character of the judicial process is to be found in Hart's account. The rules of adjudication assist in providing the legal system with a dynamic or creative quality, and serve also to confine the operations of the courts within certain rule-based limits. According to Hart, a theory of law such as Gray's, which asserts that "the law is what the courts say it is" confuses the finality of the judicial act with a supposed infallibility. Using the analogy with a game, it is in one sense true that for the purposes of the game the score is what the scorer says it is. The scoring rule, however, remains constant before and after the scorer's pronouncement and the function of the scorer in the game is to apply the rules which govern the scoring to the best of his ability. A game of "scorer's discretion" would be a different game altogether, and a highly uncertain one at that. Even though a rule may have a furry edge, it still has a core of settled meaning.

Oliver Wendell Holmes

While Gray's attention is specifically directed at the character of the judicial decision, he still remains an analytical jurist, concerned with analysing the nature of law. Holmes, on the other hand, adopted a more sceptical attitude. His scepticism can be traced through to the work of more modern American legal writers, and consists in the attention paid to the uncertainty of law when considered merely as a set of rules. It is characteristic of the work of these writers that they show a tendency to minimise the normative or prescriptive nature of law and exhibit, rather, a marked insistence on a strictly pragmatic approach to law.

An element of uncertainty in the law as it is applicable to social problems is by no means a necessarily bad thing, for the adaptability of the content of positive law to changing economic and social conditions is naturally to be welcomed. As Holmes said: "The law embodies the story of a nation's development through many centuries, and it cannot be dealt with as though it

[31] See *General Theory of Law and State*, pp. 150-152.

contained only the axioms and corollaries of a book of mathematics."[32] "The life of the law," he said, "has not been logic: it has been experience." This celebrated dictum is applicable to a great deal of the work which has come after him, and it furnishes a key to the understanding of this work. The life of the law, as a description of the path of the law through the labyrinth of social and economic development, is clearly referable to the practical administration of the content of positive law. It is, moreover, in this light that another of Holmes' best-known assertions must be understood: "The prophecies of what the courts will do in fact, and nothing more pretentious, are what I mean by the law."[33]

In the words of Bodenheimer,[34] Holmes "regarded law largely as a body of edicts representing the will of the dominant interests in society, backed by force." There is a remarkable resemblance between this method of expressing the power within a legal system with the one possible interpretation of Gray's notion of the "real rulers of society." The views of both Gray and Holmes appear to represent the type of characterisation of such power which is likely to result from an approach such as theirs which diverts attention away from a study of the normative character of the concept law, in the direction of a study of how *laws* operate in fact.

Llewellyn and legal rules

One of the principal characteristics which many later American writers share with Holmes is a preoccupation with the making of laws, or at least of judicial decisions. This characteristic tendency is also reminiscent of Gray[35] in that it shows a concern with the source of authoritative pronouncements within the institution of the positive legal system. Its effect on an analysis of the nature of law such as Gray's is to skirt the normative influences on the character of law. In later writings, such as those of Llewellyn, which make a cleaner break between the character of law and its content, a similar effect is produced: the surrounding facts which combine to influence the action of legal officials are given even

[32] *The Common Law*, p. 1.
[33] *The Path of the Law*, p. 173.
[34] Bodenheimer, *Jurisprudence*, (1962), p. 115.
[35] And, indeed, of Austin's concern with the *making* of laws by a sovereign; see *supra*. Chap. 4.

more attention than the positive legal rules around which those influences operate.

In one sense it can be thought of as "realistic" to emphasise the factors which ultimately dictate the specific outcome of judicial action. However, in any analysis of the *character* of law, an account which concentrated so much attention on the factual context of the judicial decision, including the tastes and prejudices of the judges themselves, would be very much a theory of last resort. With regard to the content of the legal rules, this marked concern with non-legal influences may perhaps be attributed, at least in part, to some conditions in the United States politico-legal system which are not to be found in legal systems which have supplied the material for some of the less radical and iconoclastic approaches to jurisprudential study.[36]

The first of these distinguishing features of the American legal system is the federal constitution of the union of states which makes an Austinian approach to legal analysis look very inadequate (though perhaps Bentham's account goes some way to avoiding this criticism). It would be a thankless and misguided task to set out in search of the "sovereign" or sovereign body in the United States system. The complex ways in which a co-operation between state and federal authorities is achieved defies any such analysis. Secondly, it is not surprising that throughout the many states can be found some notable variations in social, political and economic conditions. Williston said in 1929 that "each State is developing a jurisprudence of its own which tends to become more and more independent of the law of other States."[37] A further feature of the greatest significance is the powerful position of the Supreme Court which, under the authority of the Fourteenth Amendment, can act as the censor even of State legislation.

In *Karl Llewellyn and the Realist Movement*[38] Twining cites a contemporary of many of the leading Realists, including Llewellyn. "Professor Max Rheinstein has suggested that three problems arising out of the American legal experience have dominated the consciousness of her jurists: the problem of adapting the common law to the circumstances of the New World; the

---

[36] For a detailed review, from which the following propositions are taken, see Goodhart, "Some American Interpretations of Law," in *Modern Theories of Law*, 1.

[37] *Some Modern Tendencies in the Law*, 1929, p. 73.

[38] *Law in Context* series: Weidenfeld & Nicholson, 1973.

problem of giving specific content to the broad formulas of the
constitution of 1787 and of adapting these formulas to meet
changing conditions; and, thirdly, the preservation of the unity
of the common law in a heterogeneous country with a multiplicity
of jurisdictions. To this list might be added two related problems:
that of modernisation of the law in the wake of the industrial and
technological revolution that swept the United States in the period
after 1870, and the problem of simplification of the sources of
law, as the legal profession and the courts became more and
more swamped by the prodigious output of legislation, regulations
and reported cases. In turn, these attempts to simplify helped to
generate a reaction based on the view that the preferred 'solutions'
did not take adequate account of the complexities of modern
life."[39] Twining adds that "the controversies between analytical
and sociological jurists and between 'formalism' and 'functionalism'
appear, at least in part, to reflect differences over the priorities to
be given to the relatively 'static' needs of unification and system-
isation and the 'dynamic' need for continuous adaptation of legal
institutions to changed conditions and values. In the United States
the complexity of its legal system and the pace of change during
the past hundred years have combined to accentuate the strain
between these competing needs. The realist movement represents
part of the radical vanguard who called for a 'dynamic' jurisprudence as a basis for bringing a greater sense of urgency to
bear on the problems of adapting the legal system to the needs
of the twentieth century."[40]

In a system of legal authority so constituted, unifying influences
are by no means as readily found as in some European systems
which have supplied the raw material for much legal positivism.
Less attention comes to be paid to the mere "paper rules," and
attention is shifted by such writers as Llewellyn to the behaviour
of law officials and especially to the actions and the pronouncements of judges. Interest in the structural character of law is
outweighed by a concern with the functional aspects of the courts
and the judiciary in the process of legal regulation. In the first
printing of *The Bramble Bush*, one of the best known of Llewellyn's
earlier works, he says of the officials of a legal system: "What
these officials do about disputes is, to my mind, the law itself."
However, in the foreword to the last printing of his book,[41] he

---

[39] *Ibid.* at pp. 1-2.   [40] *Ibid.* at p. 8.
[41] Oceana Publications, New York, 1960, p. 9.

acknowledges that these words amount to no more than "a very partial statement of the whole truth." He admits that it is one of the obvious functions of the law to exercise some degree of control over legal officials, and even to guide them in situations where control would be out of place or impossible. Such a description of the judiciary is most reminiscent of Hart's expression "rule-governed operations."

Llewellyn maintains that it is important to see that there are certain regularities in what officials do about disputes—regularities which make it possible to predict what they and other officials are likely to do in the future. His version of what is commonly known as "rule-scepticism" can be seen in his exhortation to find out not only what the judges *say*, but also what they really *do*. The concept of the law in a state of flux is one which has exercised a primary influence on modern American legal writers, acutely conscious of the way in which the provisions of the law have all the time to be adapted to the ever-changing needs of society. The same kind of observation can be found in books on this side of the Atlantic on the judicial process. For the American Realists, however, it is the doing that really counts; the saying consists in the rules, and the part which the rules do play in the doing of things is to be found in their partial assistance in the prediction of future judicial action. The rules can do no more than fulfil this partial role, for "if wishes were horses, then beggars would ride."

Both Llewellyn and Hart use the analogy of the rules of law and the rules of a game, but different consequences are inferred which vary with the type of approach to law taken by each writer. Hart indicates that the finality of the judgment of the scorer—comparable with that of a judge—means that, for the purposes of the game, the score is what the scorer says it is. This is so, however, on the basis of a scoring rule, and it is the duty of the scorer to apply this rule to the best of his ability. According to Llewellyn, on the other hand, the games are few in which the rules are always observed, and we therefore come to see the officials of the legal system functioning like umpires in their attempts to see that the rules are observed. The umpire, like the judge, may not always see a breach of the rules, and he may be partial, stubborn, ignorant or ill-tempered. Moreover, all these aspects of the centrality of the courts' place in the system may exercise an influence which is, in the opinion of Llewellyn, of vital importance in the process of judicial decision: they may influence the finding of facts. And it is on the legally relevant facts that the judicial decision operates. With this aspect of the law's operation in mind, the even more radical and iconoclastic approach of Frank may now be considered.

Frank: the fact-sceptic

Realism was described by Llewellyn as an effort at more effective legal technology. In a storm in a teapot it was mistaken by some for a philosophy of law, and this it was not. The movement towards a realistic approach to law is not, however, without connection with legal theory. In his book *Law and the Modern Mind*,[42] Frank examines a number of features in the theories of law which have been considered in the previous chapters.

His position with regard to the creative function of the judicial decision can first of all be demonstrated with reference to his treatment of codification. According to Frank, codification cannot create a body of rules which will exclude judicial innovation and guarantee complete predictability. Of the German Code of 1900 Frank said: "It produced not certainty, but sterile logic-chopping."[43] It is significant, he says, that people who believe in an all-sufficient code also espouse the "command theory" of law; and in a passage which is typical of Frank's exuberant iconoclasm, he classifies both ways of thinking as a child's dream, a "hopelessly oversimplified analysis of the nature of law."

Nor did Gray's account of the judges as lawmakers succeed in satisfying Frank. For Cardozo, another celebrated American judge, Gray was too radical in saying that statutes do not constitute law but only sources of law; if the statute is clear, there is no room for judicial legislation.[44] According to Frank, on the other hand, the rules created by the judges' actions are no more law than the statutes are law; rules are merely words and those words can come into operation only by means of a fresh judicial decision. Indeed, Frank goes as far as to say that our sources of law, in order to represent a true picture, will have to include such considerations as favouritism and prejudice among the members of the judiciary, and forgetful, ignorant or stupid witnesses. It is clear by this stage, however, that the insistence on a realistic

---

[42] 1st ed. 1930; first English edition Stevens, 1949.
[43] *Ibid.*, p. 188.
[44] Cardozo, *The Nature of the Judicial Process.*

approach to the description of law is in effect identifying the rules of law themselves with the administration of justice within the framework provided by the rules.

The opinions expressed by Holmes found great favour with Frank when *Law and the Modern Mind* was written. He is described by Frank as "the completely adult jurist." Frank agreed with Holmes when he said that "general propositions do not decide cases"; and though Holmes' view of the law as the "prophesies of what the courts will do in fact" was limited to the point of view of the "bad man" who wants to know "the law and nothing else," this attention to prediction and the material on which it depends, was enthusiastically pursued by Frank. While some of his predecessors had examined the part played by rules in judicial action, Frank emphasised that the vast majority of cases, which never go beyond trial at first instance, depend ultimately on the influences which condition the fact-finding process at the lower level. It was this factor which led Frank to criticise Cardozo for his concentration on elements in the administration of law which really concern the appellate process. "For Cardozo," said Frank, "a two per cent tail wagged a ninety-eight per cent dog."

It was Holmes who originated the so-called "prediction theory" of law, and Frank happily espoused this doctrine in 1930. By 1949, when he wrote *Courts on Trial*, Frank was saying that even Holmes' method of prophesying was uncertain. The apparently mundane factors upon which Frank concentrated his later attentions are evidence of the way in which it is possible to take a study of law's operation towards a purely factual, non-normative science. But, at the same time, it is abundantly clear that by this stage of argument we have moved away from any attempt at explaining the *nature* of law, and in the direction of an assessment of all the many factual conditions which may conceivably have a bearing on the content of the positive law and the disputes which arise in connection with it.

A final word

A particularly significant feature of the "fact-scepticism" which permeates Frank's work is the way in which it discloses the importance of the personal element in all processes of choice and decision. Such choice, and the responsibility for decision, are features upon which all the American realists lay great stress.

In a choice between alternatives, the person making the decision will almost certainly be influenced by what he thinks ought to be the right result. It is here, perhaps, that some of the elements of reason and justice which were referred to in Chapters Two and Three can best be found a place.

CHAPTER 9

SOVIET LEGAL THEORY

I

Introductory

EVEN a short introduction to legal theory such as the present would be incomplete without at least a brief outline of the juristic thought and juridical institutions having their origin in the works of Marx and Engels. Despite the title of this Chapter, the theories of law about to be discussed are not peculiar to the Soviet Union, or U.S.S.R., but are common to the countries of Eastern Europe. This area of jurisprudence is alternatively known as Socialist Legal Theory, and sometimes as Communist Legal Theory. However, as will be seen shortly, the expressions "socialist" and "communist" assume specific and different meanings in Marxian doctrine and its offshoots, and they will therefore be confined in the present discussion to their own appropriate contexts.

Soviet legal theory is substantially different from other theories and philosophies of law which have been discussed in earlier Chapters. While natural law doctrines have aimed in various ways at the establishment in society of fundamental and sometimes unchanging values, it can hardly be said that any reasonably-sized community at the present day represents the practical implementation of natural law ideas. Doctrines of natural law have had their greatest effect on systems and communities which have sought to improve on their existing state or which have encountered some major practical problem which natural law can help to solve. Modern Positivism, in its various forms, relies largely if not wholly on existing juridical institutions upon which and out of which an analysis of law and legal system may be drawn. This form of legal analysis is founded, therefore, on the legal system. The main distinguishing mark of the Soviet experience is that a legal system has been based upon a philosophy, namely the political and economic philosophy of Karl Marx and his successors.

The Soviet legal system can therefore be assumed at the outset of discussion to partake of a different character from that of the systems of Western Europe and the United States, those which have provided the raw material for some principal analyses of law dealt with in earlier Chapters. This is, indeed, the case in practice, for the juridical institutions of the Soviet system must conform in substance to Marxist doctrine if they are to be accorded any function and place at all in the community. Such conformity, together with the vagaries and uncertainties which the administration of Soviet justice is prone to experience when seen through Western eyes, will be mentioned in more detail shortly. It will also be seen that the administration of justice may be rendered doubly uncertain by the fact that Marxist doctrine is susceptible to more than one interpretation. Furthermore, differences in interpretation of the original doctrine (not all of which was worked out in the fullest theoretical or practical detail) have arisen both *a priori* and as a result of political pressures to produce a theory of law suited to the political rulers of a given time. Marxist legal theory has experienced many varieties and stages since its original conception and especially since the revolution of 1917, so much so that both the legal theory and the juridical institutions of the Soviet bloc rank equal as fields of study with systems and legal analyses having a much longer history.

Marx and Engels

One of the earliest documents of great importance in the development of communism in general, and of socialist and communist legal theory in particular, was Marx' *Communist Manifesto*, about one thousand copies of the original text of which were printed in London in 1848[1] when Marx was just under thirty and Engels a couple of years younger. At the time, few people apart from these two regarded the document as of any importance. Within their relationship, which proved to be a strong partnership, Marx provided the philosophy and the determination to influence men's lives, and Engels provided both money (at the outset) and, more important, some substantial first-hand experience of social and economic conditions in the industrial Lancashire of the early 1840s.

The argument of *The Communist Manifesto* is simple and is characterised by the early sentence: "The history of all hitherto existing society is the history of class struggles." In the search for a direction and an object for an economic philosophy which

[1] For more detail, see *Marx/Engels: The Communist Manifesto*, ed. A. J. P. Taylor; Pelican Books, 1967.

already existed in embryonic form, Marx fastened readily on the experience provided by Engels. "When Engels described conditions in Lancashire and subsequently took Marx on a visit there, Marx realised that he had found the key to historic change. The driving force was not in men's minds, but in the system of production."[2] In some of his leading assertions about the paramount influence of class struggles on social development, Marx made many assumptions. Extreme examples are some of the universal generalisations which he made about the state of world society based on the Lancashire cotton industry. Nevertheless a great number of Marx' assumptions or, perhaps more reverently, predictions about the progress of class development and economic evolution have proved absolutely correct. Marx is now an acknowledged master in the history of communist thought—an accolade which, incidentally, Marx himself never doubted even in his obscure years.

Since class struggle lies at the base of social conflict and social and economic development, the typical stages of a community's development must be listed. In a very primitive stage of the exploitation of men by men there is slavery, an institution nowadays roundly and universally condemned—though not so as recently as two centuries ago in this country and in the United States of America. Slaves are regarded in some historical stages as little more than things, and this state of affairs evidences a complete exploitation by the dominant class of slaves as they would their horses or their fields. The next typical stage in social development is the feudal system based on landholding and property and the domination of the serfs. Such a community has a more sloping gradation from the top to the bottom than the sharply-divided hierarchies of early times, but the "slope" is nevertheless a very steep one. The rise of a merchant middle class betokens the beginning of the bourgeoisie, and it is this stage of social and economic development which characterises all advanced modern non-communist communities. In this development of society the tool of economic domination has changed from landholding in the feudal sense to capital, such capital being nevertheless often represented by proprietary influence. Although, for Marx, the Lancashire cotton industry represented capitalism, and although he thought himself to be living in an age of fully-developed capitalism, when in fact capitalism had at that time hardly started, Marx was substantially

---

[2] *Op. cit.* at p. 18.

accurate in his foresight of the characteristics of a bourgeois-dominated system of capitalist exploitation.

The final stage of development, according to Marx, is the socialisation of society leading to the stage of perfect communism when all capitalist and bourgeois elements have been eliminated. This final stage may come about as a result either of evolution or of revolution, the latter necessitating a positive and probably violent catalyst which the former does not. Marx being, as he was, the originator of the doctrine which now possesses an enormous number of ramifications in the theory and practice of social administration, the stage of perfect communism was but dimly perceived as a Utopia at the very end of a dark tunnel full of social and economic struggles. Even the stage of socialism, which succeeds the system of bourgeois capitalist exploitation and precedes the eventual goal of perfect communism, was not worked out in any great detail in the writings of Marx himself. The way was left open, therefore, for the wide and sometimes contradictory variations in post-revolutionary thought which have been alluded to.[3]

Marx, Engels and the State

For Marx, law represents what he calls a *superstructure* which is used in bourgeois capitalist systems of regulation in order to further the ends of the economically dominant and exploiting class at the expense, in terms of labour and production, of the suppressed class—the proletariat. He saw the normative order of capitalist societies as a cloak for economic domination by a minority ruling group, and assumed that the concepts of state and law were therefore, by their very nature, tools for the maintenance of such exploitation by systematic coercion. It is as though Marx was unable to perceive (or at least steadfastly refused to perceive) law as a normative phenomenon, the character of which could be the subject of juristic cognition without any necessary reference to the material content of particular laws.[4] As distinct from the *superstructure* so designed by the exploitating class to protect and

---

[3] It may be noted that *The Communist Manifesto* is only a mere twelve thousand words in length, and it is therefore hardly surprising that Marx' views on social and economic development should find only relatively undetailed expression within the confines of this particular work.

[4] In this, a perhaps surprising parallel may be drawn between Marxist legal theory and some aspects of modern American legal realism; *c.f.* Chap. 8, pp. 173-178, *supra*; also p. 202, *infra*.

further its own interests—referred to by Marx as *ideology*[5]—
the reality of society or *infrastructure* lies in the economic relations which permeate it. Marx not only categorised the rise to
power of the proletariat as a characteristic stage of social development succeeding the overthrow of bourgeois capitalist domination;
he expressed its occurrence as a scientific necessity, verifiable
according to objective social laws.

In contradistinction to a more familiar usage of the expression
ideology, and one which Western observers are wont to direct at
what they see as a politically-dominated concept of the nature of
law, Marx asserts the non-ideological nature of the socialist state.
This form of state reflects the reality of objective social laws,
according to Marx, and the transition from bourgeois capitalism
to the dominance of the proletariat is not merely a division
between societies differing in degree, but a stage at which the
community changes *in kind*.

It will, of course, be asked: If Marxism conceives of law and
state as tools of exploitation, characteristic of capitalist suppression, why is there still talk of law, and of a socialist state, after
the proletariat have assumed power? The answer to this question
given by Marx himself involves nice distinctions, and ambiguity
in this area of his doctrine has both perplexed and aided Soviet
legal theorists, according to their objects and their integrity. In
a perfect communist society there will be no state, because there
will be no need for one, and the existence of law and state would
connote the continuence of class struggles and economic conflicts
which would by then, by definition, have ceased to exist. However
in the stage of socialism which precedes communism, there will
still be laws and there will still be a state of a sort—frequently
referred to as a "semi-state." It will be a semi-state only, since
its aim will be different in kind from that of the state in the
traditional sense; but it will nevertheless partake of the nature
of a state in some respects, systematic coercion or at least its
possibility being a necessary adjunct to the moulding of social and
economic relationships in the direction of communism.

In the period of transition between the overthrow of the capitalist
system and the achievement of complete communism the traditional
concepts of "law" and "state" are fashioned to particular Marxist
ends. In terminology which would signify to the Western observer

---

[5] For a detailed discussion of Marx' usage of the expression 'ideology'
see Kelsen, *The Communist Theory of Law*. Stevens, 1955, Chap. 1.

the very opposite of what they mean, legal theorists in socialist countries maintain that the "state" aspect of the transitional "semi-state" is, in contradistinction to the ideological capitalist state, a non-ideological adjunct of the proletarian dictatorship. It is declared to be non-ideological since such a concept of state is merely a means to an end, a necessary tool in the fashioning of communism, to be used only insofar as it is necessary in order to protect the authority of the economically-dominant proletariat against invasions of any remaining capitalist elements in society. As and when such adverse elements are eliminated, the semi-state, together with laws, will wither away. It will be noticed that it is *laws* which are expressed to be in the process of atrophy, and not *law*; for it is inconceivable that the character of law, or law as a concept, could "wither away."

However, Marxist doctrine identifies the content of law with its character and switches, sometimes almost imperceptibly, from one meaning of the term to the other. A major contradiction[6] in the Marxist theory of the state thus arises, since the state is conceived of as at once the coercive machinery for the maintenance and also for the abolition of exploitation.

II

Soviet legal theory

The literature developing and commenting on Marxism is, of course, enormous. Just as it was said of Bentham that his analysis of the nature of law occurred almost as *obiter dicta* in the course of his total literary output in many major fields of study, the same may be said of legal theory in relation to the writings of Marx. For Marx, also, the nature of law had to be conceived in a manner appropriate to his philosophy as a whole. However, while Bentham had given a prominent place to legal regulation in his overall contribution to social reform, the very opposite happens in the philosophy of Marx. The principal object remaining law in a socialist system is, paradoxically, to provide for its own withering away. In one of his best-known works, Engels, after asserting that during

---

[6] The Marxist concept of dialectics, taken over from Hegel, accommodates such contradictions as phenomena inherent in the nature of things, and thus inherent in what can still, according to Marx, be asserted as objective social reality.

the transition period of the dictatorship of the proletariat the inter-
ference of state power in social relations becomes superfluous in one
sphere after another and becomes dominant of itself, says:
"Government over persons is replaced by the administration of
things and the direction of processes of production. The state is
not 'abolished' (as the anarchists demand), it withers away."[7]
The superfluousness of the state (or semi-state) and of the law will
occur in the normal course of events, and, once the proletariat
has assumed control over the means of production within a community, such laws as remain will be merely necessary evils. They
will be used to snuff out bourgeois capitalist reaction and then
immolate themselves on the same funeral pyre when they cease to
be any longer necessary.

The Communist Manifesto was produced some considerable
time before the stirrings of revolution really began to manifest
themselves in Russia. It is not altogether surprising, therefore,
that Marx and Engels should provide no clear and definitive
picture of the future of the law in the period of the dictatorship
of the proletariat. In the spirit of his notion of dialectics, of the
notion that contradictions are to be found even in natural reality
which cannot be explained away or glossed over by a mere philosophy, Marx noted that the period of transition prior to the
achievement of socialism will not be perfect. During the transition period of the dictatorship of the proletariat there will still be
defects, and the law of the "socialist state" will be infected with
an evil of bourgeois society, namely inequality. "These defects (the
inequality of the law) are inevitable in the first phase of communist society, when, after long travail, it first emerges from
capitalist society. The law can never be on a highter level than
the economic structure of society and the evolution of civilisation
conditioned by this structure.

The time at which the Communist Manifesto was produced, and
the social and economic conditions which formed the background
for its argument, meant that the origins of socialism and communism manifested themselves in a manner which left many am-
biguities unresolved and which provided no very definite direction
for the practical implementation of doctrine. In the approaches
to law which are now to be outlined, the juristic aspect of Marxist
doctrine is provided with the direction which it originally lacked.

[7] Engels, *Anti-Dühring*, p. 302.

Lenin and the State

The first and basic work of the Soviet theory of the State (essentially connected with the Soviet theory of law) is Lenin's *State and Revolution*, published in 1917.[8] Lenin stresses the revolutionary character of Marxian doctrine. He restricts the possibility of the "withering away" of law and of the state to the *socialist* state, and insists that during the transition period of the dictatorship of the proletariat there will be a definite need for the state and law in order to eliminate reactionary elements within the community. So far from a process of withering away commencing immediately after the system of bourgeois capitalism has been overthrown by revolution, Lenin declares: "The dictatorship of the proletariat produces a series of restrictions of liberty in the case of the oppressors, the exploiters, the capitalists. We must crush them in order to free humanity from wage slavery, their resistance must be broken by force, it is clear that where there is suppression there is also violence, there is no liberty, no democracy".[9] Against an anticipated riposte that such a situation will produce effects the very opposite of a free and democratic socialist society, Lenin adds that "this period inevitably becomes a period of unusually violent class struggles in their sharpest possible forms and, therefore, the state during this period inevitably must be a state that is democratic in a new way (for the proletariat and the poor in general) and dictatorial in a new way against the bourgeoisie."[10] To the extent, then, that the period of the dictatorship of the proletariat evidences a socialist state characterised by democracy for the previously suppressed classes, the concept of "withering away" of the state is applicable at the very outset of the post-revolutionary situation. Nevertheless, the admissibility of contradictions even within objective social laws leaves the way open for Lenin to advocate, quite within the bounds of orthodox Marxist doctrine, the violent overthrow and suppression of a certain section of the community by means of the coercive methods at the disposal of the developing socialist state. The coercive power of the proletarian state is to be exercised, says Lenin, only against the former bourgeoisie. As soon as that bourgeoisie is completely abolished the coercive machinery of the state will disappear. The difference

---

[8] Lenin, *Collected Works*, Vol. XXI—2; New York, 1932; p. 149 *et seq.*
[9] *Op. cit.* at p. 153.
[10] *Op. cit.* at p. 177.

between the capitalist state and the proletarian state is explained by Lenin as follows: "Under capitalism we have a state in the proper sense of the word, that is, special machinery for the suppression of one class by another . . . . During the transition from capitalism to communism suppression is still necessary; but it is the suppression of the minority of exploiters by the majority of exploited. A special apparatus, special machinery for suppression, the 'state' is still necessary, but this is now a transitional state, no longer a state in the usual sense."[11]

Thus Lenin, by "reinterpretation" of some aspects of the original Marxist doctrine, bridged the possible gap between theory and the practical exigencies of the pre-revolutionary situation in Russia. He was a practical politician rather than a philosopher, though substantial reliance was placed on the communist philosophy in order to substantiate the claims of the revolutionaries. Lloyd describes Lenin's approach as follows: "Some of the more fervent prophets of the new order did indeed envisage the instantaneous accomplishment of the disappearance of the state and of the law with the successful outcome of the revolution. Lenin, however, adopted a more hard-headed and realistic approach, by recognising that even a successful revolution could not result in the immediate elimination of all the apparatus of the state and the panoply of the law. It would take time for a totally classless society to emerge, and though therefore Lenin did not abandon the Marxist conception of the ultimate withering away of the state when such a society has been obtained, he still recognised the need, during an interim period when class conflict had still to be eliminated, and the surviving elements of the bourgeoisie extruded, for the apparatus of the state and coercive law to be retained."[12]

Legal theory in the soviet state

The few years following the revolution of 1917 were characterised by disorganisation and disorder. So-called people's and workers courts functioned in an unsystematic manner and palm-tree justice was dispensed by *ad hoc* tribunals. A system of the "administration of things" could not be attained overnight, and during the period of the New Economic Policy, introduced by Lenin to meet

[11] *Op. cit.* at p. 220
[12] Lloyd, *Introduction to Jurisprudence* (3rd ed.), Stevens, 1972, pp. 634-5.

the economic realities of the period, it was recognised that some form of legal regulation was necessary. Otherwise, order was not to be substituted for chaos. The period became known as one of "revolutionary legality" in which any remaining forms of legal coercion would be subordinated to economic and social necessities until such time as they finally disappeared altogether.

The most prominent representative of Soviet legal theory, in its earliest phase of development was Pashukanis. Impressed by the social and economic necessities reflected in Lenin's insistence on the temporary maintenance of a revolutionary legality, Pashukanis conceded that the coercive power of the state must remain in order to prepare conditions for the ultimate withering away of the power of government. However, as soon as relationships in the Soviet system had begun to settle themselves into some kind of order, Pashukanis developed a completely Marxian doctrine which stood in total opposition to any bourgeois concept of law.[13] "Under a guise of superficial equality, Pashukanis saw all law as nothing but a cloak for bourgeois class interests, and for him law was necessarily a capitalist institution."[14]

Pashukanis took the Marxist view of all law as the tool of bourgeois economic exploitation to its logical conclusion, and purported to survey some of the laws and institutions of non-communist societies in a way which made them all appear to have been produced to foster and preserve such exploitation. "In order to inject into the theory of law the strongest possible dose of Marxism, Pashukanis imitates Marx' economic interpretation of political phenomena by reducing, in the field of jurisprudence, legal phenomena to economic phenomena in general, and in particular to economic phenomena which can exist only within a capitalist system of economy based on the principle of private property in the means of production. He rejects the definition of law as a system of norms as 'ideological.' "[15] It could be said that Pashukanis was influenced by Marx in the same way that Marx had been influenced by the Lancashire cotton-mills.[16]

As time went on, however, and the period of the dictatorship of the proletariat was supposed to be giving way to a socialism in

---

[13] See, generally, E. B. Pashukanis: *The General Theory of Law and Marxism*; see Babb & Hazard: *Soviet Legal Philosophy*, 1951, p. 111 *et seq.*
[14] Lloyd, *op. cit.*, p. 636.
[15] Kelsen, *The Communist Theory of Law*, pp. 89-90.
[16] For Marx' assumption, see *supra*, p. 183.

which law and the state could eventually wither away, doubts began to be expressed in political circles as to the advisability of letting go the reins of coercive state machinery. Again in the spirit of dialectics, according to which contradictions are considered to be part of natural reality a new doctrine began to be propounded which turned the course of Soviet legal theory in a substantially different direction from the one which it had so far been taking, uninterrupted.

It began to be feared that a loosening of the coercive restraints which had so far been preserved might put the incipient socialism into the greatest danger. The expression "capitalist encirclement" had already been used in orthodox Marxist doctrine, though in a frequently ambiguous manner. The term could be interpreted to refer either to the remaining bourgeois capitalist influences within the socialist community—"encirclement" in a metaphorical sense; or it could be interpreted to mean the geographical (and also metaphorical) encirclement of non-socialist and therefore invidious communities. Up to his death in 1924, Lenin had believed that world revolution was imminent, and this influenced his acceptance of Marxist doctrine with regard to the eventual disappearance of law and state after the period of the "semi-state", the period of transition, had ceased to exist. Apparently in a natural extension of this attitude, Pashukanis had gone on to discuss the period *following* that with which Lenin had been immediately concerned, though to which Lenin made obvious reference.

In 1936, the year of Stalin's constitution and the time at which the attainment of socialism was declared, revolutionary legality gave way not to socialism without law but to "socialist legality." The period leading up to this declaration was one of the coincidence of apprehension at letting go the restraints and the desire of some principal elements within the political leadership actually to strengthen and reinforce the methods of state coercion and legal regulation.

Socialist legality

The new direction given to the notion of "capitalist encirclement" produced a transition from the temporary revolutionary legality of the proletarian dictatorship to a conception of a more permanent and stable form of socialist law. As Lloyd put it, ". . . although the Marxian concept still remained desirable and could be expected ultimately to be achieved when the whole world had attained a classless situation,[17] for the time being, while Soviet socialism existed solely on a national basis, surrounded by capitalist powers, there would remain the need for the protection of the state and for the concept of stable law. So far as the Soviet Union was concerned, the socialist society had been achieved and the transitional period to socialism could be regarded as terminated, since there was no longer any class warfare in that society, all hostile elements having been eliminated. This, however, was not to be regarded as ushering in a withering away of the state and the law, but on the contrary there were to be established legal institutions on a socialist basis."[18]

The political motivation behind the new strengthening of legal control came from Stalin himself, who left it to his Commissar of Justice,[19] Andrei Vyshinsky, to work out a philosophy of law which would bring the new concept into line with orthodox Marxian doctrine. It had been the principal contention of Pashukanis that "law" reached its highest (and at the same time most undesirable) development under capitalism; that law was synonymous with a capitalist ideology which was to be avoided at all costs in a socialist society. The concept of socialist legality connoted, however, a justifiable form of normative regulation directed at the strengthening of the socialist community, especially against attack from without. Vyshinsky condemned Pashukanis for fostering a doctrine of law which would be an inadequate instrument of the proletariat in its struggle for socialism. Far from actually advancing the cause of the socialist community, Pashukanis' doctrine of law would, said Vyshinsky, actually harm it. It was, furthermore, only a short step from this proposition to Vyshinsky's allegation that Pashukanis and all those who adopted his reasoning were to be condemned as traitors.

One of the principal features of Vyshinsky's analysis[20] is that law is openly and expressly presented as an effective instrument of the policy of the Soviet government, directed at the abolition of capitalism and the realisation of socialism. An example of the

---

[17] The assumption of Lenin having been that world socialism leading to communism would occur in a relatively short time, see *supra*.

[18] Lloyd, *op. cit.*, pp. 638-9.

[19] For the institution of the Procuracy or Commissariat or Ministry of Justice, see p. 201, *infra*.

[20] If so it can be called. For detail, see Soviet Legal Theory, *op. cit.*, p. 303 *et seq*.

extreme language which accompanied the *volte face* in Soviet legal theory is the following declaration by Vyshinsky, taken from his address delivered to the First Congress of the Sciences of Soviet State and Law in Moscow in 1938 : [21] "Over a period sufficiently (and unfortunately) long, the trend of our science of law has not been in accord with the interests of the cause of socialist building . . . . Over a series of years a position almost of monopoly in legal science has been occupied by a group of persons who have turned out to be provocateurs and traitors—people who knew how actually to contrive the work of betraying our science, our state, and our fatherland[22] under the mask of defending Marxism—Leninism and championing orthodox Marxism and the Marx-Lenin methodology. These persons directed their energies to holding back the development of our juristic thought and to perverting the essence of our Marx-Lenin doctrine concerning law and state. These persons strove to dash from the hands of the proletariat and the toilers of our land the Marx-Lenin doctrine of law and state which proved to be so potent an instrument in the struggle with the many bestial foes of socialism." Passages such as this, which permeate the work of Vyshinsky, are full of clichés and repetition; and insofar as any reasoning lies behind his assertions it is frequently tautologous and often contradictory. A political movement thus came to be represented as a science, and it was during the period of the influence of Vyshinsky, under Stalin, that Soviet legal theory reached its lowest ebb.

According to Vyshinsky, "a theory of law is a system of legal principles on the basis whereof the entire science of law—and all the branches of that science (irrespective of their definitive content) are built. Clearly the working out of these principles cannot have its inception in the norms of positive law: on the contrary, the norms of positive law—like all positive law as a whole—must be built in conformity with the principles established by a legal theory."[23] Though Soviet jurists, under which generic term Vyshinsky may for present purposes be included, have constantly denied any connection between the Marxist identification of objective social laws and doctrines of natural law, anyone could be forgiven for taking the basis of the foregoing passage from

[21] For a vigorous attack on Vyshinsky's purported "science" of law, see Kelsen, *op. cit.*, Chap. 7.

[22] A term which became fashionable in the period during which most concern was expressed over "capitalist encirclement" of hostile countries.

[23] Soviet Legal Philosophy, *op. cit.*, p. 323 *et seq.*

Vyshinsky's writings to be a natural law standpoint.[24] In the strong words of Kelsen: "What is most amazing in this theory of the bolshevik Vyshinsky is that it is exactly of the same type as that bourgeois theory which the Soviet writers have derided and ridiculed more than any other theory: the natural law doctrine, which, just as Vyshinsky, rejects a mere theory of positive law because of its 'sterility and impotence' and which, precisely in accordance with Vyshinsky's recipe, works out, or pretends to work out, principles of law 'from life', that is, from nature in general and from the nature of society or, what amounts to the same, from the social relationships in particular; with the only difference that these principles are the ideal norms of capitalist law."[25]

In the writings of Vyshinsky, in clear support of the political leadership which desired for its own ends to strengthen its hold on the people, the "withering away" of law in Soviet society is put off yet again. Soviet law as a socialist normative order will wither away only in the last phase of communism. The Soviet leadership had now, as it were, got it both ways, for they were (so long as Vyshinsky's declarations were accepted as representing the true development of Marxism) able to justify whatever restraints they liked by reference to the very protection of the people who were now, in effect, being exploited.

Though there can be no doubt that Pashukanis' interpretation of the Soviet law in the period of transition as an assimilated and adapted bourgeois law accorded completely with Marx' own doctrine, and that the doctrine, enunciated by Marx and Engels, of the withering away of the state after the transition period was equally applicable to law, nevertheless this position was unacceptable to the Soviet government and to Vyshinsky. According to Vyshinsky: "It is a crude perversion of Marx' doctrine of law[26] for the Pashukanises, the Bermans, and others of their ilk to assert that the transition to developed communism was conceived by Marx not as a transition to new forms of law but as the withering away of juridical form in general—as emancipation from this legacy of the bourgeois epoch which was destined to out-

[24] For the nature of Soviet legal theory as compared with other trends which have been discussed in earlier Chapters of this book, see *infra*, p. 198, *et seq.*

[25] Kelsen strenuously denies that his own *Pure Theory of Law*, with its central notion of the basic norm, has any basis in natural law; see *supra*, p. 124, *et seq.*

[26] If anything, Marx' doctrine had not been a doctrine of law but rather a doctrine of non-law; Vyshinsky's perversion is manifest.

live the bourgeoisie itself. Such a proposition would be acceptable if, but only if, the transition from capitalism to communism were without a transitional period, which is unimaginable without descending into utopianism."

In his address to the 1938 Congress, referred to above, Vyshinsky does include some element of juristic analysis, albeit directed at a justification of the Stalinist position. "Law is neither a system of social relationships nor a form of production relationships. Law is the aggregate of rules of conduct, or norms, yet not of norms alone, but also of customs and rules of community living confirmed by state authority and coercively protected by that authority. Our definition has nothing in common with normativist definitions; normativism starts from the completely incorrect notion of law as 'social solidarity' (Duguit) or as a norm (Kelsen), which is a final integration of the content of law (and with no reference to the social relationships which actually define that content). The error of the normativists is that when they define law as an aggregate of norms they confine themselves to that element, conceiving of the legal norms themselves as something closed in and explained by themselves." The difference between Duguit and Vyshinsky is, in reality, simply one of ideology, while the account of Kelsen's theory is a misinterpretation.[27] The notion of law as the *aggregate* of norms is the very antithesis of what Kelsen set out to achieve via his concept of the basic norm as a scheme of interpretation for the legal quality of physical acts and relationships.[28]

Soviet legal theory since Stalin

As soon as the Stalinist era of the perversion of law to dubious socialist ends, of the suppression of politically inconvenient elements within socialist society and of the indiscriminate use of the secret police in the elimination of "crimes against the state," had ended, Vyshinsky fell from favour. It became increasingly accepted that his doctrine was a distortion of original Marxism—that the state is essentially an instrument for the domination and exploitation of one class by another—for this was precisely the function

[27] For an analysis of Kelsen's analysis of the nature of law, see *supra*, Chap. 6.

[28] Vyshinsky's criticism is more readily applicable to Austin's version of the Imperative Theory of Law, but he would only be in the company of many capitalist jurists.

of the state during Stalinist era. After the death of Stalin in 1953, anti-Stalinist jurists brought Soviet legal theory back nearer to orthodox Marxism. Vyshinsky was denounced because his views favoured the "cult of personality."

The more liberal political climate permitted the development, under Khruschev, of the notion of an "All-People's State," of a society based on voluntary social and economic co-operation rather than force, on persuasion and example rather than upon coercion. Though Vyshinsky's doctrine continued to exercise some influence for a period following the death of Stalin, by the time of the publication of the 1961 Communist Party Programme the time was ripe for a plan to "socialise" the administration of justice and the use of legal machinery specifically to eliminate anti-socialist tendencies in the community. People's patrols and comrades courts are but two of the institutions whose very name evidences the atmosphere of the new approach. The object—the transition from the socialism which had been declared at the time of Stalin's Constitution of 1936 into complete communism—remained true to orthodox Marxism, while the means by which it might be reached were certainly much less the antithesis of Marx' doctrine than the dictatorial doctrines of Vyshinsky.

Contemporary legal thought in the Soviet Union[29] is characterised by the fact that the notion of law, in the spirit of original Marxian doctrine, is discussed as a secondary consideration, the primary consideration being the actual problems which confront the socialist state on the road to communism. It was hardly surprising, in retrospect, that doctrines such as that of Vyshinsky should have come into existence when it was remembered that the primary object of attention of legal theory was the notion of law, considered as a phenomenon as such even *before* the problems were examined, in the solution of which a form of normative regulation could play a specific and restricted role.

Law in the Soviet Union is now conceived as just one of many available sources of guidance along the road to communism. Law is now treated as something which can provide an educative influence on the community. The norms of Soviet law are said to *express* the will of the Soviet people and the policies of the Communist party, and though "a rigorous and undeviating adherence to and execution of Soviet laws" by authorities and citizens alike

[29] For a survey of contemporary attitudes, see Lloyd, *op. cit.*, pp. 643-645 and p. 675 *et seq.*

is insisted on,[30] compulsion is regarded as an instrument of last resort in case the positive influence of education in the ways of socialism should founder. Socialist legality is conceived of as a sort of collective consciousness on the part of the whole people of the ideals of socialist society on its way to communism. To the extent that the practice of Soviet justice measures up to what is claimed in theory,[31] the present spirit of socialist legality could be said to represent in practical form the dichotomy between the "two moralities" described by Fuller in *The Morality of Law*.[32] The "morality of necessity" is characterised by standards which must be met as a *minimum* for the furtherance of social ends within a community, while the "morality of aspiration" signifies a striving towards increasingly better conditions in a situation where men aim, not at a minimum, but as high as they are capable. The preservation of a minimum set of standards within a community is apt to lead to stagnation if all that is done is to keep the peace according to the *status quo*. The "morality of aspiration" is that which can lead a society forward in a dynamic way, a way which, in fact, modern Soviet legal theory is anxious to express.

This climate has enabled the views of Pashukanis to be partially rehabilitated, though of course since emphasis is now primarily on the problems which have to be solved by socialism rather than on the specific ability of law to solve them, such rehabilitation includes only those aspects of Pashukanis' doctrine as are suited to the gradual attainment of communism by means of all justifiable methods which present themselves. In answer to the question: Why should socialism need law more than does capitalism, Ioffe and Shargorodsky[33] answer that, while under capitalism, law is a stabiliser, under socialism law is needed to build the society and to develop productive forces. However, law by itself is not enough, and the general socialist consciousness, the attention to socialist legality, is necessary. "Merely to enact the very best of legal norms is inadequate. Only adherence to socialist legality can assure a situation in which regulation by legal norms is actually implemented in life." Such is the awareness that law may act as an

---

[30] See *Soviet Law and Government*; International Arts and Sciences Press Inc., Vol. IV, No. 2, at p. 13 *et seq.*

[31] Trials and detention of leading authors, and the imprisonment of dissidents in institutions for the criminally insane, leave substantial doubts, to say the least, as to the coincidence of theory and practice.

[32] Revised edition, Yale University Press, 1969, Chap. 1.

[33] Soviet Law and Government, *op. cit.*, Vol. II, No. 2, p. 3.

influential adjunct to education in socialist consciousness that recent writers[34] have placed great emphasis on the need to publicise laws in a manner which will make everyone aware of their content and their purpose: "The goal pursued by the establishment of any norm should be clear to the very broadest strata of the population."[35]

Communism—the goal of socialist society—remains even yet a distant vision, though many of the problems in the tunnel down which Marx first looked have now been surmounted. It now seems, in retrospect, that Khruschev went a little too quickly along the road to communism than was good for the Soviet socialist state, in a manner similar to Pashukanis' desire to make rapid progress towards communism once the immediate problems of the post-revolutionary transition period had been overcome. The problems which still confront the socialist society are now, it appears, to be solved by a wary and careful approach to the improvement of the socialist condition, rather than with an eye to the rapid attainment of the end in view. That end, communism, is now being sought by more pragmatic and less doctrinal methods than have been used in the development of the socialist semi-state.

III

Theory and system

The accounts and analyses of law which have been examined in earlier Chapters may roughly be divided, for reference, into three: natural law doctrines, positivism, in various forms and with a variety of purposes, and realism. As has been mentioned, natural law elements in Soviet legal theory were strenuously denied by Vyshinsky, and this influence is in fact generally denied by Soviet writers, including also those whose views are in opposition to those of Vyshinsky. Though there might, to Western eyes, appear to be a distinct similarity between the ideal elements in natural law philosophies and the realisation of "objective social reality" in Marxian doctrine; and though the vices of man's acting against his nature may seem similar in kind to those of his acting against objective social laws, any such connection is denied by Soviet legal theory.

[34] *E.g.* Golunsky in *Soviet Law and Government*, Vol. 1, No. 1, p. 13.
[35] *Ibid.* at p. 18.

It has sometimes been said by Soviet writers that, since no type of law other than positive law is recognised in the socialist state, Soviet legal theory partakes of positivism. To this it is always added, however, that the definition of positive law includes a necessary reference to the *social substratum* of law, since social background and economic function are essential additions in Marxist legal philosophy to general methods of the identification of norms. As distinct, therefore, from the accounts given by the positivist approaches which have been examined in earlier Chapters, the sources of socialist law include all the law-configurating factors in society, that is to say, both the formal and the material influences on the existing positive law (or rather *laws*). One such factor, alluded to before as the "socialist consciousness" within a community, is the will of the people, and in particular of the dominant forces within society which act as guides and organisers for the progress of socialism. Law, including both its formal and its material sources, is conceived of as a matter of social engineering.[36] It can therefore be said with confidence that Soviet legal philosophy, in its concern with *laws*, as distinct from *law* as a phenomenon, is concerned with a subject-matter very different from that of most other theories considered earlier in this book. Their concentration on the socialist *content* of laws and the Marxist condemnation of the *character* of law in the traditional sense as a tool of bourgeois capitalist exploitation are connected only by an ideological[37] assumption on the part of Marx and his followers. The nature of all law, whether it be that of a capitalist or a socialist community, that of a state or a "semi-state," remains and always will remain normative. The content of laws will vary with time and place—and ideology—but the character of law will remain constant. It is no solution to the major problems of legal theory to say that law is always directed towards an undesirable socio-economic end and is therefore itself undesirable. There is as much point in asserting that law should and will wither away because it has often been used to certain vicious ends as to argue that philosophy should and will wither away because its products have on occasion, in the opinion of some men, led others astray. This is not to say, of course, that the communist goal of the

[36] An expression coined by the American jurist Roscoe Pound, and one which expresses also a principal subject of discussion of modern American "realist" jurists.

[37] Also in the traditional sense!

withering away of law is unworthy of attainment, but simply that more worthy, social reasons may be adduced to justify a withering away than a mere dogma that capitalist positive *laws* are undesirable. Modern Soviet juristic thought is clearly aware that a concentration on the functional aspect of laws, rather than a recourse to dogmatic deductions from just one among many premises of original Marxian doctrine of society, is the most beneficial study from a socialist viewpoint.

In the light of the relative lack of attention now given by Soviet legal writers to abstract generalisations about the nature of law, a comparison may be drawn between Soviet legal theory and American legal realism. Both are concerned with social engineering, with getting jobs done in society; both are concerned to concentrate on policies and principles, in addition to the "paper rules."[38] In socialist legal systems judge-made law is not recognised as a formal source of law, but rather as an important social and material source, in much the same way as the directives issued by certain executive agencies.[39]

The People's Power

Though lines of persuasive authority are certainly recognised as important material sources of law, no system of judicial precedent as we know it exists in socialist legal systems. If such were recognised as an independent source of law, this would be an invasion of a principle of the greatest importance in socialist systems: the principle of the completeness and indivisibility of the people's power. If exploitation is to be eliminated, the will of the whole people[40] must be preserved, if only in name, as a principal value. The legislative, executive and judicial organs of the people's power are all answerable to their electing agencies among the people, as well as to their respective superiors in the hierarchy of each organ (or branch) of state (or the people's) power. Though the incidence of this principle of dual responsibility varies from one

[38] See *e.g.* Dworkin: Is Law a System of Rules? referred to in Chap. 5, p. 105, *supra.*
[39] See, further, David & Brierly, Major Legal Systems, Part II, title I.
[40] The concept of the people's power is, of course, still the mainstay of Soviet institutions, even though the administration of socialist society is recognised to be in the hands of a minority group, Khruschev's notion of an All-People's State having been dismissed as "hare-brained".

organ to another, the concept evidences a system of checks and balances within the constitutional structure of the Soviet state reflecting the ideal of the socialist community.[41]

The Procuracy

In the jurisprudence of non-socialist legal systems the separation of powers is commonly regarded as an integral part of the Rule of Law. The notion of the separation of powers as employed by Montesquieu connotes the separate though related existence of legislature, executive and judiciary. The principle of socialist legality dictates the very opposite of such a separation, at least to the extent that the "areas of activity" (as they are called) *within* the people's power should not be regarded as separate sources of authority, but rather as different manifestations of authority all emanating from a common source. The concept of socialist legality is a reflection of the completeness and indivisibility of the people's power, and both are concerned with the material content of legal norms rather than with their form. On the other hand the Rule of Law is frequently, though not always, concerned with the *form* of law, with forms of lawmaking and formal sources of control. Socialist legality is not satisfied by an assertion that justice may be seen to be done unless it actually is done in accordance with the material principles of socialism.

In addition to the legislative, executive and judicial areas of state activity there exists also a fourth organ, namely, the Procuracy or Commissariat of Justice. Though the equivalent term 'Ministry of Justice' exists in some non-socialist legal systems, the office of procurator and its connotations in the area of socialist legality are peculiar to Soviet systems. Within this area of authority there is no system of dual responsibility, and only the Procurator General, or Commissar of Justice, is elected. The Procuracy has wide and varied powers to institute and terminate judicial proceedings, to act as prosecutor or as defence, as well as to maintain a general survey of the administration of socialist law. The object of this further area of activity is to ensure, in the name of the people, the maintenance of socialist legality in the material content of regulations and norms which affect members of society. The political

---

[41] Here again, with the reservation that their ideologies differ, a comparison may be made between constitutional theory in socialist systems and in the U.S.A.

influence on the particular requirements of socialist legality is clear
from the fact that the Procurator-General takes part, as a matter
of convention, in the meetings of the Central Committee of the
Communist Party.

The relative independence of the Procurator-General and his
subordinates has as its object the frank and objective assessment
of state activity with a view to its operating properly in the development of socialism. Its dependence on political opinion is justified
in Soviet legal theory ultimately on the ground that the so-called
"politics" of socialist government are concerned to reflect and im-
plement objective social laws and are a necessary part of the
modern development of orthodox Marxian doctrine.

Conclusion

The conclusion of this Chapter on Soviet legal theory provides
a fitting conclusion for this brief comparative survey of some
major developments in legal theory as a whole. The development
of legal theory in the world before Marx took two-and-a-half
thousand years to produce a complete cycle from the metaphysics
of early natural law doctrines to the down-to-earth pragmatism
of modern realism. Marxist legal theory, taking its starting point
in allegedly objective social laws, some based more in assumption
than others, has developed a pragmatism substantially akin to
modern American "realist" methodology, having gone through
a sort of positivism[42] en route, in a mere century. However, when
the claims to our attention of some of the analyses of law discussed in earlier Chapters are remembered, it may be doubted
whether the material aims of socialist law and legality can supply
us with a satisfactory account of the nature of the concept of law.

[42] In an attenuated and perverted form in the writings of Vyshinsky,
supra, p. 192, *et seq.*

INDEXES

INDEX OF CONTENTS

INDEX OF JURISTS